BALANCING ACTS

Behind

the Scenes

at London's

National Theatre

BALANCING ACTS

NICHOLAS HYTNER

Alfred A. Knopf · New York · 2017

THIS IS A BORZOI BOOK
PUBLISHED BY ALFRED A. KNOPF

www.aaknopf.com

Knopf, Borzoi Books, and the colophon are registered
trademarks of Penguin Random House LLC.

Library of Congress Cataloging-in-Publication Data
Names: Hytner, Nicholas author.
Title: Balancing acts : behind the scenes at
London's National Theatre | Nicholas Hytner.
Description: First American edition. | New York :
Alfred A. Knopf, 2017.
Identifiers: LCCN 2017016630 | ISBN 9780451493408
(hardcover) | ISBN 9780451493415 (ebook)
Subjects: LCSH: Hytner, Nicholas. | Theatrical producers and
directors—Great Britain—Biography. | National Theatre (Great
Britain) | Theater—England—London—History—21st century.
Classification: LCC PN2598.H96 A3 2017 |
DDC 792.02/33092 [B]—dc23 LC record available at
https://lccn.loc.gov/2017016630

Jacket photograph by Matthew Williams-Ellis/Alamy
Jacket design by Chip Kidd

Manufactured in the United States of America

First American Edition

Contents

BALANCING ACTS

Introduction

In a National Theatre rehearsal room, Michael Gambon has been wrestling for three days with Alan Bennett's new play *The Habit of Art*. Michael has given many prodigious performances at the National, most recently Falstaff in Shakespeare's two *Henry IV* plays, though there were occasional memory lapses which he covered with Elizabethan rhubarb. I had a couple of letters complaining that my production had made Sir Michael incomprehensible, to which I replied politely, although he's a famous hoaxer so he may have written them himself. One of them compared him with suspicious pomposity to that admirable Shakespearean and model of clarity, Simon Russell Beale.

He now seems much less confident than he was as Falstaff. He's playing an old actor who is struggling with the part of the poet W. H. Auden to Alex Jennings's Benjamin Britten in a play about Auden and Britten within a play about a theatre company putting on the same play. Alex has an almost mystical faith in the great tradition of British acting, so he's urging Michael on. With them on stage is Frances de la Tour, who in the face of life's absurdities has an eyebrow permanently raised and a voice permanently tuned to deadpan. She's playing a stage manager, and I'm sure that she can nurse Michael through anything that goes off-piste.

But at the moment he can barely get to the end of a sentence.

And then, suddenly, the blood drains from him. He staggers, and falls into a chair. We call for help, an oxygen tank is hurried into the room, then a stretcher. Michael is wheeled out, the oxygen mask over his face. One of the stage managers goes with him in the ambulance to St. Thomas' Hospital. As he's carried into A&E, she asks him whether there's any message he'd like her to take back to the rehearsal room.

"Don't worry about those bastards," he says. "They're already on the phone to Simon Russell Beale."

And as he speaks, I'm with Alan Bennett and the rest of the company recasting the part. Simon Russell Beale is doing something else, probably making a documentary about Renaissance choral music: he is as erudite as he is audible. So he's not in the running. But once we know that nothing serious has happened to Michael, we barely have a thought for him. We're in the canteen, overlooking the river. Tourist boats glide under Waterloo Bridge, and glum office workers stare at computer screens in the building next door, while we make a list of actors who are available for the part, all of them distinguished, none of them immune to our brutal assessments of their suitability. By the end of the day, Michael has been advised to withdraw from the play, and I've called Richard Griffiths, an actor renowned for his delicacy and wit, but also for his immense girth. Alan has already written lines to justify the casting of a fat actor in the part of Auden, who, although dissolute, was not even plump.

You start with a vision, and you deliver a compromise. And you're pulled constantly in different directions. So although you want the actor who plays W. H. Auden to be as much like W. H. Auden as possible, you know that the play will work best with an actor who can remember what the playwright wrote.

You know that what works generally trumps all other considerations, and you also know that if you care only about what works, you'll end up with something slick but meretricious.

You want a play to be challenging, ambitious, nuanced and complicated. You also want it to sell tickets.

You want playwrights to write exactly the plays they want to write. You also want what they write to reflect your own image of what your theatre should stand for.

You want your theatre to vibrate with the rude, disruptive energy of the carnival. But in your heart of hearts, you recoil from the chaos: you seek intimations of celestial harmony.

You want to look into the abyss, and make sense of human misery. But you flinch from pretension, despise self-importance, and take refuge in irony.

You want Shakespeare to be our contemporary. You also know him to be writing very specifically about a world that is separated from our own by four hundred years.

You want to tread a tightrope between all your conflicting impulses, to find poise and balance. But you despise yourself for your caution; you want your work to be full of jagged edges and careless abandon.

So when Richard Griffiths picks up the phone and says, "It may interest you to know that you have called me from my exercise bike," you dismiss the unrealistic thought that he may be thinner than he was when you last saw him, because you know it doesn't matter. You explain to him the pickle you're in, and you aren't surprised that it doesn't occur to him to remind you that you might have asked him to play W. H. Auden in the first place. But Richard is always a model of good grace, and he says he'll start on Monday.

Monday comes, and Richard is stuck in traffic on the A40. He calls to say he'll be half an hour late. He's one of the world's great raconteurs, but his stories never have a destination and they go on for hours. And we're now two weeks behind, which is why Alan Bennett says plaintively from the back of the room, "Start rehearsing as soon as he arrives or we'll be here all morning with Traffic Jams I Have Known."

So that's what we do. And *The Habit of Art,* though not as popular, or probably as good, as Alan's previous play, *The History Boys,* turns out to be worth a couple of hours of the audience's time, as it is provocative, funny, touching, sad and original. The playwright, the actors and I have spent the short rehearsal time left to us trying to reconcile our high ideals with what's achievable. We want to make art, and we know we're in show business. It's one of the balancing acts that the National Theatre, and this book, are about.

❦

Michael Gambon was back four years later, in 2013, for the National's fiftieth birthday, formidable in a scene from Harold Pinter's *No Man's Land,* in the part originally played in 1975 by Ralph Richardson. He and Derek Jacobi, who played John Gielgud's part with all the finesse of his predecessor, were part of a two-hour celebration of the National's history, which brought together actors from all of its five decades in a programme of scenes from many of its most memorable productions, broadcast live by the BBC. Michael and Derek recorded a brief and irreverent introduction to Pinter, admitting that they had no idea what his plays were about. They wouldn't have dared if he'd still been alive.

There was never a chance that the fiftieth-birthday celebration could in a mere two hours balance the need to do full justice to the range of the National's achievements against the need to deliver a good show. But as much as a single evening could, it touched on most of my preoccupations.

It started as the National itself started at the Old Vic Theatre in 1963, with Act 1 Scene 1 of *Hamlet,* and Shakespeare haunts these pages as his plays haunt me. I was afraid that *Hamlet* might be too high-minded for an opener, but "Who's there?" is an unimprovable first line; and when Derek Jacobi, who played Laertes in the 1963 production, appeared in armour as the Ghost, he was a reminder that high-minded can also be showbiz gold.

Hamlet himself doesn't appear in the first scene of *Hamlet,* but later in the evening, Simon Russell Beale stood on the vast Olivier stage, as vulnerable and lonely as he was in 2000. "I have of late, but wherefore I know not, lost all my mirth." Adrian Lester and Rory Kinnear had only finished their run of *Othello* a couple of months earlier. Their gripping account of the climax of Othello's descent into jealousy gave way briefly to a tape of Laurence Olivier and Frank Finlay in the legendary 1964 production, recorded live at the Old Vic. Time turned somersaults.

Olivier was the National's founding director, and, according to many of those who saw him live, its greatest actor. Archive footage of his stage performances is a spectral counterfeit of what it must have been like to be there. But a few days before the show his wife, Joan Plowright, returned to the Old Vic to film a scene from George Bernard Shaw's *Saint Joan,* fifty years after she'd first played it. She asked if she could stop if she forgot or stumbled over her lines. I said we could stitch her performance together from as many takes as she wanted. The cameras rolled, and the years rolled back. She did the whole thing in one take. A young guy on the camera crew had no idea who she was, and no idea that she was playing a girl who was going defiant to the flames, but he was still in tears.

Among the biggest regrets of my twelve years as the National's director is that I found nothing for Maggie Smith, who, like Joan Plowright, was part of Olivier's first company. She was aware of the irony when I asked her to be in the birthday show: irony is one of her special subjects. But she suggested a short, enigmatic speech from George Farquhar's *The Beaux' Stratagem.* She said she remembered it because when she played Mrs. Sullen, it took her so long to work out what it meant. I didn't believe this: in a rehearsal room, she's always several steps ahead of everyone else. At the party after the show, she spoke to William Gaskill, *The Beaux' Stratagem*'s director in 1970. He admired how still she'd been. "You told me not to move my hands," she said, pleased that he'd noticed. More than forty years on, she still remembered his note, maybe because it was so practical and unpretentious, and a lesson in how a director should talk to an actor. Judi Dench arrived one afternoon to rehearse Cleopatra's elegy for Antony, after a gap of more than twenty-five years. "Any notes?" she asked, when she'd finished. How do you give notes to someone like Judi Dench? Or Helen Mirren? Are any of us really up to Maggie Smith?

My years as the National's director brought me into the kind of contact with theatre directors that I would never otherwise have had, as we rarely see each other at work. Actors know everything about all of us, but will only under extreme provocation spill the beans. I've watched many of the most celebrated British actors at work, and I'm still trying to crack the mystery of how they do what they do. Many of them were there for the birthday show, but two survived only in grainy video: Paul Scofield as the composer Salieri in *Amadeus* (1979) and Nigel Hawthorne as the king in *The Madness of George III* (1991), who both grabbed the audience by the throat.

The evening was studded with scenes from modern classics that were first produced at the National. *Rosencrantz and Guildenstern Are Dead* (1967), *No Man's Land* (1975), *Bedroom Farce* (1977), *Amadeus* (1979), *Arcadia* (1993) and *Copenhagen* (1998): major plays by playwrights— Tom Stoppard, Harold Pinter, Alan Ayckbourn, Peter Shaffer and Michael Frayn—whose work is the backbone of the British theatre. Central to the National's identity are the new plays that take the temperature of the nation. Peter Nichols's *The National Health* (1969) was the first of them, the NHS no less emblematic of the nation's health then than now. Howard Brenton and David Hare's *Pravda* (1985) was a prophetic account of the debauching of the British press by a proprietor eager to stick two fingers up to the British establishment, and happy to shaft his readers. Nobody who saw Anthony Hopkins lope onto the empty Olivier stage as the Rupert Murdoch avatar Lambert Le Roux will forget it. Luckily, Ralph Fiennes hadn't seen it, or he might not have agreed to give his own terrifying performance.

David Hare's gift of second sight was on display again in a scene from *Stuff Happens,* which in 2004 interwove verbatim reportage with informed speculation in a gripping drama about the build-up to the Iraq War, with Alex Jennings uncanny as George W. Bush. Tony Kushner's *Angels in America* (1992) had its British premiere at the National, before it played New York, and was as comprehensive in its anatomy of contemporary America as anything we produced about ourselves.

It was harder to chip fragments from many equally striking plays. Some of them were too challenging to sell many tickets, but the box office is an imperfect measure of success. Still, I'm eager to explore what made *War Horse* (2007) such a phenomenon, and why *One Man, Two Guvnors* (2011) made so many people laugh. What *is* funny? How do you do comedy? And what part should musical theatre play in the National's repertoire? Richard Eyre's production of *Guys and Dolls* (1982) marked a sea change in the way the London audience looked at the Broadway golden age. Trevor Nunn's gorgeous *My Fair Lady*

(2001) was the climax of a series of incisive re-evaluations of classic American musicals.

The first new musical I programmed as the National's director was Richard Thomas and Stewart Lee's *Jerry Springer—The Opera* (2003), which married low entertainment to high art even in its title. The theatre has been finding ways to test the boundaries of taste since Aristotle suggested that comedy had its origins in phallic parades. There will always be a part of me that would prefer to be at the Wigmore Hall listening to a Haydn string quartet, so I'm glad that *Jerry Springer* did without the phallus, but it was still as blithely offensive as it was musically literate.

Many of the *Jerry Springer* company reappeared in a scene from *London Road* (2011), by Alecky Blythe and Adam Cork, based on testimony from residents of Ipswich caught up in the trial of a serial killer, and evidence, if it were needed, that musicals can be as far-reaching in form and subject matter as any other theatrical genre. The immense range of the entire evening was answer in itself to one of the questions I asked myself throughout my years as director: what is the National Theatre for?

There were two scenes by Alan Bennett, who has entrusted his plays to me for the last twenty-five years. Working on *The History Boys* (2004), about history, literature, education and eight clever schoolboys, was as good a time as I've ever had in the theatre. Most of the original company came back, though not, to our great sorrow, Richard Griffiths, who died only a few months before the reunion. Alan Bennett played Richard's part, the teacher everyone wishes they'd had. He didn't efface memories of Richard, but he landed an enormous laugh that Richard never got, because ten years previously, neither Richard nor I had understood the line properly. "It used to drive me mad," said Alan. "Why on earth didn't you tell me?" I cried. The history boys, all of them at least fifteen years too old for school, jeered triumphantly.

The show closed with the final speech from *The Habit of Art* (2009). As a National Theatre stage manager, Frances de la Tour remembered the move from the Old Vic to the intimidating new building of the South Bank. But there was no need to be frightened:

Because what's knocked the corners off the place, taken the shine off it and made it dingy and unintimidating—are plays. Plays plump, plays paltry, plays preposterous, plays purgatorial, plays radiant, plays rotten—but plays persistent. Plays, plays, plays.

Backstage, we created a temporary green room in one of the rehearsal rooms. School benches were lined up in front of a big screen so that the cast could watch the show. Members of the 2013 company sat with members of the 1963 company, colleagues on equal terms. Actors who will be around for the National's centenary in 2063 shared a bench with Maggie Smith and Judi Dench. They'll be able to tell actors whose parents aren't yet born that they were there.

The green room was the place to be: even during the dress rehearsal it was a magnet for everyone involved in the show. I decided I'd slip out of the auditorium for twenty minutes during the performance and run backstage. But I'd bought a new suit and, determined to show everybody how thin I still was, I didn't want to spoil its line with my wallet. So I came without it, and had to borrow somebody else's pass card. Halfway through the show, I slid out inconspicuously, and ran to the pass door. The card didn't work.

I pushed hard at the door, but it wouldn't open. On the other side, down the stairs, was the green room, but I was locked out of my own theatre. I started to beat at the door, in a fury of frustration and disappointment. Harder and harder I battered the door, hammering with my fists at a reinforced glass panel, which suddenly shattered, though as it was reinforced it didn't give way, and I still couldn't get through.

I retired hurt, though the new suit still looked sharp, and I slunk back into the auditorium. It seemed like a brutal reminder that the clock was ticking on my twelve years at the National, so I told nobody what I'd done until, eighteen months later, I fessed up during the farewell speech at my leaving party. Out in the crowd, a contingent from Security nodded gravely. They'd known all along. I'd been caught on CCTV.

It's Monday morning first thing. I've been in the job a couple of years. I'm in my office on the fourth floor, which has a view over the Thames to Somerset House, and though I'm growing used to it, I'll never get used to the noise of the recycling van collecting last night's empties from the goods entrance below my window. The National Theatre regularly appears on lists of both the ten most loved and the ten most loathed buildings in London. I love its uncompromising exterior; I love the concrete fly towers when they're etched sharp by the sun against a blue sky, and even when they go soggy like an egg box in the rain; I love the buzzing, purple-carpeted foyers; but I'm not crazy about the vast rubbish bins that occupy one of the best river frontages in Europe.

On my desk is the current repertory chart: for each of the National's three auditoria, the next eighteen months are divided into slots for six or seven shows to play in rep: around twenty shows every year. The top of the chart looks good. We've planned promising shows for all three theatres: the 300-seat Cottesloe, the 900-seat Lyttelton and the 1,150-seat Olivier. Nine months in, gaps start to appear. By the bottom of the chart, there's next to nothing. Choosing the repertoire and shepherding it onto the stage are at the heart of my job.

In the office next door, Nick Starr is already hammering at his keyboard. As director of the National, I'm its chief executive; but Nick, its executive director, runs the building and the organisation, while I manage the writers, directors, actors and designers whose attachment to the theatre is more intermittent.

"You busy?" I ask.

"Board papers," he says.

Nick has an encompassing grasp of the National's business, but behind his managerial nous is the student idealist who volunteered at the Half Moon, a radical fringe theatre that twenty years ago was where the action was.

"Still nothing in O3," I say, waving the rep chart, meaning that the third slot in the Olivier hasn't been filled yet.

"What happened to *Oedipus at Colonus?*" he asks.

"I got another letter from Scofield, apologising for being so enthusiastic in his first letter," I say. I would have loved to bring Paul Scofield back to the stage one last time, and for a few tantalising days, it looked as if he would play the dying Oedipus in Sophocles' strange valedictory tragedy, but he's decided against it. "I'm afraid I responded in a moment of euphoria at being invited by you to do it." Without him, there's no point in doing the play.

"How was Friday night?" I ask. Nick has been to see a show at a theatre for which neither of us has much time, because nothing that reaches its stage seems to bear any relation to the world as it actually is.

"Entirely self-referential," he says, "ridiculous." We spend ten satisfying minutes slagging off stuff we don't like.

I leave his office and go down the corridor to the casting office and catch up on which actors have accepted our offers, and which have turned us down. Then I move on to the literary office, where the shelves groan with thousands of scripts, arranged alphabetically by author from Aeschylus to Zweig: old plays we've done, plays we might do, successive drafts of new plays that we've commissioned. I ask whether the play we're expecting from a young writer we all admire has come in yet. It hasn't, which makes me even more nervous about the gaps in the chart. Then everyone tells me what shows they've seen over the weekend, and we do some more slagging off.

"There's a meet-and-greet in Rehearsal Room 2 at ten o'clock," says my assistant Niamh Dilworth when I return to my office. On the first day of rehearsals for a new show, the acting company and the creative team gather to meet colleagues from every department in the National: stage crew, lighting, props, costume, front of house, marketing. As I go downstairs, there's an announcement on the tannoy. "Would the darlings on the Lyttelton crew please go to the stage?" Linda Tolhurst at stage door has discovered that English National Opera has issued new guidelines to its staff about acceptable forms of theatrical address, and darling isn't one of them. She is now like a dog with a bone.

In Rehearsal Room 2, the stage managers have marked the outlines of the set for the new show on the floor. The sixty people who have gathered for the meet-and-greet hover on the edges of the mark-out, as if it would bring bad luck to step into it. Everyone gathers in a large circle. It's my job to welcome the new company of actors, the director, the designers, and the playwright if the play is new, though this morning's playwright is Henrik Ibsen. I say how excited we are to be working with them, which is always true. It's even truer today, as this show is the first to be directed at the National by Marianne Elliott, whose work has bowled me over at the Royal Exchange Theatre in Manchester. Marianne addresses the circle; she's inspiring, and staggeringly well prepared. I'm already looking forward to the opening of the show, six weeks later.

By now, it's time for me to go to my own rehearsal, if I have one. I direct maybe two shows a year (after twelve years as the National's director, I'd done twenty-six). But if I'm not in rehearsal, I go back up to the office.

"Could Nick Hytner call extension 3232? Thank you, darling," says Linda on the tannoy, as I climb the stairs. 3232 is Lucinda Morrison, head of press. Lucinda and I go to the ballet together when she isn't quietly feeding the arts press the stories we want them to tell, but this morning she says the *Daily Telegraph* is after 1,500 words about why the government should support the arts. "But I've written that piece at least fourteen times already," I say. Lucinda says I haven't written it for the *Telegraph* yet, and the case can't be made often enough. I say I'll write it as soon as I can.

Beneath my window, a saxophonist has started to play "Moon River" very badly to the passers-by on the South Bank. He will keep this up all day, every day, until the day I leave. Another of the stage managers puts her head around the door. I rely on them to be my moles: if there's trouble in rehearsal, I want to know. In Rehearsal Room Three, a director and a playwright are locking horns. I'll talk to the director later, and I'll probably take the playwright's side in whatever tussle they're having, because in the end, it's her play.

I pull up the weekend's show reports on my computer screen.

They include box-office results for our shows at the National, in the West End and on tour, as well as anything that struck the stage managers as noteworthy. In the Olivier, "the understudy was excellent as the Fish Woman this afternoon but the Gypsy was very late on as he was in the wrong place and couldn't find his heather. We had to cut the Knicker stall."

I have a meeting with a young playwright, who wants to write an ambitious new play for the Olivier; it's an entirely convincing pitch, so we commission it. Then I push through the pass door at the end of the corridor outside the office into the sepulchral dark at the back of the Olivier, to see how the technical rehearsal for the next show is going. It is during the tech that tempers sometimes fray: a show that has been painstakingly created over six weeks in a rehearsal room is forced onto the stage, all its design and technical components suddenly thrust onto the actors over two or three days before its dress rehearsal. I'm in time to see a heavy wall descend slowly from the flies and shudder to a halt six feet above the stage. "Is it stuck?" the director calls from the stalls. I don't hang around to find out: the final run-through of this show in the rehearsal room worried me, but there's nothing I can do about it until I've seen it in front of an audience at its first preview tomorrow.

In a windowless studio beside the lift on the fourth floor, Wendy Spon, the head of casting, brings in five actors at twenty-minute intervals, to audition for a part in my next production. I talk to them a little, ask them to read from the play, work with them on what they've read. Their lives are an endless parade of rejection; directors sit safely in judgement, though very few of us are wiser or more expert than the actors we judge. A candidate walks into a room, and often if she doesn't look right, she's finished before she's opened her mouth. She's a victim, maybe, of the director's lack of imagination. He wants someone stockier, or brasher, or more like Julia Roberts.

Some of the actors this morning, all of them men in their twenties, can't conceal their nerves: as they read, their eyes keep darting towards me as they try to work out whether they're hitting the target. They give it everything they've got under the harsh fluorescent lights, but four of them are simply wrong for the part: I probably haven't described accurately enough to Wendy what I'm looking for, or maybe I'm only discovering the part through seeing it done by good actors who don't nail it. So the audition process is constructive for me, but a painful injustice for the four actors. I've seen the fifth on stage in another show, so I'm eager to meet him, which could be why he's the first who seems not to care what impression he makes. His name is Rory Kinnear, and when he reads the part, he's totally immersed in it, so I ask him to play it.

When I return to the office, a group from Marketing are waiting with proofs for the next leaflet. Niamh reminds me that I have lunch with a potential donor. I groan, but Niamh knows how to cheer me up: she tells me that over the weekend, Security found a famous actor up to no good with an autograph hunter in the underground car park. I'm usually the last to know about this sort of thing, so I run down the corridor to share it with everyone else. It turns out that I'm the last to know again.

The potential donor is staying at the Savoy hotel, and I walk across Waterloo Bridge, looping and re-looping a tie. She's American, and an admirer of President Bush. I steer the conversation onto how theatre can transform the lives of disadvantaged young people, and how anxious we are to extend the reach of our Learning Department. The potential donor is all in favour of the transformation of young people's lives, as long as it isn't big government doing the transforming. I keep quiet about the money the National receives every year from the Arts Council.

I return to the theatre through the Espresso Bar, and buy coffee from Jay Miller, who will soon leave to turn an old factory in Hackney Wick into a theatre of his own called the Yard. Behind the National's bars, selling programmes, tearing tickets are an ambitious army of young people who are tomorrow's writers, directors, actors and producers. Back on the fourth floor, one of the production managers wants to see me about the designs for a show that goes into rehearsal in a couple of months. Production managers are responsible for delivering designs to the stage on time and on budget, and these designs are much too expensive. I think the show would benefit from a less extravagant set, so I tell the production manager to stand firm, happy that I can use the budget to nudge the show in the right direction, without having to engage the director and designer in another awkward conversation about why I don't like what they're doing.

Outside the office I hear Niamh fighting off someone from Development who wants to brief me about a fundraising event later in the week. "He has to go to a run-through. Come back tomorrow," says Niamh, whose ferocious gatekeeping is belied by her infectious cackle.

The run-through is in Rehearsal Room 1, next to the workshops, so I spend a few minutes with the scenic artists, carpenters and prop makers. Up on the paint frame is a vast and gorgeous cloudscape. Next door in props, someone is working with punctilious delicacy on a severed head. I tear myself away and go into the rehearsal room, where the actors are warming up as light streams in from the high windows. It's my first sight of a show that started rehearsals four weeks ago, and I'm impatient to see how it's come together. I sit with a gaggle of dressers who are there to work out when they're going to be needed backstage for quick costume changes. At the end, I'm expected to give perceptive notes to the director, who this afternoon is Howard Davies, laughter and fierce conviction fighting for possession of his sky-blue eyes. But his productions never need any intervention from me. "It's great," I tell him, though he's already worrying about everything he thought was less than great.

Jeannette Nelson, the head of Voice, follows me back upstairs to the office, wondering whether I'd been able to hear the actor who has come back to the theatre after three years on television. Jeannette is serene and sane even when actors are losing their heads, and helps them find vocal reserves they never knew they had. The actor was excellent, but I tell her I'll check him out again when the show moves into the Lyttelton.

Nick Starr is in his office with Lisa Burger, the finance director. I slump onto his sofa. "Howard's show is terrific. Any ideas yet for O3?" I'm still worrying about the vacant third slot in the Olivier, but Nick and Lisa are onto next year's budget, so we're soon talking about O2 next year and O1 the year after that.

"And what about the goods entrance? And the rubbish bins? Anything in the budget for that?" I ask, not for the first time.

"It would cost millions," says Lisa, "but one day we'll do it."

And I believe her, because she knows where to find the money, and if she can't find it, she and Nick know how to raise it. I tell them I want to see another preview of the new play in the Cottesloe before it opens on Wednesday. Most shows at the National have around six previews before they open officially to the press, and it is during previews, when everyone involved in a show can gauge how it connects with an audience, that much of the most valuable work is done. Scenes are cut or rewritten, performances are adjusted, sound and lighting improved. So Lisa, Nick and I go down to the canteen to grab something to eat with the actors, ushers, dressers and technicians. The neighbouring building is deserted: everyone has left work to play with their children, argue with their partners or watch TV. At the National, we're fuelling up for the evening shows.

The play in the Cottesloe has much improved, so I have a cheerful drink with its cast in the green room, where in defiance of puritan good sense there's still a bar, though the days when the actors downed a few pints before going on stage are long gone. And although some of them are starting to fret about the last train home, none of us would swap our lives with the office workers' next door.

I can remember day after day like this, though maybe I'm merging many Mondays into one, as I kept no diary, and this book isn't an exhaustive account of what happened when. But I spent twelve years as director of the National, thinking about what to put on its stages, about what made an evening in the theatre good and about what was good about the theatre. And I rarely thought alone. I talked, my colleagues talked back, they shaped my thoughts, and they allowed me to tell them their ideas were terrible knowing that ten minutes later I'd play back to them the same ideas as my own. If a lot of what follows is the result of grand larceny, I stole from the best, and the balancing act I will never be able to perform is the one that does justice to how much I enjoyed it.

PART ONE

Set-up

National Identity

2001

At university, I realised I couldn't write and I couldn't act. I could time a laugh, though not always appropriately. As a tyrannical general in *The Queen and the Rebels,* an intense play by Ugo Betti, I brought the house down, to the despair of the director. There were legions of mediocre writers and actors in Cambridge, eager to insert themselves into the student theatre scene by calling themselves directors. That's all you had to do: call yourself a director. Drama wasn't on the curriculum, so the undergraduates had it to themselves, which may be why so many of them have thrived in the professional theatre. If you had the nerve, you pitched an idea to a committee of your fellow students, and you hustled them into giving you a show. The happy few were given a giant Meccano set.

In the bar of the ADC Theatre, which was one of the many places you could put on a play, was a signed photo of Peter Hall, the first director of the Royal Shakespeare Company and the director who led the National into its new building on the South Bank. "To the ADC—with thanks for giving me the opportunity to learn by my ghastly mistakes." Nobody taught you to direct. If you wanted to learn, you had to keep a ruthless eye on yourself. Then, after three years, you tried to repeat the same trick all over again, this time with the professionals, and find yourself an apprenticeship. University graduates have arrived in London and infiltrated the theatre for more than four hundred years. The so-called University Wits of the 1590s included men of genuine talent, like Robert Greene, Thomas Nashe and Christopher Marlowe. Among those who bypassed a university education were Shakespeare and Ben Jonson, so it doesn't seem to have been a prerequisite. I was the fifth director of the National, and the fourth who went to Cambridge and read English. Olivier managed without.

The University Wits muscled into a business that lived or died at the box office, and had a hard time surviving if it didn't entertain. They sneered at the uncultivated excesses of the vulgar players, and hit the audience over the head with the range of their classical learning; but they still courted popular success with tales of the rise and fall of swaggering heroes, like Marlowe's *Tamburlaine the Great*. These days, their successors are less learned than Marlowe, but like him we have to reach out to the multitude. The Elizabethan court provided patronage, but not much in the way of subsidy. The queen paid the actors when they performed at court, but the bulk of their income came from ticket sales on the South Bank. When the French and German courts got interested in the theatre, they gobbled it up whole, funded it lavishly, and used it as an instrument of princely prestige. French and German state theatres are still funded almost entirely by government. They are accountable to ministries of culture, and are ambitious, demanding and superbly scornful of popular taste. Our theatre still tries to juggle substance with pleasure. Like the Elizabethan players, who rubbed shoulders with the bear pits and the brothels, we are part of the Entertainment Industry.

❧

I served most of my apprenticeship in opera houses, so I learned early how to manage vast casts on huge stages. Then I directed everything from the Christmas panto to Elizabethan tragedy in repertory theatres in Exeter, Leeds and Manchester. Afterwards I bounced like a pinball from Friedrich Schiller's *Don Carlos* to Alan Bennett's adaptation of *The Wind in the Willows*; from *Miss Saigon*, a musical with its heart on its sleeve at the enormous Theatre Royal, Drury Lane, to Ben Jonson's Jacobean satire, *Volpone,* at the intimate Almeida. "Hail the world's soul, and mine!" cried Volpone, flinging open his chest of gold, while the tills rang at Drury Lane.

Richard Eyre, successor to Laurence Olivier and Peter Hall, asked me to be an associate director of the National in 1988. My memory of our first meeting is coloured by the account of it in his evocative diaries: I was gossipy and opinionated, he was wry, generous and shrewd. I reminded him of Jean-Louis Barrault, which is the nicest thing anyone has ever written about me. But I always felt he saw me more clearly than I saw myself. He made space for me to become a better director, I watched him do the same for all the other associates, and only gradually realised that his manoeuvres were as much for the National's benefit as for ours.

Under his leadership, the repertoire was wide enough to celebrate the gap between art and show business even as it tried to close it. I directed new plays by Alan Bennett and Joshua Sobol, a musical by Rodgers and Hammerstein, and *The Recruiting Officer.* In 1994, when Richard announced a three-year countdown to his departure, I couldn't imagine taking the National in a different direction. He seemed to be running it as well as it was possible to run it; and, no more solipsistic than any other busy theatre director, I must have thought that as I was getting my shows onto the stage, there wasn't much that needed putting right.

So I didn't apply to succeed Richard, and neither did any other of those thought eligible at the time. I'd just made a movie, *The Madness of King George,* so I got myself an American agent, and told myself how interested I was in American popular entertainment. This added up to an uncomfortable attempt to make American movies, though I shrank from the kind of scripts that would actually have provided popular entertainment, and soon found myself directing Shakespeare in New York.

In a significant act of public service, Trevor Nunn stepped into the breach at the National Theatre. He was, and remains, a mighty figure in the British theatre. He needed the National far less than it needed him, and he was unlucky to start in 1997. During the 1990s, government-funded theatres were told to charge what the market could bear. Ticket prices rose, which meant theatres took fewer risks, which led to the mainstream audience losing its appetite for risk. At the National, *Guys and Dolls*, which at the time had seemed like a groundbreaking attempt to redefine a great musical in the same way that we redefined great plays, was followed by a large part of the canon of Broadway classics. They were all good productions, but there were too many of them, and they took up too much space in the repertoire. The new Labour government wasn't ready yet to increase investment, so the National needed them to boost the box office; and in any event, Trevor loved them. But they fed the suspicion, never altogether fair, that the National was playing an unadventurous repertoire to a greying, conservative audience.

Few theatres were able to programme large-scale new plays, so the young generation of playwrights was herded into a network of tiny black-box studio theatres. In rooms on top of pubs, there was an explosion of creative energy that played to an enthusiastic coterie devoted to New Writing, always capitalised as if to emphasise its special status. I was exhilarated by how much the new playwrights had to say, and by how they said it. But I started to wonder why they couldn't work on a larger canvas, and whether new plays could be dragged back into the limelight, which is where they were in London in 1599 and at the Restoration, in Dublin and New York in the mid-twentieth century, in London again in 1956. Now, even at the Royal Court, for decades a magnet for playwrights, much of the most exciting stuff was happening in the tiny Theatre Upstairs, in front of no more than ninety people a night.

Meanwhile, two small theatres had seized the initiative in the classical repertoire. Under the direction of Jonathan Kent and Ian McDiarmid, the Almeida Theatre was mining a vein of rarely performed European classical plays, impeccably mounted and beautifully cast. At the Donmar Warehouse, Sam Mendes was producing revelatory re-evaluations of plays and musicals from the recent past, as well as the classics.

Jonathan, Ian and Sam were all shrewd showmen. They attracted to their theatres actors who would once have headlined a long West End run, but who now gladly accepted a tiny weekly salary in exchange for a short engagement that didn't interfere with their schedule of film and television work, which is how they made their livings. It was all upside for the audience that managed to get in. The cognoscenti who were savvy enough to book ahead were treated to a string of superb productions of fascinating repertoire. The downside was that actors and directors were increasingly reluctant to expose themselves in big theatres: they now preferred to work in miniature. And there seemed to be a real danger that the entire theatre, new and classical, was withdrawing from the larger public, and from the wider cultural conversation. Just as in the early 1600s the English court developed a taste for tiny indoor theatres that excluded the groundlings, so a new court was created in the small, uncomfortable auditoriums of the Donmar and the Almeida. The tickets themselves were not expensive, but the only way that you could be sure of getting hold of them was by writing a cheque and joining up as a supporter. The shows were terrific, the audience congratulated itself that it was there, and everybody in the charmed circle was happy.

By 2000, after my dalliance with American show business, the charmed circle seemed like a wonderful place to be. Jonathan, Ian and Sam were old friends, and, still hopping from gig to gig, I was happy they wanted me to work with them. Jonathan and Ian sent me an intriguing new play by Nicholas Wright about a washed-up old actor who trained boy players in the London theatre of the 1630s. *Cressida* was doubly attractive because Jonathan and Ian had become restless with the exclusivity of the Almeida, and had taken a West End theatre, confident that their flamboyant programming and casting no longer needed the protective confines of their Islington home. Responsible for delivering their West End season was their executive director, Nick Starr, who was planning director at the National in the 1990s, when I was one of Richard Eyre's associates. He already knew that he wanted one day to return to the National, and he knew, before I admitted to it myself, that I did too.

᭤

Backstage plays are enchanting to those of us who make our lives in the theatre, though they usually play less well in London than they do in New York, perhaps because show business is a better reflection of the American experience than of our own. "You're going out a youngster but you've got to come back a star," says the director to the chorus girl in *42nd Street,* which is an apt enough metaphor for the American Dream; over here, we back warily into the limelight, ambition shrouded in self-deprecating irony. We're suspicious of the rampant individualism of *A Star Is Born.* But *Cressida*'s central role was written for Michael Gambon, so it was never going to be a problem to persuade the London audience that it was worth their time. And Nick Wright was less interested in coming back a star than in what happens when the new star throws out the old rules of engagement. In *Cressida*'s best scene, Michael Gambon teaches a fourteen-year-old boy how to play Shakespeare's Cressida, the part he played himself thirty years ago, when *Troilus and Cressida* was new. The boy has his own ideas about how to act. He thinks that the old actors are artificial, and that he can do it more realistically. Gambon shows him why the old way of doing things, the strange old gestures that look like so much posturing, conceal a deeper truth. In many of the great stories about acting, the new generation stuns the audience by appearing not to act. The young actor says to the old actor, "I don't believe you." The old actor says, "I don't understand you."

It was the first time I'd worked with Michael Gambon. He's a big man with long, exquisite fingers: an extraordinary combination of brute power and feline delicacy. He looks like he could chop down a forest in the morning, and weave lace in the afternoon. In fact, he restores seventeenth-century duelling pistols, which is only a step away from making lace. In *Cressida,* Michael Legge and Daniel Brocklebank, who played his pupils, were scarcely out of their teens. They pressed Gambon for everything he could tell them about acting. Like the kids in the National Theatre's fiftieth-birthday show, they never took their eyes off the old pro. Gambon watched them from the wings and hung out with them in the pub after the show. "What do these beginners know that I don't know?" is what he was thinking. Good actors never think they're good enough.

The actors in *Cressida* effortlessly reached the back of the 900-seat Albery Theatre. Michael Gambon has the voice and personality always to be in close-up however far you sit from him. In 1983 he gave a shattering performance in Arthur Miller's *A View from the Bridge,* in the smallest of the National Theatre's three auditoria, the 300-seat Cottesloe. I saw it again after it moved to the 1,200-seat Aldwych Theatre in the West End. The performance was still astounding, and the circumstances were preferable. The mid-century classics of the American stage were written for Broadway in its pomp, a great public arena, prey to the commercial imperatives of the box office, but for a brief golden age hospitable to dazzling balancing acts of ambitious popular theatre.

It was on one of these that I had my eye for the Donmar. *Orpheus Descending* was not one of Tennessee Williams's commercial hits, and it is not as perfectly achieved as *The Glass Menagerie* or *A Streetcar Named Desire.* Even so, it doesn't need to be reined in and reduced in scale, but I thought it would be up Sam Mendes's street, and I was flattered by his invitation. Sam was about twenty-three when I first met him, another University Wit, straight out of Cambridge. Even then, he was perfectly poised between confidence and humility. I was at a party with my friend and contemporary, the director Declan Donnellan. Declan, like me, had taken his time to build a career. Here was Sam, fresh from a production of *The Cherry Orchard* with Judi Dench in the West End. "We'll all end up working for this fucker," I said to Declan, after he'd mysteriously charmed us into submission. "Why don't I want to kill him?" Twenty-five years later, I still don't, even after his Oscar and billion-dollar James Bond. We often take in a show together like a couple of old matinee ladies, then gossip over dinner about who's up and who's down in the London theatre.

Back in 2000, he was keen on *Orpheus Descending.* So, to my delight, was Helen Mirren, who had played the queen in *The Madness of King George.* Helen later had no problem playing Racine's Phèdre to a crowd of 14,000 in the ancient theatre at Epidaurus. Now, in front of a mere 250, she played Lady Torrance, a shrivelled captive to her dying husband in a dry-goods store in a small town in the Deep South, whose inhabitants have sucked out whatever was left of her soul. Heat and light arrive from nowhere, like magic: Val Xavier wanders into the store looking for work, a wild boy wearing a snakeskin jacket and carrying a guitar. He electrifies Lady: they make love and she comes back to life.

If you direct somebody else's play, your job is to be useful to it. If you have nothing to say about it, if it means nothing to you, if you think that all you need to do is get out of its way, you end up draining the life out of it. But directors too determined to use a play as a vehicle for their own preoccupations can send it down a dead end where it locks its audience out. When you discover a personal stake in a play, you need to balance your connection to it with your need to connect it to its audience. The better the play, the easier that becomes: the connection you thought to be entirely personal is in fact universal. You sit in the theatre and realise that you're not alone in your terror at the dry-goods store you think you're making of your interior life. You feel the collective longing for the beautiful blues singer in the snakeskin jacket, you let him show you briefly a life on the wing, and you grieve together at his inevitable destruction.

The only thing wrong with *Orpheus Descending* was that so few people saw it. The Donmar was packed, sold out before the show opened. To play it in front of 1,200 people would have taken actors with the vocal technique, charisma and imagination to project without looking as if they're projecting, and Helen would barely have broken into a sweat. And although the show would have lost some of its intimacy, it would have gained the kind of intensity that comes from communality. As it becomes less exclusive, the theatre re-enters the cultural bloodstream. I no longer wanted to make theatre for the kind of people, like me, who were part of the club. It was frustrating that *Orpheus Descending* was for members only.

So I was elated when Trevor Nunn suggested that I came back to the National in 2001. And not long after he asked me back, he announced that his tenure as director had only two years left to run. I started thinking about which plays I should do for Trevor, and at the same time, I finally started thinking about what I could do with the National Theatre. But although I could imagine choosing its repertoire and guiding it creatively, I knew enough about everything else to know that I needed an executive director to do the rest of the knowing for me.

At which point, Nick Starr called, and we started a conversation about the theatre that has still not stopped. I told him about the kind of work I wanted to bring to the National's stages. He told me that he wanted to reorganise how it was brought to them. At no point then or since did either of us feel that our spheres of activity were distinct. I've watched dysfunctional relationships between artistic and executive directors bring performing arts companies to their knees, but I trust Nick's judgement on a new play as much as I trust it on the management of a building. Both of us are strong-willed and voluble. Our social lives don't overlap very much. But professionally, it works better than most marriages, because neither of us is remotely protective of our patch. We welcome the other's intrusion into it.

Soon after starting to talk to Nick, I met with Christopher Hogg, the National Theatre's chair. He was meeting with everyone who might be a candidate for the directorship, and everyone who might have an opinion on who the candidates should be. I warily put myself in the latter category. Chris Hogg wasn't fooled. He took tiny notes of our meeting in a precise hand that matched the scrupulous courtesy of his manner.

❧

Trevor Nunn and I quickly decided that I should direct one new play and one by Shakespeare. *The Winter's Tale* hadn't been done at the National for a while, and I had a hunch that it was a different play to the one I'd generally seen. I turned out to be partially right, which is the best you can ever hope for with Shakespeare, and it laid the foundations for the way I approached Shakespeare through the next twelve years. Meanwhile, I wanted to find a big public play for the 900-seat Lyttelton Theatre that brought the energy of the 1990s black-box theatres onto the main stage: a declaration of intent. If there wasn't a big audience at the National for the raw, sometimes violent, often exciting world of New Writing, I didn't want to be its director.

So I went into the National's Literary Department and asked if there was anything new looking for a director. The literary manager, Jack Bradley, pulled from the shelf a play called *Mother Clap's Molly House* by Mark Ravenhill. I'd never met Mark but I knew two of his previous plays, *Shopping and Fucking* and *Some Explicit Polaroids*: startling reports, frequently brutal, from the front line of 1990s consumerism. *Shopping and Fucking* started life at the Royal Court Theatre Upstairs, the Vatican of black boxes, strictly reserved for votaries of New Writing. It became an unlikely West End hit. The title must have helped, but the real reason for its popular success was that Mark's voice reached beyond the coterie that gathered in the studio theatres, so he was exactly the kind of playwright that I wanted to see at the National. I wondered whether I'd be the right director for him: in photos he looked dour and forbidding, though there was a dark mischief, and a sexy underbelly, to his plays that made me wish I got out more.

Mother Clap's Molly House more or less had me by the time I'd read the title. It was based on fact. In eighteenth-century London there were around forty molly houses, where men met to have sex with other men, wear women's clothes, and call each other by women's names. There was a gay scene stretching from Covent Garden to Moorfields, where you cruised on a path known as Sodomites' Walk. One of the molly-house owners was called Margaret Clap. She and several of her customers were had up for keeping a sodomitical house. "I went to the Prisoner's house," said one Samuel Stevens, in evidence. "I found between 40 and 50 Men making Love to one another, as they call'd it. Sometimes they would sit on one another's Laps, kissing in a lewd Manner and using their Hands indecently." Mother Clap was pilloried and jailed; three of the mollies were hanged for sodomy.

Most of what we know about the molly houses comes from court records of prosecutions for the "detestable crime," which you could use to write a harrowing play about the oppression and marginalisation of gay men. Mark hadn't written it. In *Mother Clap* he appeared to be channelling the celebratory bawdy of the early eighteenth century. Blithely thrusting himself back to the 1720s, Mark extolled not just sex, but the money his heroine was able to make out of it. In the second half, he intercut the molly house with a contemporary sex party. The modern gays were soulless sensation-seekers, and the contrast with the joyful communion of mollies was not to their advantage.

Over the twelve years I ran the National, I was responsible for producing more than a hundred new plays. I admired all of them, but I sometimes went ahead with plays I didn't particularly like. I suspect *Mother Clap* wasn't Trevor Nunn's cup of tea, but he embraced it without hesitation. His enthusiasm was an example I carried with me throughout the next twelve years.

Mother Clap was scheduled to open at about the same time the National's board was due to choose its new director. A play in which a wily old brothel keeper decides that "arse will always triumph over cunt" became part of my job application.

❦

The Winter's Tale went into rehearsal six months before *Mother Clap,* and I was in more familiar territory. I was keen to move on from what I found unsatisfactory about the Shakespeare I'd recently directed in New York. At Lincoln Center Theater, the world for *Twelfth Night* was exotic, unreal and seductive. I was swept away by the miraculous reconciliation of the twins Viola and Sebastian at the end of the play, which seems always in performance to offer a glimpse of numinous perfection. I thought I could capture it in the way the play looked.

Though many of the performances were touching and true, Bob Crowley's amazing set turned out to be the best thing about the show. Throughout my career, it often has been: Bob's poetic imagination is matched by his perspicacity, so he's been the perfect friend and confederate. But on *Twelfth Night,* I failed to perform one of the most basic Shakespearean balancing acts: there is no act of grace in any of his plays that is not rooted in the here and now. Instead, I made a world in the image of the lovesick Orsino:

> Away before me to sweet beds of flowers:
> Love-thoughts lie rich when canopied with bowers.

It wasn't that I failed to recognise how self-indulgent Orsino was, or how lacking in self-knowledge. Paul Rudd nailed Orsino's vanity with the alluring wit that has since made him a movie star. But the production was too eager to match his absurd high fantasy. The play's tough scepticism was present only in theory. In practice, it was swamped by the show's glossy exterior.

I was determined not to repeat the same mistakes with *The Winter's Tale,* a play even keener in its intimations of grace than *Twelfth Night.* In its final scene, the dead Hermione, the object of her husband Leontes's violent and irrational jealousy, is resurrected from the dead in a scene of transcendent benediction.

Except she isn't. She never died in the first place. She pretended to be dead for fourteen years, hidden by her friend Paulina from her husband. When Paulina presents Leontes with a lifelike statue of Hermione that miraculously comes to life, it isn't a miracle at all: it's a scam. None of this is to deny that the effect is miraculous, nor to pretend that the tale the play tells isn't fantastical: it taps into a profound, unconscious longing for reconciliation. But in 2001, impatient with the gorgeous extravagance of the world I'd imposed on *Twelfth Night,* it seemed that the secret of *The Winter's Tale* was that it located the possibility of the supernatural in concrete reality.

It starts with Leontes's sudden and crazy descent into murderous jealousy. In an unexplained flash, he's convinced that his wife has been having an affair with his best friend, Polixenes, and that the child she's carrying isn't his. Some commentators offer this as the play's first implausibility, evidence that the playwright is no longer interested in the psychological exactitude he once brought to the jealousy of Othello. They see it as a problem that needs solving, maybe by inventing a fanciful stage world where mad jealousy coexists with an abandoned baby, storms at sea and "Exit, pursued by a bear." But jealousy doesn't seem to me to require explanation. It can happen as instantaneously as it happens to Leontes, just because. It can be, maybe usually is, mad.

I asked Alex Jennings to play Leontes, and told him I thought it might be a play about the kind of people we knew, in the kind of world we knew, which was where we'd try to find magic. We didn't, of course, know any kings or queens; and in the world we knew, nobody had power over life and death. Every production of Shakespeare asks its audience to make an imaginative leap between what it sees and what the play is asking it to take on trust. If you put on stage, as we did, a marriage and a home that are reflections of the modern audience's own world, you're asking them for a free pass on a power structure more familiar to its original audience; though even in 1611, you would have had to be well over seventy to remember the last time a king of England put his wife on trial for her life.

Alex, Claire Skinner as Hermione and Julian Wadham as Polixenes, all in early middle age, all of them parents or about to be, approached the emotional and psychological maelstrom of the first half of *The Winter's Tale* as if it was something that might happen to them. I asked the audience to believe that a happy marriage in our world can spiral out of control in a second; Alex and Claire brought terrifying lucidity to its collapse, so it wasn't a stretch. Then I asked them to believe that a husband in our world can have his wife hauled off to jail, which was awkward, though it was made easier by the furious incredulity of Deborah Findlay's performance as Paulina. I would return to the challenge of bridging the gap between Shakespeare's world and our own repeatedly during the next twelve years. The solutions can only ever be partial.

Many audiences come to Shakespeare seeking secret harmonies; I do too. But I think he is a less sentimental playwright than the one those audiences want. The apparent resurrection at the end of *The Winter's Tale* cannot fail to move. It suggests another life where our sins are forgiven, our mistakes are put right and the dead are restored to us. Just before Paulina unveils her fraudulent statue, she urges her spectators:

> It is required
> You do awake your faith.

I envy those who hear in this an affirmation of their own religious faith. But Hermione's resurrection is in fact a carefully prepared work of performance art. And after fourteen years, she can't quite manage a replay of what she was before she apparently died. When Leontes first sees the statue, he says:

> Hermione was not so much wrinkled, nothing
> So aged as this seems.

And when he finally touches her, he gasps: "O, she's warm!" The play insists on the reality of flesh and blood, and on the damage time does to them, which I find infinitely more affecting than an exhortation to believe in miracles.

❧

Nothing about *The Winter's Tale* felt like a last word. As soon as I'd done it, I wanted to argue with it. But I headed straight for the molly house, where Mark Ravenhill turned out to be nothing like his photo. Sweet-natured and quick-witted, he didn't bother with the guarded mating dance that is almost mandatory for a playwright and a director who are new to each other. We got on immediately. Some playwrights have written their last word before they let anyone read their play. Pinter, famously, was exact to the last comma. But Mark was wedded to nothing in the first draft of *Mother Clap*. He rewrote it, and went on changing it until the last preview.

Rehearsing a play is an act of imagination, but I'm often taken aback by the range of experience of even the smallest company of actors. The contemporary sex-party scenes seemed hardcore to me, but none of the actors, most of them straight, turned a hair at the stage direction: *Phil is fucking Josh over the sofa. Josh sniffs from a bottle of poppers. There is a porn video playing.* Josh was Dominic Cooper, not long out of drama school. Phil was Con O'Neill. Neither was embarrassed, though Dom was vaguely interested in whether the sofa would conceal the business end of the action. It did, mostly.

In 1980, the National had staged Howard Brenton's play *The Romans in Britain*. In its most famous scene, a Roman soldier raped a young Druid priest. Its director, Michael Bogdanov, found himself at the Old Bailey, the subject of a private prosecution by Mary Whitehouse, the champion of so-called moral rearmament, for "procuring an act of gross indecency." The judge threw the case out after the trial descended into farce: something to do with a prosecution witness mistaking a thumb for a penis. But it was no joke that Michael Bogdanov might have gone to prison.

The fleshy, consensual pleasures of *Mother Clap*, where the sex scenes were actually about sex, had little in common with *The Romans in Britain*, where rape was a metaphor for colonial oppression. But a mere twenty years later, it never occurred to me that I'd be put in the dock, though I had no idea how the National's audience would respond either to the sex in *Mother Clap*, or to its sexual politics. It was way ahead of the game in its delight in sexual and gender fluidity. It seemed blithely unbothered by promiscuity.

"Oh, Ma, I get bored so easily," says the most loved-up of the mollies as he's getting ready to cheat on his current boyfriend. "Do you think that's bad? Am I a bad 'un?"

Debbie Findlay, censorious in *The Winter's Tale*, was now all indulgence, the mother everyone wishes they had. "No, love. In't none of Mother's children bad. I in't here to judge."

Here, if the audience was up for it, was a vision of forgiveness as encompassing in its way as the last scene of *The Winter's Tale*. But towards the end of the play, Mother Clap wearies of the relentless partying, and she retires to the country with a straight transvestite called the Princess and two of the mollies. In 2001, it felt like the play was throwing down a gauntlet: in the new century, it said, we don't just want to love in any way we choose, we want our own marriages too, and our own families.

❦

"As a nation we think we know who we were, but we need to find out what we're becoming," I finally wrote to Chris Hogg, "so it's a tremendous time to be a national theatre." The possibility of rejection is gruesome to theatre directors, who spend their careers doing the rejecting, and I'd never run anything more complex than a rehearsal room; but I thought I knew what the National Theatre should be, so I came off the fence and told the board I wanted to run it, and what I'd do with it.

We talk passionately about renewing our audience; we wonder how we can attract a more heterogeneous crowd. We worry about marketing, ticket prices, image. It all matters, but in the end it's only on our stages that we can galvanise new audiences.

A colony of playwrights emerged in the 1990s, many of them finding ferocious life in diverse corners of their own communities. What they had in common was an unabashed desire to reach out to their audience and entertain them. We must challenge them now to paint on a larger canvas.

None of this is to deny our responsibilities as a classical theatre; but after twenty-five years on the South Bank, it's hard to think of many unarguably great plays, particularly from the English repertoire, that haven't been done here. We've arrived at a place where we can start to trudge through the canon again with a weary sigh, or we can dedicate ourselves to its rediscovery in the context of our overarching curiosity about what makes the classical repertoire speak now.

I'm urged on by the example of the first theatres to make the move to the South Bank, not to occupy a site of national importance but to escape one of the periodic crackdowns by the city fathers on "the uttering of popular, busy and seditious matters." And yet our theatre was never so national as it was 400 years ago: a whole society gazing hungrily into the poets' mirror, an "inordinate haunting of great multitudes of people, specially youth, to plays, interludes and shows," everyone in London having a really good time.

The self-confidence of the Elizabethan theatres was nothing to do with their official status—they were daring, disreputable and sceptical of authority. We share with them an audience thirsty for adventure, anxious to discuss what it means to be part of a society that's in a state of permanent reinvention, and looking for a really good time.

This was fine as far as it went, and the rest of this story is bound to reveal a shortfall between the intention and the execution. But even as I sat down to write it, I was aware that if audiences didn't have a really good time at *Mother Clap,* the egg would be hard to scrape from my face. At the dress rehearsal, around fifty people sat silent as the grave in the circle, so the omens weren't good. But I cheered up as I watched the crowd gather for the first public preview. They looked right for the play: young, funky, a lot of them gay, and they seemed to have a ball. *Mother Clap* seemed to point the way towards a carnival of provocative, enjoyable new shows. Maybe I had underestimated the allure of the conjunction of bodice and hairy chest, but as one molly lured another from the path of virtue, the show struck a universal chord. How wonderful it would have been, everyone thought, to have discovered the ways of the world with these mollies! Or maybe that was just me.

⌒〜⊙

A week after *Mother Clap* opened, I was interviewed by the National Theatre's board. There were five other candidates for the job. I remember nothing of the interview. I do remember that Chris Hogg called me the same evening to offer me the job.

2

Imaginary Forces

2002

At the press conference announcing my appointment, someone asked why the National Theatre's board had selected as its director yet another white, male Cambridge graduate. I came pre-armed with a sound bite: "I'm a member of several interesting minorities." It got a laugh, but it didn't bear examination: I had only two minorities in mind (gay, Jewish), and they both flourish in the performing arts. So I turned the spotlight on the audience, accusing it of being too white, middle-aged and middle class. Furious letters poured in from patrons who had no problem at all with the idea that the theatre should be run entirely for the benefit of the white, middle-aged middle classes, many of them pointing out that I was guilty of being all three.

Nick Starr was appointed executive director four months later. His predecessor, Genista McIntosh, had agreed to stay on long enough to ensure that I had a say in who succeeded her. She knew as much as there was to know about the National, and left us with a comprehensive analysis of what needed putting right. It boiled down to: the current operating model isn't working; the audience isn't there anymore for the traditional repertoire of high-minded classics and groundbreaking new plays; and we're dependent on frequent and uninterrupted runs of Broadway musicals, which are the only reliable way of filling the house, almost invariably with the white, middle-aged middle classes. This didn't seem to her, or to us, what the National was for.

The idea of a British national theatre on the continental model was proposed first by the critic William Archer and the playwright George Bernard Shaw at the end of the nineteenth century. There were many false starts; even sixty years later it wouldn't have got off the ground if Laurence Olivier hadn't been willing to sacrifice his film career for the vision of a company dedicated to the kind of repertoire that was standard in the great European state theatres.

In the absence of a purpose-built house for the first thirteen years of the National Theatre's existence, Olivier took temporary occupation of the Old Vic, a Victorian music hall, its bricks and mortar steeped in the rough and tumble of popular entertainment. The Old Vic was inherited in 1912 by Lilian Baylis, an idealist who was partly motivated by the desire to get the working man out of the pub and into the theatre, where she felt the works of Shakespeare would set him on the path to sobriety. In this she was certainly deluded, but her way of thinking still dominates public policy on the arts. The great work of the past is performed not for its own sake, but instrumentally, as a means to an end. The end changed several times during my twelve years: economic regeneration, social diversity, international prestige, whatever bee was in the government's bonnet, though it was never, as it was for Lilian Baylis, fewer drunks on the street at closing time. God helped her run the Old Vic. She would tell an actor wanting to play Romeo that God preferred to see him as Tybalt. God wasn't keen on actors who asked for wage rises, so she turned most of them down. Despite, or maybe because of, her relationship with the Almighty, the work she produced, without government support, was by all accounts of an astonishingly high standard. She kept ticket prices low and attracted the best actors of her day, Olivier included.

When Olivier accepted the invitation to lead the National Theatre at the Old Vic, he brought to it his experience both of Lilian Baylis's instrumental populism and his own seasons as a commercial actor-manager in the West End, where he'd given many of his most celebrated performances. And he appointed as literary manager Kenneth Tynan, the *Observer*'s theatre critic, to help him identify the kind of plays that you might find in a French or German state theatre.

The National had no charter. There is no founding document that announces what kind of work it should do, and who it should do it for. The nearest they had in 1963 was a handbook, published in 1908, by the playwright and director Harley Granville Barker, in which he proposed a Shakespeare Memorial National Theatre that would:

> keep the plays of Shakespeare in its repertoire; revive whatever else is vital in English classical drama; prevent recent plays of great merit from falling into oblivion; produce new plays; produce translations of foreign works both ancient and modern.

Nearly a century later, this still described the repertoire I'd proposed in my application, though I would have added to it the aspiration that the National Theatre should examine the constituent parts of its title, and explore both the state of the nation and the boundaries of the theatre.

⌒~⌒

"I know I have to start with Shakespeare," I said to Nick Starr. "But not *Hamlet*."

The first three directors of the National all opened their accounts with *Hamlet*, and I never doubted that Granville Barker was right to put Shakespeare at the top of the agenda, but I wanted to start with the play that seemed most likely to speak as if it was written yesterday. In 2002, this was *Henry V*. British troops were involved in military action against the Taliban in Afghanistan. At the time, I thought this was justifiable, so I didn't have a doctrinaire anti-war agenda, but I thought I could explore through Shakespeare what it felt like for the country to be at war. I had no idea, obviously, that *Henry V* would open within weeks of the invasion of Iraq, although by the autumn of 2002, five months before the Iraq War, I described it, in the *Times*

Literary Supplement, as "a play about a charismatic young English leader who commits his troops to a dangerous foreign invasion for which he has to struggle to find justification in international law."

"And there's another reason for kicking off with *Henry V,*" I said to Nick, "and that's ticket prices."

As ticket prices had risen during the 1980s and early '90s to compensate for a drastic reduction in government funding, a huge potential audience, including those most likely to respond to Granville Barker's ambitious repertoire, could no longer afford the arts. We thought we would find the audience to support the work we wanted to do if we could charge them less to see it; but reduced box-office receipts would spell financial disaster. The reason this didn't seem like an open-and-shut case for despair was that, except for the musicals, the box office was already feeble. *The Winter's Tale* had been barely half full. In fact, unless a musical was playing, the Olivier Theatre never seemed to be much more than half full. So we had to ask ourselves whether we'd be selling the other half of the house if the tickets cost half as much. What if we sold one hundred percent of the house at half price and meanwhile spent less on staging the shows? Wouldn't we end up doing better?

And while I wondered how to produce an ambitious repertoire cheaply enough in the Olivier to justify huge cuts in ticket prices, here was Shakespeare's Chorus talking about staging Agincourt at the Globe:

> Can this cockpit hold
> The vasty fields of France? Or may we cram
> Within this wooden O the very casques
> That did affright the air at Agincourt?

Over the years, designers had filled the Olivier with some impressive vasty fields. Act 4 of *The Winter's Tale* was a rural music festival, revellers pitching their tents in a big grassy meadow. The Chorus suggested a different design strategy:

> On your imaginary forces work.

A battle cry for the whole theatrical enterprise: use your imagination!

> Suppose within the girdle of these walls
> Are now confined two mighty monarchies . . .

Suppose. Suspend your disbelief. How much would it bother you if we emptied the stage of scenery, and in exchange charged what it cost to see a movie—say, £10? You may even prefer it: stripped back, the Olivier stage is a beautiful and harmonious space, where you may find it very satisfying to

> Piece out our imperfections with your thoughts.

So how many shows could we do like this? Could we do a whole season of them? If I did *Henry V* on a rock-bottom budget, I might be able to persuade the directors and designers of the other plays to do the same; and in exchange we'd deliver them full, enthusiastic houses who'd be up for whatever we wanted to give them, because they'd be able to afford it.

I couldn't shake my conviction that the National needed to be the big, public alternative to the studio theatres. Its response so far to the success of the superb classical work at the Almeida and Donmar theatres had been to produce superb small-scale classical work of its own in the 300-seat Cottesloe, which only added to the growing reluctance of actors and directors to rise to the Olivier and the Lyttelton. So I issued a self-denying ordinance in the Cottesloe: no more famous classics—new and experimental work only. I stuck to this for twelve years, making only occasional exceptions for plays from the far reaches of the repertoire and *Twelfth Night,* directed by Peter Hall to celebrate his eightieth birthday. I rejected productions that could have been wonderful; but withholding the easy option forced directors and actors to develop their stamina for the main stage.

෨৩

The avalanche of new plays in black boxes all over London made it easier to imagine that we could fill the Cottesloe with them. I asked

to read everything that was sitting neglected on the Literary Department shelves. Two plays stood out. The first, *Scenes from the Big Picture*
by Owen McCafferty, a sweeping survey of contemporary Belfast,
was made up of a succession of scenes too intimate for the Olivier:
it needed twenty-one actors in a small theatre, the kind of play only
the National could afford to do. And it might have been written as
part of the project to investigate the nation that I'd promised in
my letter to Chris Hogg. So might Kwame Kwei-Armah's *Elmina's
Kitchen,* set in a cafe in Hackney's Murder Mile, another corner of the
nation under-represented by its National Theatre. Soon after I was
appointed, Martin McDonagh, whose play *The Cripple of Inishmaan* I
had directed in the Cottesloe in 1996, sent me *The Pillowman.* Maybe
it had less to say about the state of the nation than some of the other
new plays, but few of them pushed so hard at the expressive boundaries of the theatre.

Meanwhile, I pursued some of the big beasts who already had
relationships with the National, pretending to them that I had a
right to be where Olivier and Peter Hall had been before me. There
was an early stroke of luck: Michael Frayn, the most versatile of great
playwrights, as funny (*Noises Off*) as he is intellectually stimulating
(*Copenhagen*), delivered a new play out of the blue. *Democracy* told the
true story of the Stasi spy who worked as personal assistant to the
West German chancellor Willy Brandt in the early 1970s. Michael
is the kind of playwright who delivers a watertight final draft: there
was nothing to say about his play except yes. It came with his regular
director, Michael Blakemore, who was one of Olivier's associates at
the Old Vic, and one of the great masters of the craft: someone else
who wouldn't need notes.

No playwright had done more than David Hare to anatomise the
nation on the National's stages. He now wanted to work with the
director Max Stafford-Clark: they were both part of the pioneering
company Joint Stock in the 1970s. Max gave David a book by Ian
Jack about the Hatfield rail disaster of 2000, and they proposed a
co-production, with Max's company Out of Joint, of a play based on
interviews and research, in collaboration with a group of actors: the
old Joint Stock method. Talking to David and Max, I felt like a frivo-

lous interloper from the wonderful world of show business, but I was growing into my skin, and starting to realise that nobody cared much about where I'd come from: they were interested in the director of the National and the patronage he brought with him.

Many prominent playwrights had nothing cooking. Alan Bennett never says what he's up to, and is always downbeat about writing another play. He told me that he'd try, but didn't sound convinced. Tom Stoppard promised something one day. Harold Pinter proposed a revival of his most recent play, *Celebration,* which he'd written for the Almeida in 2000. I wondered whether he didn't think that, at thirty minutes, it was rather short. Harold suggested it could be done, as it had been at the Almeida, in a double bill with one of his early one-act plays. I didn't dare ask him why the National should want a reheat of an Almeida show, so I prevaricated, and told him it was an interesting idea. Peter Hall could have said no to his face: I wasn't yet up to it.

Several playwrights accepted a commission for the Olivier and Lyttelton theatres, but none of them would have anything ready for 2003. A major plank of my platform—the promise to lure the new generation of playwrights into the big theatres—was looking shaky. I was apprehensive about an invitation from a group of eight young playwrights called the Monsterists: I assumed from their title that they'd asked me along to rough me up. They said their objective was to encourage theatres to produce monster new plays, which I told them was my objective too. Why should Shakespeare be allowed twenty actors, they asked, and living playwrights think themselves lucky to have six? No reason at all, I said. Write the plays! If they're good, we'll do them. They doubted I'd put the National's money where my mouth was, but they let me go without doing me any harm. Although none of them made it into the 2003 line-up, four saw their plays produced in the Olivier by the time I'd finished: Richard Bean, Moira Buffini, David Eldridge and Rebecca Lenkiewicz. At least two of the others had plays in the Cottesloe. Job done, the Monsterists have now disbanded.

⌒∽◯

There were no new plays for the big theatres, but by the middle of 2002, we had committed to a big idea to win back the audience that could no longer afford us, and to lure in the audience that had never given us a chance. We'd offer them tickets that cost no more than they'd pay to get into a West End cinema: a £10 Season in the Olivier with four shows, two-thirds of the seats at £10, the rest at £25. Nick Starr estimated that at a hundred percent (nearly always theoretical), we'd make as much money as we'd take from sixty-five percent at normal prices, which was where the National's budget was traditionally pitched. The shortfall between a hundred percent and what we might expect to take, maybe eighty percent, would be covered by reduced production costs, and sponsorship. So we needed a sponsor.

And we needed the actors and directors who could make the classical repertoire feel like it was new. At the Old Vic, Laurence Olivier formed a permanent company of actors. It was possible in 1963 to identify and hang on to a National Theatre Company, among them Olivier himself, Joan Plowright, Maggie Smith, Robert Stephens, Billie Whitelaw, Derek Jacobi and Michael Gambon, carrying a spear. When the company moved from the Old Vic to the South Bank in 1976, there were three theatres to fill and the maintenance of a permanent acting company became impossible. Trevor Nunn tried to restore it in 1999: an exceptional ensemble of thirty-eight actors appeared in six plays. But the world had changed. There are too many opportunities outside the theatre, and after a year, the thirty-eight seized them, and went their own ways. I didn't regret the change: I wanted to create a repertoire too diverse in style and subject matter for a single acting company. Many of those who appeared during the first year came back later, including Roger Allam, Simon Russell Beale, Alex Jennings, Paterson Joseph, Adrian Lester, Helen Mirren, Margaret Tyzack and Zoë Wanamaker. There was a recognisable core to the company, but there was nothing permanent about it. There were too many actors I wanted to include.

A repertoire of twenty plays can't be dreamed up alone, so I solicited suggestions from anyone who understood that it was my habit to dismiss something out of hand before hailing it a stroke of genius

ten minutes later. For the Olivier £10 Season, I needed shows that
were robust enough to thrive on an appeal to the audience's imagination, without expensive visuals: a four-play manifesto. I had Shakespeare, so now I wanted a foreign classic, a modern classic (in the
absence of a new play) and an undemanding summer treat, which
Granville Barker would have thought unnecessary, but what the hell,
I'd promised in my letter of application to give the audience a really
good time. Alex Jennings suggested that restoring *His Girl Friday* to
the stage could make for a good time. The 1940 movie was based on
Hecht and MacArthur's *The Front Page,* with the reporter Hildy Johnson, who in the play is a man, re-sexed for Rosalind Russell. "Why
would we want to stage the movie when we can do the play, which is a
masterpiece? It's a ridiculous idea," I said to Alex. "Because it's just as
funny, much sexier, and why shouldn't Hildy Johnson be a woman?"
said Alex. "And I'd be very good as Walter Burns." "Genius," I said,
ten minutes later.

Over coffee in Soho, the director Richard Jones suggested *Tales
from the Vienna Woods,* a fascinating panorama of pre-Nazi Vienna by
Ödön von Horváth. "Who'll come? Where's the audience for pre-
war Vienna?" I thought. Then I remembered the £10 ticket, and the
new audience that would be able to afford it. "Terrific idea," I said.

Howard Davies floated *Waiting for Godot,* the Olivier stage empty
of everything except a tree and two tramps. He reread the play
and thought better of it, to my secret relief: I dreaded having to sit
through endless performances of it. Habit, as one of the tramps says,
is a great deadener, and over the years I've become immune to their
drollery. Deborah Warner, a Beckett devotee, later suggested *Godot*
again, with Maggie Smith and Judi Dench as Vladimir and Estragon.
I'd have sat through that as many times as it took for Godot to turn
up, but it was a waste of time taking it to the Beckett estate, who are
famously intransigent about casting.

Then Mark Ravenhill reminded me of David Mamet's *Edmond,*
a short, violent fable set in New York. "It's a studio play, isn't it?" I
said, though I'd never read it. When I did, I thought that although
its twenty-three short scenes were all small in scale, it was driven
by a kind of mania, which in the right hands could fill the Olivier.

Kenneth Branagh thought so too, and Zoë Wanamaker was on for the Rosalind Russell part in *His Girl Friday*. So in the Olivier we had a wide-ranging repertoire; we had leading actors; and we had a £10 ticket, though we still didn't have the money for it.

We had auspicious plans for the Lyttelton. Tom Stoppard's *Jumpers* was written for the National in 1972 and had a leading role for Simon Russell Beale. Katie Mitchell, a director whose work I admired partly because it was so unlike my own, was eager to do Chekhov's *Three Sisters,* the only indisputably great play of the season. *Henry V* was lurid hack work in comparison: a sequel to three better plays, unsubtle and emotionally shallow, though I came to respect it far more than I thought I would. Howard Davies suggested Eugene O'Neill's epic *Mourning Becomes Electra,* a huge play for which the Lyttelton might have been designed. Actors fight to work with Howard; it was no surprise that he persuaded Helen Mirren to be in the O'Neill, though that made her participation in the season no less of a big deal.

So far, the repertoire might have come from the Granville Barker playbook. Shakespeare (tick); revive whatever else is vital in English classical drama (not yet, but it was on the cards for 2004); prevent recent plays of great merit from falling into oblivion (*Jumpers, Edmond,* tick); produce new plays (entire Cottesloe repertoire, tick); produce translations of foreign works both ancient and modern (*Three Sisters, Tales from the Vienna Woods,* tick; Katie Mitchell already talking about Euripides). It felt like a serious, considered response to my brief: a substantial balancing act. But pulled as always in the opposite direction, I worried at the same time that it was all too worthy. An evil spirit whispered in my ear: *boooring.*

I thought I had one ace up my sleeve. Back in 1990, when I was one of Richard Eyre's associate directors, I'd volunteered to direct a big family show in the Olivier. I suggested *The Wind in the Willows*; Richard set me up with Alan Bennett. The family audience couldn't get enough of it, and although Granville Barker had nothing to say about children, no contemporary National Theatre can afford to ignore them. But I saw no reason why we should bother anymore with the kind of stories our grandparents loved: there was a stirring corpus of contemporary literature for young readers.

Jack Bradley, who had found *Mother Clap* on the Literary Department's shelves, asked me whether I'd read Philip Pullman's trilogy *His Dark Materials*. I hadn't, but I knew enough about it to know that it sounded unstageable, which was a plus. "Lyra and her dæmon moved through the darkening hall," it began, and as I read it I already fancied putting a dæmon on stage, even before I knew what it was. Later, Lyra makes friends with an armoured polar bear, and who wouldn't want to see one of them? Later still: "her harsh voice was drowned by a million whispers, as every ghost who could hear cried out in joy and hope; but all the harpies screamed and beat their wings until the ghosts fell silent again." I thought, like the tap dancer in *A Chorus Line,* "I can do that." Two children from parallel universes stand on the brink of hell, face down spectres and cliffghasts, watch the death of an unimaginably old man who may be God, and fall in love. "Get the rights," I said to Jack. Philip Pullman had been an English teacher, and knew enough about making plays to be relieved that we weren't asking him to write ours, though he offered his help if we wanted it. I asked Nicholas Wright to make the adaptation; as it took shape through a series of workshops, Philip's ideas were always less reverent about the original than anyone else's. Part of Nick Wright's mandate was to give us a script that called for the exploitation of the Olivier's stage machinery, a miracle of 1970s engineering. It had fallen into disuse, though was lovingly maintained by the National's Engineering Department who toiled underground like the Nibelungs over their gold, waiting for it once more to see the light of day. I scheduled *His Dark Materials* to follow the £10 Season, partly as an antidote to its austerity. It demanded a staging of extravagant theatricality. "How will we afford it?" I asked. "We need to find £1.5 million to balance the year's budget," said Lisa Burger, the finance director.

❦

Trevor Nunn became director of the National a few months after the Labour victory in the 1997 general election. After twenty years of dwindling funding, Nick Starr knew exactly when to strike, and wrote to the Arts Council reminding them of a request made in 2000 by Trevor Nunn and Genista McIntosh for an extra £1 million to cover the cost of maintaining the building, which was granted, and an extra £1.5 million for the repertoire, which was not. By 2002, when the National's grant was £13.5 million, the government had started pushing money the Arts Council's way, and Nick was fluent in Official Artspeak. He promised that a re-energised programme and the £10 ticket would together tackle "the pressing need for artistic and audience regeneration." This hit the target at the Arts Council, who committed to giving us the raise from 2004, and was a resolute partner throughout the next twelve years. But we were still short of £1.5 million for our first season.

When we explained our problem to Chris Hogg, he shrugged and told us that in the light of the promised raise in 2004, we could assume that the board would pass a £1 million deficit budget for 2003. We could view it, he said, as a vote of confidence in our ambition. Floored, I found myself struggling with my inner Thatcher. I was viscerally terrified of running a deficit. We met him in the middle and settled for a £500,000 deficit and a spending squeeze, enjoying the irony that Chris, a renowned captain of industry, was more relaxed about it than we were.

But there still was no declaration of intent as disruptive as *Mother Clap*. And with six months to go, there was a gap in the schedule that cried out for one: the very first slot in the Lyttelton, to play against *Henry V* in the Olivier and *Scenes from the Big Picture* in the Cottesloe. Maybe we could do *Le Bourgeois Gentilhomme,* I suggested: Molière could be a riot in the hands of the right director. Or Bulgakov's *Molière,* that's pretty wild. Nobody was convinced, least of all me, so I took the train to Edinburgh, to see if there was something on the Fringe that I could plunder.

The first night I was there, I went to a show I'd already seen twice in embryonic form at the Battersea Arts Centre, where Nick Starr was on the board. Back in August 2001, he'd taken me to one of BAC's scratch nights, when its director, Tom Morris, used to introduce work in progress and ask the audience to hang around in the bar afterwards and say what they'd made of it. BAC was, and still is, the home of physical theatre, devised theatre, puppetry, immersive theatre, musical theatre: theatre that's made by theatre makers more often than it's made by playwrights. I didn't know the theatre makers anything like as well as I knew the playwrights and I wasn't that keen on the term theatre maker, though over the years I started to use it more often, probably under Tom's influence. At BAC he was like a brainy P. T. Barnum, shouting "Roll up! Roll up!," loud and posh, pulling in the crowds to any amount of crazy stuff, unstoppable in his enthusiasms. I lured him to the National as quickly as I could.

Before the scratch night, he told us we were about to see the first act of an opera about the talk-show host Jerry Springer. Its composer, Richard Thomas, was at the piano. Stewart Lee, a hero of the stand-up circuit, had helped write the lyrics. There was a cast of eight, all of them tremendous singers, which they needed to be as it started like Bach's Mass in B minor, except they were singing "Jerry" instead of "Kyrie," and they followed it with a solemn fugue:

> My mom used to be—
> My mom used to be—
> My mom—
> Used to be—
> My mom—
> Used to be my dad!
> Used to be
> My dad
> Used to be my dad!
> Snip Snip!
> Used to be Dad!
> Snip!

There followed sixty perfect minutes: a garish episode of *The Jerry Springer Show* set to music of astonishing operatic panache. By the time it returned to BAC in February 2002, word had got out, and it ran for three sold-out weeks. The first half was still sensational; the new second half, which saw Jerry go down to hell and host a chat show with Jesus, Satan and a handful of other biblical celebrities, was weaker, though it perked up when God appeared as Elvis.

In the bar after the show, I told Richard Thomas and Stewart

Lee that I'd never had a better time in a theatre, and gave them a list of reasons why it wasn't suitable for the National. The reasons must have been terrible, because I can't remember any of them. I imagine I thought it was so rough and scabrous it would flourish better elsewhere; and with only a handful of singers and a piano, it felt small-scale.

In the Edinburgh Assembly Room six months later, the rudimentary staging was by Stewart Lee. There was a proper band and a chorus, so for the first time there was a big TV studio audience to sing the opening fugue. There must have been 400 people in the audience, but the show felt like it could have played to 4,000.

"Have yourselves a good time," sang Jerry's warm-up man early in the show, echoing the very part of my manifesto that drew me to Edinburgh in the first place. The Edinburgh crowd went wild, and so did I.

"What have I done?" I wailed at the interval. "I'm having the best time I ever had, so is the crowd, and I turned it down!" The second half was still a mess, but I couldn't have cared less. I tracked down Richard, Stewart and his agent, who doubled as their producer, and I ate crow. We got the show, which was as lewd as a phallic parade.

There seemed at last to be a real balance of old and new, of serious and irreverent, of shows that looked outwards at the world and inwards at the soul, a repertoire that took seriously both the "National" and the "Theatre" in our title. There was at least one horrible flaw. Not one of the new plays was by a woman. The National's record in commissioning and staging female playwrights for the first forty years of its existence was miserable. There seemed to be nothing available in 2003 that was immediately producible. That situation changed in the Cottesloe in 2004 and continued to improve. During the last two years of my tenure, there were sixteen new plays by women and fourteen by men. But it took too long.

◈

By the start of 2003, the £10 Season was on the way to paying for itself through reduced expenditure and what we assumed would be bigger houses, but it was a massive risk, and it still needed a sponsor. We thought we had a big bank in the bag, but just before we announced the season and put the £10 tickets on sale, it withdrew. We went ahead anyway, and held our breath. Not all the donors on our Development Council saw the point of the £10 ticket. Some of them worried that well-off patrons would be able to get in for less than they could afford. Short of means-testing the audience, I didn't know what I could do about that. The deputy chair of the Council, Susan Chinn, whose eyes seemed to sparkle with secret amusement at the vehemence of her fellow benefactors, pulled me aside after a couple of them had worked me over. She said I should meet her friend Lloyd Dorfman, the founder and chief executive of the foreign-exchange company Travelex.

Lloyd turned out to be a fervent lover of the theatre. He and his wife, Sarah, had been quietly sponsoring the performing arts for years, and he was ready now to swing Travelex behind a major sponsorship. I was already in rehearsal for *Henry V,* the first £10 show, when in early March, Travelex told us that they were in for £300,000 a year. A week later, coalition forces invaded Iraq, and almost immediately, Travelex suspended all new spending. I couldn't blame them: their business was foreign exchange and the world had stopped travelling. I buried myself in rehearsals. As I staged the siege of Harfleur, British troops entered Baghdad. A couple of days later, after working on the battle of Agincourt, I called Lloyd. "The war's ended," I said. "I thought it might be worth checking in." It was. By the end of the first £10 Season, Travelex had virtual copyright on the £10 note. Their sponsorship was widely imitated, nationally and internationally. A substantial provision of cheap tickets became standard in all London theatres. Travelex stuck with us throughout my directorship and into the next, a record-breaking long-term relationship.

With rehearsals under way and the budget balanced, I felt confident enough to tell the government what it was paying for, and why it was worth paying for it. I wrote in the *Observer* that it would be churlish not to acknowledge the Labour government's impressive injection of cash into the performing arts, but that it was time to ask again what we were here for. I wanted to reframe the debate about investment in the arts, to move on from its supposed instrumental benefits and to find a better way of talking about it.

> We didn't get the hang of it during the lean years. We tried talking the Thatcher government's own language: it made economic sense to invest in the arts because it was an enormous invisible earner, pulling in the tourists, regenerating inner cities, earning back a fortune in VAT, the lot.
>
> Now we've learnt to speak the language of access, diversity and inclusion. We share the aspirations of the New Labour arts agenda. We all of us want to play to as wide a public as we can find. But there is a real danger in a relentless and exclusive focus on the nature of our audience. Performing artists, once under attack for apparently not paying their way, are now in the dock for attracting the wrong kind of people.
>
> There's evidently a thing called the young audience and everybody accepts that it's a good thing. And there's also a white, middle-class, middle-aged audience and it's a very, very bad thing indeed. Until recently, the National Theatre's audience was getting worse reviews than some of its shows. Then somebody noticed some kids in the house with studs through their noses, and the reviews looked up.

I might have said that one of the audience's worst reviews had come from me, but I left that out, and drew attention instead to how difficult it was to attract new audiences because arts education in state schools was so low on the list of their priorities.

> It seems absurd to invest so heavily in the arts and so little in introducing kids to the lifetime's pleasure and fulfilment that is available to them. We are disenfranchising a vast swathe of our future audience, and it isn't fair on them. They won't all like everything they're introduced to, and that's fine. I was introduced at school to all sorts of things I hated, football for a start. It's not compulsory to like classical music, theatre,

or dance, but unless their mysteries are uncovered, you don't stand a chance of deciding for yourself. Our schools deserve to have returned to them the wherewithal to give their kids space to discover their souls.

Twelve years later, drama and music teachers were a vanishing species in state schools. In 2015, the Education Secretary advised teenagers against studying the arts and humanities, "which will hold them back for the rest of their lives." But in 2003, I didn't feel like I was swimming against the tide when I moved into a major key and sang about art's intrinsic value, building to my standard feel-good climax.

The best reason for the state to help pay for art is because a vibrant society thrives on self-examination. Simply, it's more exciting and fulfilling to live in a society actively engaged in wondering what's beautiful and what's truthful. The healthy state builds not just monuments, but the resources for its citizens to discover for themselves values that transcend the marketplace, and to have a really good time.

3

A Really Good Time

2003

Giving the audience a good time must have been high on Shakespeare's agenda when he wrote *Henry V.* At least three other Henry V plays ran in London during the 1590s. Shakespeare borrowed a lot from the only one to survive, *The Famous Victories of Henry V: Containing the Honourable Battle of Agincourt.* He must have known what the public wanted from the Henry V franchise: to cheer the English, jeer at the French, and bask in the glow of "this star of England."

Henry V has often been used to take the temperature of the nation when it has been at war, but its belligerent patriotism coexists with its insistence on the bloody consequences of armed conflict, and I have never seen a jingoistic stage production of it. Still, the Olivier film hovered over all of them: the play has never been more necessary than it was in 1944, when it summoned the country to arms. Olivier had to do considerable violence to the text to bend it to his pugnacious ends, cutting everything that tarnished the king, but in the context of the imminent Allied invasion of France, who can doubt his urgency, or his honesty? Responding to current events, he employed Shakespeare as a scriptwriter. During 2002 it became evident that I had to do the same. On 16 March 2003, the day before we went into rehearsal, George W. Bush and Tony Blair announced that they would bypass the UN Security Council and go to war with Saddam

Hussein. The invasion started three days later. It would have been perverse not to play *Henry V* as a contemporary text.

Adrian Lester was Henry. I'd admired him since he played Rosalind in a mind-bending, all-male production of *As You Like It* by Declan Donnellan in 1991. He looks, sounds and moves like a war leader, but brings subtle refinement and intellectual precision to everything he does. The play begins with a council meeting. The king needs rock-solid legal justification for the invasion of France. He's in icy control, cueing the Archbishop of Canterbury to give him the answer to the question that matters: "May I with right and conscience make this claim?" The archbishop obliges him, at tortuous length, with an analysis of the ancient Salic law governing succession to the French throne:

> There is no bar
> To make against your highness' claim to France
> But this, which they produce from Pharamond,
> "In terram Salicam mulieres ne succedant,"
> "No woman shall succeed in Salic land."
> Which Salic land the French unjustly gloss
> To be the realm of France.

There's nearly a hundred lines of this stuff, and the king is as gratified as Tony Blair must have been when the attorney general delivered to him the notorious justification in international law for the invasion of Iraq. The serpentine archbishop handed copies of an elaborately produced dossier around the Cabinet table, and referred to it repeatedly as he explained England's right to take military action. The audience, force-fed by news media on UN resolutions and dodgy dossiers, caught on instantly.

Plays, particularly Shakespeare's plays, change all the time. When Olivier made his film, who was interested in the justification of the cause? The cause spoke for itself, so Olivier cut the archbishop to the bone, and mocked what was left, though he was at his imperious best a few minutes later, when he sent the French ambassador packing after the delivery of the dauphin's insulting gift of tennis balls.

Jacques Chirac, the anti-war French president, gave Adrian Lester an unexpected bonus when, days before we opened, he sent half a case of inferior claret to Tony Blair for his birthday.

A large portion of the play turned out to be about presentation, the king spinning first the build-up to the war, then the initially perilous progress of the campaign, then its aftermath. I kept insisting that the play wasn't about the Iraq War, that Agincourt was a parallel reality, not the thing itself. Tony Blair was not in power through hereditary succession, and the then archbishop, Rowan Williams, was not a member of the War Cabinet: it would be hard to imagine a prelate less likely to speak untruth to power. But as we worked on the play, we gained a vivid impression that Shakespeare was writing for us, now. We lost its corollary: the indisputable truth that Shakespeare was writing for his own audience, then. A serious loss, but not a permanent one: there's always next time.

This time, there was no avoiding what the play had become. On only the fourth day of rehearsal, the papers were full of an address given on the border of Iraq by Colonel Tim Collins of the 1st Battalion, Royal Irish Regiment, to the men he was leading into battle:

> We are going to liberate Iraq, not to conquer . . . There are some who are alive at this moment who will not be alive shortly. Those who do not wish to go on that journey, we will not send. As for the others, I expect you to rock their world . . . If there are casualties of war, then remember that when they got up this morning and got dressed, they did not plan to die this day . . . You will be shunned unless your conduct is of the highest order, for your deeds will follow you through history.

In the safety of the rehearsal room, we worked on another rhetorical tour de force:

> he which hath no stomach for this fight,
> Let him depart, his passport shall be made . . .
> This day is called the feast of Crispian:
> He that outlives this day and comes safe home

Will stand a tiptoe when this day is named . . .
And gentlemen in England now a-bed
Shall think themselves accursed they were not here.

Whether or not Colonel Collins had Shakespeare in mind, Adrian had Colonel Collins in mind when he crouched on top of a jeep to give the St. Crispin's Day address.

Colonel Collins's speech was recorded in shorthand by Sarah Oliver, a British journalist. At the start of rehearsals, Penny Downie, who played the Chorus, ran with the idea that she too could report on the action as if embedded with Henry's troops, but we soon realised that the Chorus, who introduces each of the play's five acts, speaks in retrospect, as a chronicler of the action and not as a participant. And we weren't the first to notice that the action she promises often fails to materialise. It's as if we're given first the approved, spin-doctored version of history, and then the messy reality. Before Agincourt, we're told to look forward to "a little touch of Harry in the night." It's not, as it turns out, an inspirational touch. Nobody "plucks comfort from his looks." He skulks around the camp in disguise, and gets right up his soldiers' noses.

Penny started the play committed to the official version of the invasion of France. Act by act, she became more and more aware of the limitations of her vision, because the action she introduced was at odds with her description of it. In a play that's so concerned with presentation, she struggled to impose her narrative on the truth. At the end, foreseeing the disaster of the War of the Roses, you felt she'd lost faith in her whole story.

Penny was a welcome presence in the rehearsal room. She wasn't the first woman to play the Chorus—Charles Kean cast his wife in 1859—but I'd always seen it done by a man. Penny brought the testosterone count down, marginally: there were only three other women in a cast of twenty-five, one of the hazards of staging a war play. The army trained every day: soon enough, some of them were squaring up to each other, an inevitable consequence of imagining themselves at war. It made it easier for me to accept that the days of hanging out with the actors after rehearsals were over. For the next twelve years, as they left for the pub, I went back through the pass door to the office.

The pumped-up cast did not erase my unease about staging a military campaign. How many of us involved now in making or watching theatre or film has personal, or even second-hand, experience of battle? For centuries, drama about war has been made by and for those who have lived through it. Shakespeare must have spoken to hundreds of soldiers, even if he wasn't himself involved in military action, as he might have been during the 1580s. Olivier was a member of the Fleet Air Arm. We who know nothing, who are required to use our imaginations, are much better advised to find suggestive metaphors for combat than to pretend we can involve an audience in full-scale reproduction.

The Chorus helped: "Suppose . . . play with your fancies . . . grapple your minds . . . work your thoughts." On the empty stage, the designer Tim Hatley provided, besides the Act I Cabinet table, a few garish reproduction Louis XV chairs for the French court, a wall that doubled as a video screen, and a couple of real jeeps. The jeeps probably gave the audience more help to play with their fancies than the Chorus intended, but they were dirt cheap, and an exciting short cut to armed conflict.

Verbal rhetoric is Henry's weapon of choice in his propaganda campaign. In our linguistically impoverished age, spin is more often the province of the film-maker, though video was still in its infancy as a theatrical language, and my use of it wasn't sophisticated. The king was often on television. He broadcast his declaration of war to the nation at the end of Act I: "We'll chide this Dauphin at his father's door." In the next scene, his old drinking crony, Bardolph, watched him briefly in the pub, before switching over to the snooker. He made his threats to the townspeople of Harfleur to the cameras; in the following scene, the terrified princess of France watched it with French subtitles. As British troops entered Baghdad, the propagandists moved up a gear: George W. Bush proclaimed Mission Accomplished a few days before we opened. We made our own Mission Accomplished video, the king, like our political masters, taking care in victory to burnish his own image.

Henry V seems constantly to probe the gap between propaganda and reality, asking whether the king is justified or wise in going to war. It asks how good a strategist he is, and how much he cares about his subjects. It asks whether his show trials and show executions are right, or worthwhile. Is he hero or war criminal? In the context of the Iraq War, the lies we'd been told to take us into it, and the self-satisfaction of its victors, Shakespeare seemed to be with us in the rehearsal room, demanding answers.

The answers were often the direct opposite of what they'd been for Olivier in 1944. War criminal? As written, the king orders the slaughter of French prisoners before he hears of the French attack on the English boys and baggage carriers. Olivier and Ken Branagh tried to load the dice in the king's favour by changing the order of play: Henry slaughtered the prisoners in response to the French attack on the English boys. It felt like a revenge attack, which doesn't make it any less of a war crime, and I'm not sure the play cares. Henry V is hero *and* war criminal, and he isn't the first or last to be both.

How much does the king care about his subjects? How justified is the war? The night before Agincourt, while he's in disguise and failing to provide much in the way of a little touch of Harry in the night, he gets into a fierce argument with his troops about whether they have a right to be in France in the first place. By the time the production opened, there can have been nobody in the audience who didn't hear the rebuke to our own leaders in the voice of the common soldier, Michael Williams:

> But if the cause be not good, the king himself hath a heavy reckoning to make, when all those legs and arms and heads, chopped off in a battle, shall join together at the latter day and cry all, "We died at such a place" . . . I am afeard there are few die well that die in a battle.

The king's overlong response was no more convincing than the increasingly desperate spin coming from London and Washington.

Just before the end of the play there is one of those scenes to which the audience traditionally looks for a kind of redemptive grace.

After all the slaughter, the victorious king woos and wins Katherine, princess of France. Audiences usually respond with delight to his charm and wit, and bask in the healing atmosphere of romance. Adrian is inescapably charming, but none of us were persuaded of the scene's charm. If you see it from Katherine's point of view, the romance goes sour. It was another scene whose meaning had completely changed. Henry can be played with wit, seductive allure, the whole works; but you can't escape the fact that the victor is insisting not just that the daughter of the vanquished marries him, but that she tells him she loves him. "In loving me you should love the friend of France: for I love France so well, that I will not part with a village of it—I will have it all mine." The king's heavy humour was lost on Katherine. She accepted Henry on compulsion, as the victim of diplomatic rape.

Henry V does not have the saving grace of self-consciousness. He is no Hamlet. But his eloquence has the power to make almost irrelevant the question of his sincerity. Gentlemen in England now a-bed, who today include almost all of us, can still be galvanised by Olivier or Adrian Lester, or by those with graver responsibilities than theirs, like Colonel Collins or Winston Churchill, who reach back to *Henry V* for inspiration. But by the time the production opened, there was such widespread suspicion of Tony Blair's rhetoric, and even of his motives, that he tainted the king by association. So we maybe missed some of Henry's characteristically Shakespearean ambiguity: although he's ruthless and out for himself, he's also the heroic embodiment of the kind of nation-builder that has only recently fallen from public favour. It was Adrian's achievement in 2003 to give theatrical presence to the king's heroism, but the audience wanted the play to discuss the kind of leader it thought Blair was, and I suppose the production encouraged them. Although Henry was brave, resolute and inspiring, nobody trusted him an inch.

Henry V wasn't the subtlest or best Shakespeare I directed at the National, but I never got closer to unmasking him as the new century's sharpest political commentator.

A few days before the first preview, I asked how big a house we could look forward to. "Really good—sixty percent," said a member of the Marketing Department. It wasn't what I wanted to hear. Really good was one hundred percent. When the first preview arrived, I was more nervous about what was going on in the auditorium than what was on the stage. I lurked behind the sound desk at the back of the stalls, watching the audience arrive, counting the house. It wasn't quite full, but there'd been a big rush in the last forty-eight hours from the kind of audience that doesn't bother to book in advance. They seemed new to us, and so was the buzz. Large numbers of them weren't middle-aged. Some of them weren't even white.

Henry V quickly filled up; it finished on ninety-six percent, and not long after, we appointed a head of marketing, Chris Harper, who persuaded the entire organisation that one hundred percent was the new normal. More than thirty percent of the Travelex audience had never come to the National before. For a tenner, they were up for anything: they seemed to sit forward in their seats, inclined to give us the benefit of the doubt. Many regulars wrote to me to say that the new prices would allow them to come more often, another welcome boost to the box office. A few were less comfortable, maybe feeling the theatre was slipping from their exclusive grasp. Some indignantly pointed out that Adrian Lester was black, and Henry V wasn't. Lucy Prebble, the office assistant, put their letters gingerly in my in-tray, and decided it was time to give up her day job, which was a good call. She had what she called a dirty secret: her new play, which opened at the Royal Court Theatre Upstairs in November 2003.

Each of the £10 shows had a budget for sets, costumes and props of £60,000, much less than half of a normal Olivier show. The head of production, Mark Dakin, was responsible for delivering the shows physically onto the stage. He and the designers ran with the brief with such panache that few people seemed to notice that we'd spent so little. And in return for our frugality, we got the new £10 audience, packed to the rafters.

His Girl Friday followed *Henry V.* Alex Jennings was right: he was very good as Walter Burns, and Zoë Wanamaker was very good too as Hildy. John Guare made a theatrical fusion of the Howard Hawks film and *The Front Page*. John's voice is one of the most idiosyncratic in the American theatre and he blows into any room on a hurricane of enthusiasm and curiosity, usually singing hits from the great American songbook, whose most obscure corners he knows as well as he knows the canon of American drama. The American director, Jack O'Brien, knows them too, and knew enough about the British theatre to ask Bob Crowley to be his designer. Bob's costumes, which cost next to nothing, looked a million dollars. Margaret Tyzack, a legend of the London stage, played a fierce old lady in a fur coat that took up a large chunk of the costume budget. A couple of weeks into rehearsals I asked her how it was going. "I love Jack O'Brien," she said. "No nonsense. He tells you where to stand, when to move, where the laughs are. It's such a relief. I haven't worked with a director like him for decades." She seemed so happy that I thought I wouldn't remind her how recently she'd worked with me. *His Girl Friday* played to ninety-seven percent.

There was never any doubt that *Edmond* would do the business once Kenneth Branagh said he'd play the title role. Ken gave a performance that seemed to shrink the Olivier into the tiny prison cell that is the last of the play's twenty-three short scenes, almost all of them duologues for Edmond and one other actor. Some leading actors are in exclusive communion with their public, their occupation of the space so complete that the rest of the company doesn't get a look-in. Ken is the opposite. In all his short scenes, he lifted the other actors. Sometimes, he appeared only to be listening, turning the spotlight on his interlocutor. *Edmond* played to ninety-eight percent, and brought us within a few seats of the theoretical one hundred.

The final £10 show brought down the box-office average: *Tales from the Vienna Woods* played only to seventy-five percent. Richard Jones was unhappy at the National. His bracing theatrical aesthetic, remote from the psychological realism of the British mainstream, split the £10 audience. But although we'd been spoiled by months of nearly full houses, the seventy-five percent houses for *Tales from the Vienna Woods* seemed to be the ultimate vindication of the Travelex ticket. At normal prices, it would have struggled to fill a quarter of the house.

❧

Many of my usual correspondents must have stayed away from *Jerry Springer—The Opera*: they left space for more than half of its audience to visit the National for the first time. Those who paid careful attention might have caught a whiff of moral seriousness in the second half, when Jerry, who has been shot in a studio brawl, goes to hell and is forced to acknowledge the devastation his show visits on the lives of its wretched guests. "I don't solve problems, I just televise them," he whines; and for a moment the show seems to be asking whether television has any responsibility for the real people it devours in the name of entertainment.

But on the whole, the show was a carefree extravaganza, an amoral marriage of trash television and high art. Richard Thomas heard opera in the inflated passions of daytime TV, and he had an outlandish gift for matching them to the right music.

"I've been seeing your best friend!" sang Steve, an enormous Puccini tenor, to his coloratura wife, Peaches.

"What the fuck, what the fuck, what the fucking, fucking fuck!" she replied, climbing the chromatic scale.

"Dirty whore! Dirty whore! Filthy, dirty, manky, skanky slut whore!" sang the chorus in gorgeous close harmony to Peaches's best friend, Zandra, who responded with a poignant solo, as if by Benjamin Britten: "I remember when we was young, we had some laughs, we had some fun, we lived on dreams, we was full of hope, until I got addicted to crack and dope! Crack and dope!"

In the 1580s, the theatres took refuge on the south bank of the Thames, after the outraged city fathers expelled them because they gave vent to forces that the authorities, spiritual and temporal, preferred to suppress. In 2003, *Jerry Springer—The Opera* was rude, disreputable and exhilarating in a way that would once have had its creators thrown into jail, but now the authorities helped pay for the theatre that staged it.

Jerry Springer and the £10 Season promised a new kind of National Theatre to a new audience. I worried in the *Observer* at the beginning of the year about judging "the success of an artistic enterprise by its ability to pull in an Officially Approved Crowd." We discovered in 2003 that the crowd follows the show, so a wide-ranging programme brings in a wide-ranging crowd. Who cares if they don't all come at the same time? For the audience that shunned *Jerry Springer* we had *Three Sisters* and *Mourning Becomes Electra,* substantial, serious productions of the kind of play that the National has always served well. On the page, *Mourning Becomes Electra* feels overripe, a kind of high-class soap opera, but Howard Davies faced down its melodramatic excesses partly by taking them entirely seriously, partly by sniffing out every opportunity the play gives its actors for self-lacerating irony. Helen Mirren, its red-hot centre, knew when to allow laughter as an escape valve. At four and a half hours, even though heavily cut, *Mourning Becomes Electra* feels in retrospect like the blueprint for the massive cycles of violence and recrimination that started to dominate long-form television a few years later, a step only from *Breaking Bad.*

Although an avalanche of trouble was about to be triggered in the Olivier, there was no less of an appetite for new plays in the Cottesloe than there was for £10 classics. In *Elmina's Kitchen,* Kwame Kwei-Armah wanted to ask questions about what was happening to his own children's generation. Elmina's Kitchen is a "one notch above tacky" West Indian takeaway run by an ex-boxer, Deli, whose son, Ashley, has started to deal drugs. "I wanna do big tings with my life." The dialogue swings from north London to full-on Jamaican patois. "Oh God, dem catch me again, I could kill a bloodclaat man tonight."

Deli was Paterson Joseph, a classical actor of massive presence, who brought tragic weight to a play that was fierce, funny and terrifying. But he was as aware as everyone else that it would be pointless to put a new community onto the National's stage and then betray it by softening its contours to make it accessible for a National Theatre audience, to whom much of the dialogue wouldn't be immediately comprehensible. White people, like me, would get it more easily in the company of people who got every word of it. And it was in any event way past time for the people who got every word of it to find out about their National Theatre.

There's an audience that will come to anything at the National, voracious for whatever it throws at them. But there's also an audience that expects everything to conform to its expectations of what the National Theatre should be. We had to develop a way of communicating in code when we described a play to them in the rep leaflet. "Experimental" was a useful turn-off. "Foul-mouthed" became less of an issue as the years passed. But most of the people who saw *Elmina's Kitchen* were those who hung out at joints like Elmina's Kitchen, which were the focus of much of our marketing. It didn't hurt that Kwame, who was then also an actor, had just come off a long stint on *Casualty*, and was a celebrity contestant in *Comic Relief Does Fame Academy*. Whatever packs them in.

The first preview audience for Michael Frayn's *Democracy* spotted him in the auditorium, and stood and applauded him at the end, a few of them shouting "Author! Author!" which I thought only happened in the movies. They looked a little sheepish about making an exhibition of themselves, but they knew their man, and had come with high expectations. *Democracy* grew in part, as Michael wrote in its postscript, from "an achievement at which I never cease to marvel or to be moved," that from the utter desolation of 1945, the citizens of West Germany "constructed one of the most prosperous, stable and decent states in Europe." In Michael Blakemore's production, the workings of the West German political system were as intoxicating as musical comedy.

After the first run-through of *The Pillowman* I told Martin McDonagh that it was the best play he'd ever written. "No, it's the best play anyone has ever written," he said. It was a joke, but as with all Martin's jokes, you could only just tell. He's an urbane and seductive collaborator, nothing like you'd expect from the cruelty of his humour. *The Pillowman* is sustained by a genuinely tragic vision of blighted lives that are, in a gathering storm of theatrical invention, redeemed by art. It's full of stories. One of them, mentioned only in passing, is called "The Shakespeare Room": "Old Shakespeare with the little black pygmy lady in a box, gives her a stab with a stick every time he wants a new play wrote." In the full version of the story, which Martin told me years earlier, the pygmy, who writes all Shakespeare's plays because he couldn't have written them all by himself, is fed up with writing to order. She writes the play she wants to write in her own blood on the walls of the box where Shakespeare keeps her locked up. It's the best play ever written, better by far than any of the ones she gives to Shakespeare when he stabs her with a stick. I can't remember how, but at the end of the story the pygmy dies, and the box with the world's best play goes up in flames, so nobody ever gets to read it. Maybe Shakespeare's relationship with the pygmy in the box is Martin's relationship with his own imagination. Somewhere, smeared in blood on the inside, is the best play ever written. I hope he keeps trying to write it.

The Pillowman ended up on Broadway, and has since been produced by theatre companies all over the world. Three more of the first six Cottesloe productions went on to play to much bigger audiences: *Elmina's Kitchen* in the West End, *Democracy* in the Lyttelton and later in the West End, and David Hare's *The Permanent Way* in the Lyttelton. Most of the new stuff got onto the main stage after all.

In the autumn, we came close to nemesis. As big as it was, it was still an act of reckless folly to try to cram *His Dark Materials* onto the Olivier stage. The three novels come in at 1,300 pages. Milton's *Paradise Lost* is their inspiration, and Philip Pullman outdoes Milton in the wild fantasy of his imagination. Squeezing his trilogy into two three-hour plays was like pouring a petrol station into a pint pot.

The novels use string theory as a launch pad, and travel across multiple universes. The two heroes are twelve: Lyra Belacqua, from Jordan College, Oxford, in a universe where every human is accompanied from birth by an animal dæmon; and Will Coulter, from an Oxford housing estate in our own universe. By the time Will makes his first appearance at the start of the second book, we are so immersed in Lyra's universe that ours seems more bizarre than hers, so it's as shocking to us as it is to her that Will has no dæmon. Lyra and Will move between universes with a knife that can divide subatomic particles and create portals in space. Lyra is on the run from Mrs. Coulter, who is the glamorous mastermind behind the mass kidnap of children throughout England; the children are taken to the frozen north and violently separated from their dæmons by the "experimental theologians" of the Magisterium, a church body that has discovered a prophecy identifying Lyra as a second Eve, and wants her dead. The novels climax in a Miltonian battle between the forces of the Magisterium and the forces of Lyra's father, Lord Asriel, a benign Satan. The Magisterium is vanquished, the Authority behind it expires, and Lyra and Will make love: a second Fall that redeems the first. When they realise it is their destiny to live in different universes, they vow to return every midsummer's night for the rest of their lives to the Oxford Botanic Gardens. They sit on the same bench, further away from each other than the furthest star in the universe.

Which is how we started and ended: two desolate young actors sitting together on a bench under a vast tree, in different universes, unable to see each other. Beside one of them was a third actor dressed entirely in black carrying a puppet pine marten: Lyra's dæmon, Pantalaimon. The two shows unfolded in flashback, which helped justify the casting of adults as children: the same two actors played Lyra and Will as twenty-year-olds and as twelve-year-olds. Casting turned out to be the very least of our problems.

I asked Giles Cadle, who had designed *Mother Clap's Molly House,* to do the sets. I guessed that the dæmons would be puppets, though I knew nothing about puppetry. Tom Morris took me to a couple of puppet shows at Battersea Arts Centre. They didn't seem like the right kind of thing, so I contacted the designer who had made the animals for *The Lion King.* Giles and I travelled to Portland, Oregon, to meet him at his workshops. Each character in Lyra's universe has a different animal dæmon, so we described them all to him, exchanged drawings, and left him to it. Meanwhile, I encouraged Giles to go to town with the Olivier. His designs made full use of the drum revolve, a monumental piece of kit that can deliver amazing visions from deep underneath the stage. Oxford, London, Arctic mountaintops, the palace of Iofur Raknison the King of the Bears, the deserted city of Cittàgazze: Giles imagined these and many more in spectacular detail. The National's technical and production teams squashed into his tiny Kilburn shopfront studio to look at the mind-blowing set model. I was their new boss, so nobody said to me, "Are you out of your mind?"

Both shows sold out almost as soon as booking opened. I had no idea how passionately the books were loved, but I kept quiet and allowed everyone to think how clever I was, though the Association of Christian Teachers was less impressed than the tens of thousands of advance bookers. "Philip Pullman actually sets out to undermine and attack the Christian faith. His blasphemy is shameless. This production is in poor taste," said its chief executive, long before it actually opened. The books seek new symbols for the life of the spirit: they attack not faith, but religious fundamentalism and its pitiless doctrines.

On the first day of a ten-week rehearsal period, the puppets arrived from Oregon. We had no idea how to use them, as it hadn't occurred to me to bring a puppet specialist onto the directorial team. Still, they looked wonderful: translucent and airy. Philip Pullman introduced himself to the company, then went off to meet his friend Rowan Williams, the Archbishop of Canterbury, a great admirer of his books whose faith somehow survived their shameless blasphemy. The thirty actors sat down to read through Part One.

It was during the table reading that I first heard myself saying, "This isn't working." Nick Wright didn't flinch, and quickly wrote something that did. "It's not working" became a mantra during rehearsals. I told the actors I wanted high-definition acting. By this I meant that our priority would be vivid storytelling, and that most of them would have very little time to establish the several characters they each were playing, so they'd need to present them in primary colours. It also turned out to mean that I'd scheduled too little time to work with them in detail on their performances, so the best they often got from me was: "That isn't working." And before they had time to ask what would work, I'd be buried in the script with Nick Wright trying to untangle some narrative knot, or running off with the technical team to work out how to get from the streets of London to the frozen north via a rusty old ship without a ten-minute pause between each scene.

At the still centre of the storm were three young actors who had been at drama school together. Anna Maxwell Martin as Lyra, Samuel Barnett as her dæmon and Dominic Cooper as Will were all LAMDA alumni. They forced me to carve out time for them, partly because almost alone in the company they were having a ball, so it was possible to have fun with them. Everyone else was sweating under their enormous bear masks, or learning synchronised witch movements, or staring blankly at their dæmon frog, scorpion or cat and wondering how to bring it to life. Anna and Sam slowly worked out how to be the same person. They wouldn't be hurried into clarity. What is the relationship between a girl and her dæmon? they asked. Is the dæmon her brother, her heart, her better nature, her worst fears, her soul? There was no easy answer: Philip Pullman's dæmons have the power of myth, pregnant with meaning, beyond rational explanation. By exploring every possibility, trying everything, taking their time, Anna and Sam went beyond high definition into something suggestive of a rich inner life. The same happened between Anna and Dom: you watched them grow up together.

Mrs. Coulter was Patricia Hodge and Lord Asriel was Timothy Dalton, and their inherent authority gave them instant access to the commanding heights of Philip Pullman's many worlds, Patricia bringing to them the cold allure of Marlene Dietrich. As experienced as they were, they were still surprised when after only three weeks I announced a run-through of Part One. After four turgid hours, while everyone else queued up for coffee, two members of the cast sat weeping in opposite corners of the rehearsal room.

"It wasn't that bad. What's wrong with them?" I asked Aletta Collins, the associate director.

"Massive affair, one of them has a partner at home, won't leave the partner, everybody's noticed except you," said Aletta.

"Nothing to do with the show?" I asked.

"No. But they're very unhappy," said Aletta.

"I've no time to worry about that," I said, and called the company together. "The show's far too long, and the dæmons aren't working. I have to move on to Part Two. Aletta can sort out the dæmons in the next room." And as I started the long trek through the second play, Aletta worked with the dæmons.

"Where did your dæmon train?" I heard someone ask, as they disappeared down the corridor. That was the problem: none of them were trained. Together, Aletta and the actors taught themselves the rudiments of puppetry. By the time we produced *War Horse,* four years later, we knew better than to be so cavalier about an ancient theatrical art.

Halfway through rehearsals for Part Two, Aletta returned with the dæmons. I tried again the first scene in Part One when Lyra meets Roger the kitchen boy, and their dæmons make friends with each other, so they realise they should, too. The puppets, once beautiful but inert, were now alive, moving and thinking as extensions of the actors who manipulated them. Russell Tovey as Roger was so delighted with his dæmon that he went on playing with her long after the focus of scene had moved elsewhere. "Russell, stop being so interesting," I snapped at him, which by then was the best most of the actors were getting from me.

When we moved into the Olivier, Giles's sets were magnificent, but I had underestimated how long it would take to get the drum revolve working again after years of neglect. The technical rehearsal kept grinding to a halt.

"Why are we waiting?" I would call from the auditorium. "How long will it take? Will someone please talk to me? This isn't working!"

As a young director, I once or twice lost my temper, which was counterproductive and discourteous. I mellowed quickly. As the technical rehearsal staggered on, I felt myself unmellow, but as the director of the theatre I couldn't allow myself to boil over, so when the palace of Iofur Raknison the King of the Bears got stuck in the flies for the ninth time, I ran up the centre aisle and banged open the heavy auditorium doors so I could let rip alone, in the privacy of the foyer. I felt my wrist give way, and howled louder than the entire company of witches. I already had a huge sty on my right eye. I was coming apart and we were only just past the interval of Part One.

We cancelled the first preview in time to let most of the audience know not to come, but it was still a terrible humiliation not to be able to give them a show. On the afternoon of what should have been the second preview, we invited everyone who worked front of house to watch the dress rehearsal. The drum revolve seized up after three minutes. Three hours later, after several more unscheduled seizures, we hadn't reached the interval. Nick Starr and Mark Dakin pulled me aside and said we'd have to cancel another show, though there was no time to stop the audience turning up to see it. "What about the children?" I wailed, but they were more interested in the safety of the actors, so I admitted defeat. Philip Pullman gamely offered to sit in the foyer and sign books for the disappointed children.

The next night I took to the stage before the show, my wrist swollen and my right eye livid, and warned the audience that the show they were about to see might stop at any moment. "I'm very sorry," I whimpered. It sometimes moved at an elephantine pace, but it didn't stop, and the thirty actors finally started to declare independence from the tyranny of the gargantuan production. At the second performance their confidence soared. But the following morning, in a piece of scheduling from a hell of my own making, we had to put Part One aside to start the technical rehearsal for Part Two. I arrived early with the production team, and watched the stage crew strike all the scenery from the night before. I started to laugh hysterically. If anyone had given me the option, I'd have cancelled the whole run.

We only just survived. Part Two opened after another lost preview, and not before Anna had threatened to lead the whole cast out on strike because Patrick Godfrey, the oldest actor on stage, got stuck behind a moving tree and was almost flattened.

Meanwhile, every time there was a break, the young actor playing Brother Jasper came quietly to the front of the stage to run through his long, sinister address to the Magisterium. He was straight out of RADA, and there was nothing I hadn't thrown at him: he was a stolen child, a gyptian, an armoured bear, a dæmon goose, a witch in a long black wig and silk skirt. Brother Jasper was his big moment, and I'd hardly had time to notice how good he was. "This kid is mesmerising," I whispered to Aletta, who already knew. Not long afterwards he told me that he'd been asked by Trevor Nunn to play Hamlet at the Old Vic. Trevor's not lost his touch, I thought, and Ben Whishaw won't be playing any more bears.

When we finally performed both plays together, it started to feel that it had been worth the agony. The audience, half of them children or teenagers, were completely swept up in the narrative. They marvelled as the drum revolve belched up Giles's mind-boggling visions, and took to their hearts the intrepid company of actors, who were never better than when I gave them the room to be quiet. "The moon is high. But the clouds are still. Two children are making love in an unknown world," said the witch Serafina Pekkala, in a shaft of golden light, as Anna and Dom played out the old story of the Fall of Man, though this time the story was not about Sin, but about Love. When they parted to spend the rest of their lives in different universes, there wasn't a heart in the house left whole.

"To see large school parties in the audience of the Pullman plays at the National Theatre is vastly encouraging," said Rowan Williams to the BBC. During a platform discussion before one of the performances, he and Philip found a lot of common ground.

"We might as well end by reminding ourselves Jesus was one of the greatest storytellers there's ever been. Whether or not he was the Son of God, he was a great storyteller," said Philip.

"Eight out of ten," said the archbishop.

❧

We brought *His Dark Materials* back the following year, by which time we all knew what we were doing, and I blushed at the memory of the impatient autocrat who had directed it in 2003. The new cast suffered none of the war wounds of the heroic originals. The staging was smoother. We all decided to forget how close we came to disaster.

Writing the introduction to my first annual report as director of the National, I reflected on the reasons why public funding of the performing arts was vital to their survival. At the very least, I wrote, subsidy ensures the stability that arts institutions need to "outlive the vanities and inadequacies of individual artists." The scars of the second cancelled preview were still showing. But I was able otherwise to report ninety-two percent capacity over the year, and in place of the budgeted £500,000 deficit, a £500,000 surplus. The annual reports of subsidised arts institutions generally find a way to flaunt their enormous statistics, and ours grew ever more tumescent as the years passed. But I'm not sure that I ever presided again over a period of such consistent creative success.

PART TWO

New Things

Ourselves and Each Other

NEW PLAYS

It's Wednesday morning at 9:30, and around twenty people squeeze into my office for the weekly planning meeting: the associate directors, Nick Starr and Lisa Burger, casting, technical, literary, learning, music, marketing. We all stare at the rep chart, and we fling ideas at each other to the sound of bottles rattling into the recycling truck on the riverfront below. The associate directors pick their moment to insinuate their pet projects into the conversation, and manoeuvre them into slots that fit neatly into their own diaries.

"*The Seagull* would work well in L2," says Katie Mitchell. She wants the second Lyttelton slot.

"Chekhov would work better in L4," I say, looking across the chart from the Lyttelton to the Olivier, where Howard Davies is directing Bertolt Brecht's *Galileo* in O2. I'm worrying about the balance of the rep: if *The Seagull* plays at the same time as another twentieth-century classic, they may cannibalise each other's audience. But the dates for L4 don't work for Katie, and Howard can't move from his Olivier slot, and we want both shows, so they stay where they are.

"Around sixty performances for each of them?" I ask. Marketing aren't keen on selling sixty *Seagull*s at full price in the Lyttelton, and I know they're right, but the next show into the Lyttelton can't open sooner because its director's dates are as fixed as Katie's. Sixty *Galileo*s won't be a problem in the Travelex £10 season, but Howard always tries to negotiate his performance numbers down as he prefers full houses to long runs. The exact numbers can be settled later, so I drop it.

Mark Dakin points out that on the current chart both shows open in the same week. He doesn't want to overload his colleagues in the Production and Technical Departments, who have to deliver them to the stage, so we separate their openings by ten days. I ask Katie whether she has any casting ideas for *The Seagull,* but she keeps her cards close to her chest, though she says she's talked to Juliet Stevenson, which makes me more cheerful about sixty performances as there are bound to be lots of people who want to see her play Arkadina.

"It's time we did a Restoration comedy," I say. "Anybody interested?" They study the rep chart and say nothing, so I sigh and say I'll take one for the team, though secretly I'm pleased to have the Restoration to myself. I pontificate about Restoration comedies I've seen and read, but they're still buried in the rep chart, so I move the meeting on from old stuff to new stuff, and everyone perks up.

"Where's the play about climate change?" someone asks. "Who's going to write that? Where's the immigration play? Why is nobody writing about the NHS? Where's the Middle East play? The play about what's happening in China?"

We try to wind playwrights up to share our sense of urgency, but most of the time, we commission them simply because we admire them and want to work with them. They pitch ideas to us, and we encourage them to write the play that sounds most interesting to us. Sometimes we say we want their next play whatever it is. Sometimes, we bring material to them and ask them to adapt it.

We're looking for the plays that answer what Tennessee Williams called "the crying, almost screaming need of a great worldwide human effort to know ourselves and each other a great deal better." We want plays that turn their gaze inward, and plays that look outward at the world; plays that speak to particular communities, and plays that transcend particularity; plays that build on the literary tradition of the English-speaking theatre, and shows that subvert it.

We hear what's going on at the National Theatre Studio, ten minutes' walk from the National, next to the Old Vic. It's where young playwrights are given residencies, and ideas are allowed time and space to develop. The director of the Studio has a large degree of autonomy: she brings in the artists she thinks can use the Studio's resources most productively, and she lets me know when I should see work in progress. In turn, I send over to the Studio shows that I think would benefit from unpressured workshop time before they go into rehearsal. I ask how Emma Rice is getting on. Emma has a legion of fans for the popular theatre she makes with her company Knee-high in abandoned tin mines and deserted factories, and she wants to make a stage adaptation of Powell and Pressburger's 1946 film *A Matter of Life and Death.* Her Studio workshop is going well, and we're keen to see what she might do in the Olivier, so we're back to the rep chart looking at vacant slots.

We talk about the plays that are due for delivery, most of them overdue. In prospect, they're all masterpieces. When they arrive, some are bound to disappoint, and we'll have to decide whether to push for further drafts, or tell the playwright that we don't want to produce a play we've been responsible for commissioning. This is always painful, particularly for the playwright, but it's never a good idea to try to force a play into being something it doesn't want to be.

But every Wednesday morning, we beat each other up about the new plays that we want to see, but nobody wants to write. In 2011, we decided that global warming could be ignored no longer. Seized by the project's self-evident necessity, we titled it *Greenland* and scheduled it before we even knew who'd write it. We decided the best way to force it onto the stage would be to persuade several writers to take part in a series of workshops, and divide the work up between them. Four playwrights were hustled into the Studio. Some exciting ideas emerged: all of them might have made good plays if the individual playwrights had been given time to write them. A mother fought her daughter over her decision to become an eco-warrior; a policy wonk and climate scientist had a stormy affair at the 2009 Copenhagen conference; a geographer fumed through a patronising Oxbridge interview; a naturalist communed with his younger self on an Arctic island, and was visited by a polar bear. The fifteen actors were excellent, and the polar bear was amazing—really amazing, easily the best thing about the show. The four writers all delivered interesting stuff but we chopped it up into small pieces, and delivered a reconstituted turkey. "Couldn't we take it off and bring *Hamlet* back instead?" asked Alex Bayley from Marketing at the planning meeting a few days after it opened, paling at the thought of all the seats he wouldn't be able to sell. We quietly pulled it and chalked one up for Shakespeare.

Greenland opened at the same time as Richard Bean's play *The Heretic* opened at the Royal Court. *Greenland* failed to make drama out of climate science, while Richard's play was concerned with what it was like to be someone who rejected current orthodoxy about global warming, and he'd written it because he fancied writing it, not because anybody had told him to. He was less interested in the science itself, which is scarcely disputable and may for that reason be beyond the reach of drama, than he was in the predicament of the scientific heretic. He enjoyed enraging the rest of us. I enjoyed being enraged, and wished the play had been at the National.

☙

David Hare is one of the few established playwrights who is happy to write to order if the order strikes him as stimulating. *The Permanent Way* started with a group of actors, who helped gather the interviews on which it was based. It consisted entirely of verbatim transcripts of those interviews, but it was assembled by a strong-willed writer who knew how and why to tell a story. "Britain, yeah, beautiful country, shame we can't run a railway," was its first line, Passenger 1 announcing that the play was going to be about what had happened to the country as well as what had happened to the railways since their privatisation in 1991. During two wrenching hours David slowly allowed the focus to switch from the causes of the four rail disasters that followed privatisation to the people caught up in them.

The final speech belonged to a character called Bereaved Widow. She wasn't identified, but she was herself a writer. "I've coined a phrase for what we feel," she said. "Those of us who've been through these ordeals. I call it hysterical friendship." Looking outward at the world, *The Permanent Way* travelled inwards, and became as much as anything a play about grief.

David planned next to write a play about the United Nations. I was still looking for a big, new Olivier play, and the failure of the UN to prevent the war in Iraq felt like a good subject. But as the post-war catastrophe in Iraq started to unfold, I said to David that a National Theatre worth its name would surely produce a play about how we got ourselves there in the first place, and that I'd like to direct it. He took no persuading. A few weeks later he gave me a title, *Stuff Happens,* after Donald Rumsfeld's insouciant response to the looting of Baghdad: "Stuff happens . . . And it's untidy, and freedom's untidy, and free people are free to make mistakes and commit crimes and do bad things." David said he'd mentioned it to his friend and fellow playwright Howard Brenton, who told him that the title was so perfect there was no need to write the play.

Ignoring this advice, he started to assemble verbatim transcripts both from the public record, like Rumsfeld's press conference, and from participants in the events that led to the war. He interviewed several major players, who were prepared to talk more openly to a playwright than to a journalist. By the time we spent a week at the Studio with a group of actors he already had some startling material. And it played well. Few playwrights take as much delight in what actors can do with their dialogue as David does. For some playwrights, actors are only good to the extent that they fulfil their preconceptions, but most are astonished by what happens when actors complete their plays for them. They know that their text is only the starting point: a show is as much the property of its actors as its writer. David is no pushover, but he always gives the impression that he can't believe his luck to have escaped Bexhill-on-Sea and run away to the circus. He went back to his study and wrote a history play, much as *Henry V* is a history play. "What happened, happened," he wrote in his programme note. "Nothing in the narrative is knowingly untrue. Scenes of direct address quote people verbatim. When the doors close on the world's leaders and their entourages, then I have used my imagination."

Stuff Happens was structured like *Henry V* too. There was an A plot—the Americans; and a B plot—the British. The tragic hero of the A plot was Colin Powell. Why, the play asked, did Powell not use his considerable power to get the war either not to happen, or to happen the way he wanted it to happen, with a full buy-in from the UN? The barons and warlords who outmanoeuvred Powell would have worked just as well in armour and chain mail: Rumsfeld, Dick Cheney and Paul Wolfowitz were as ruthless and crafty as any of the dukes of Suffolk, Somerset or York. Maybe the play reinforced a widely held suspicion that Powell was as much a victim of the rush to war as an instigator; but George Bush was given a radical reinterpretation. Sure, he had a problem with language, but in Alex Jennings's lethal performance there was a core of cunning that constantly threw off balance those who treated him as a fool. A speech lifted directly from the public record can seem stupid on the page, but behind Alex's apparent opacity was steel:

> I'm the commander—see, I don't explain. I don't need to explain why I say things. That's the interesting thing about being president. Maybe somebody needs to explain to me why they say something. But I don't feel like I owe anybody an explanation.

When the A plot and the B plot intersected, Bush quietly wiped the floor with Blair. Paul O'Neill, Bush's Treasury Secretary, described their meetings as "me talking and the president just listening." David's Bush used silence as a weapon, Alex timing every pause just to the point where his interlocutor started to sweat, then offering a platitude. The British never knew where they were with him. Blair, played with desperate anxiety to please by Nicholas Farrell, chattered on, driven by the success of his humane interventions in Kosovo and Sierra Leone, wilfully blind to the fact that humane intervention wasn't even on Bush's radar.

Opponents of the war, expecting an orgy of self-affirmation, were wrong-footed by interventions in the action by unidentified chorus members. One of them rounded on the Olivier audience:

> How obscene it is, how decadent, to give your attention not to the now, not to the liberation, not to the people freed, but to

the relentless archaic discussion of the manner of the liberation. Was it lawful? Was it not? How was it done? . . .

Imagine if you will, if you are able, a dictator in Europe, murdering his own people, attacking his neighbours, killing half a million people for no other offence but proximity. Do you really then imagine, hand on heart, that the finer feelings of the international community, the exact procedures of the United Nations would need to be tested, would the finer points of sovereignty detain us, before we rose, as a single force, to overthrow the offender?

But David has a showman's sureness of touch. He was telling a story the audience thought it knew, much as the Globe audience thought it knew the story of Agincourt in 1599, and he played like a cat with its expectations. Where was Dick Cheney, the wicked Uncle Abanazar? Why did Desmond Barrit sit behind the Cabinet table, oozing contempt for Powell, the UN and the British, but saying so little? Because David waited until halfway through the second half for Cheney to explode. If *Stuff Happens* were a musical, Dick would have the eleven o'clock number.

Tony Blair? I've read his stuff. I've heard him talk . . .

He knows what he wants: he wants to build some new world order out of the ruins of the World Trade Center. He wants the right to go into any country anywhere and bring relief from suffering and pain anywhere he finds it. And I don't . . .

We don't need him. And as of this moment he's bringing us nothing but trouble . . . It's a good rule, when the cat shit gets bigger than the cat, get rid of the cat.

Des Barrit brought the house down with a scene behind closed doors, and therefore imaginary, but to the audience it had the reek of unvarnished truth.

Twelve years and tens of millions of pounds later, on 6 July 2016, the Chilcot Report into the Iraq War was finally published. David convened a rehearsed reading at the National Theatre on the night of its publication. The only line in the report that I wished we'd had twelve years earlier was Blair's in a letter to Bush: "I will be with you, whatever." But the reading confirmed that *Stuff Happens* got it right, and that getting it right was only part of its achievement.

David rose to the occasion again in 2009, when I asked him if he could make sense on stage of the 2008 financial crisis. "Can we explain to a theatre audience a financial system so complex that the people who were supposed to be running it didn't understand it?" I asked him. Again he went out and talked to the major players—bankers, investors, bond traders, politicians, regulators and journalists— and wrote *The Power of Yes*. One of its performances coincided with a visit to the National of a group of theatre directors from the rest of Europe, who would in normal circumstances have been dismissive of the British theatre's aesthetic conservatism. But they were impressed and perplexed that there was such a hunger for a play that performed a straightforward public service by helping audiences to understand something they didn't understand before they came to see it.

In the hands of dramatists less expert than David, verbatim theatre quickly palls: the theatrical and narrative structure of a verbatim play needs no less cunning than a thriller, and I've sat through too many that simply roll out the transcripts. But the director Nadia Fall wanted to give a theatrical voice to the marginalised young people who had taken to the streets of London in the summer of 2011, looting shops, and setting them ablaze in a spasm of unfocused rage. During the next two years, she got to know the inhabitants and staff of a high-rise hostel for vulnerable young people in east London. They told her their stories, she recorded them, and shaped a play out of them called *Home*. The inhabitants and staff came to a midweek matinee. Most of them had allowed Nadia to record them without fully grasping why she was so interested, and they were elated that they had not only been listened to, but had been turned into something other people bought tickets to see. They cheered each other on as their alter egos appeared: Nadia had persuaded them to tell her what was too painful to tell their fellow residents. No audience emerged knowing themselves and each other better than the hostel residents. We had tapped into one of the theatre's primal functions: to give dignity to the stories of our lives by performing them for each other.

All the best advocates of verbatim theatre are uncompromising in their adherence to the words their subjects have used, but Alecky Blythe is hardcore. I saw a couple of her shows outside the National where the actors wore visible headphones that relayed an edited tape of the original testimony, so that every inflection, stumble and pause of the recorded witnesses could be accurately conveyed to the audience. Both shows had a weird, compelling authority.

One day in 2010, there was a speed-dating session at the Studio for writers and musicians, to set the ball rolling on some new musical theatre; the two who hit it off most enthusiastically were Alecky and the composer Adam Cork. Adam wanted to write the score for a verbatim musical. "It sounds certifiable, but let me know when you have something worth listening to," I said. A few months later I heard the first act of *London Road,* based on testimony from the residents of London Road, Ipswich, and others involved in the fallout from the serial murders of five sex workers in 2006. Adam had worn Alecky's headphones, and drunk her Kool-Aid. He composed music of startling beauty and complexity that embedded every inflection, repetition, stumble and pause into a beautifully structured whole. He and Alecky found in apparently grim material an unexpected story of resilience and community, as the murders brought together the inhabitants of the road where the murderer lived and the women who walked the kerb. It bowled me over. I thought it would bowl over one of the associate directors, Rufus Norris, too, so I sent Alecky and Adam to play it to him.

The show they delivered in 2011 was one of the very best we ever produced, and though I suspected it would have appeal for the cognoscenti only, we had to transfer it from the Cottesloe to the Olivier to satisfy public demand. When the real residents of London Road came to see themselves, they were as amazed as the residents of the east London hostel, particularly by the way their words had been transformed into song. They were more secure in themselves than the kids in the hostel, so they had notes. There was a cardigan that came in for particular stick: the original of the character who wore it insisted that he wouldn't have been seen dead in it.

☙

London Road provoked some unwelcome coverage when I foolishly described it before it opened as a musical about the Ipswich murders. The general perception is that musicals get produced in the West End for money: they're show business, not art. If we'd announced *London Road* as music-theatre or experimental theatre with music, the response from the local Ipswich press might not have upset the families of the murdered women so much. It looked as if we were going to make something tawdry out of their grief. Alecky, whose integrity matches her creativity, sought out the families and tried to reassure them. Still, it was one of the few occasions when I wished we hadn't made the news pages.

I was much more robust about the commotion that surrounded Howard Brenton's *Paul* in 2005, a play that put us in the vanguard of a national debate about faith. In *Paul*, Yeshua survives his crucifixion, and is rescued by his followers, who engineer for him a chance encounter outside Damascus with Saul, the zealous persecutor of his followers. Saul believes that Yeshua has risen from the dead. The rest of the play follows a familiar trajectory: Saul changes his name and preaches Christianity with the same zeal he once reserved for its persecution. In the final scene, when he lies with Peter in a Roman jail awaiting execution, Nero visits them. "Death cults always give the state problems," says the emperor, before offering a sardonic rationalist's guide to the rise of Christianity.

But *Paul* is also an awed acknowledgement of the mysterious fruits of religious faith from a playwright who doesn't share it, but who, as the son of a Methodist minister, understands it. After Nero leaves their cell, Peter confronts Paul with the truth: that the resurrection "was a story." But Paul chooses to believe in miracles, and so, in the end, does Peter. And the play's audience, even the convinced non-believers, are asked to accept the direct link between irrational faith and the power of Paul's teaching, particularly in a spontaneous sermon to the Corinthians.

> Though I command language both human and angelic—if I speak without love, I am no more than a gong booming or a cymbal clashing.

The ghostly echo of the King James translation suggests how impoverished humanity would have been without the faith of one of its great spiritual leaders, even if his faith was based on an illusion.

To many believers, the play's refusal to accept that Christ rose from the dead was neither here nor there. Their faith had survived generations of secular scepticism, and they were stirred by the play's incarnation of the inspirational power of Christian teaching. Most of the offence was taken before the play opened. Its content was described in an anodyne press release about the new season, a couple of the papers picked up on it, and within days I had received literally hundreds of letters, most of them identical and some of them copied laboriously and signed by young children. None of my correspondents had read the play, but all of them were outraged, and they all demanded its cancellation. Some of them were praying strenuously for me.

Conor McPherson's *The Seafarer* opened less than a year after *Paul*. Four drunks hole up in a disgusting house in Dublin to play cards. Through a haze of alcohol emerges a Christmas fable of self-harm and redemption, as steeped in Catholic terror as *A Portrait of the Artist as a Young Man,* but much funnier. One of the drunks brings a friend with him who turns out to be Satan. Another of them ends up playing poker for his soul.

Conor's plays bring the most sceptical audience face-to-face with the supernatural. In hell, says the Devil,

> there truly is no one to love you. Not even Him. (*He points to the sky.*) He lets you go. Even He's sick of you. You're locked in a space that's smaller than a coffin. And it's lying a thou-

sand miles down, under the bed of a vast, icy, pitch-black sea. You're buried alive in there. And it's so cold that you can feel your angry tears freezing in your eye lashes and your very bones ache with deep perpetual agony and you think, "I must be going to die . . ." But you never die.

The family of old drunks see the Devil off. It turns out they love each other, and love is their salvation. As the Devil leaves the house, "the light under the Sacred Heart blinks on. The first rays of dawn are seeping into the room."

I am less interested in plays that mirror my own way of looking at experience than in playwrights who dumbfound me with their conviction and authenticity, so I was as much moved by *The Seafarer* as I was by *Paul.* The National Theatre has no responsibility to be fair and balanced in its approach to anything: journalism is not its business. Still, at the planning meeting every Wednesday morning, we weren't much concerned with whether we agreed with a play. Challenged once by an arts reporter about the perceived left-wing bias of those who make theatre, I should have rejected the attempt to corral the creative arts into categories that are no longer adequate even as an indication of political belief. Instead, I said I'd be delighted to produce a right-wing play if someone would write a good one. Boring scripts poured in, all of them monomaniacal about making some point or other, none of them remotely theatrical. Plays that make points rarely are. A hundred pages that worshipped at the altar of Margaret Thatcher were no more unstageable than the hagiography of Nelson Mandela that arrived a few months later. I turned down both plays because as drama they were dead. Mrs. Thatcher's tedious devotee chose to assume that he was the victim of political bias.

I was always delighted to upend expectations, but for others it was an article of faith that we had an ideological agenda. To commentators on the rebarbative right, we were blasphemous, cowardly leftists who happily abused Christianity but didn't have the guts to take on Islam. In fact, nobody was much interested taking on either, but several dramatists were fascinated by the causes and consequences of their deformed fundamentalist offspring.

Richard Bean was the third Monsterist to have a play with a huge cast in the Olivier: *England People Very Nice* was his 2008 comic odyssey through four waves of immigration to London. First the French Huguenots, then the Irish, the Jews, and the Bangladeshis arrive in Bethnal Green. Each new arrival, fleeing persecution and poverty, is greeted by violent hostility over housing, jobs, religion and culture. In the pub, Ida moans about the French:

> Fucking Frogs! My grandfather didn't die in the English Civil War so's half of France could come over here and live off the soup.

Ida, Laurie and Rennie, two cockneys and a Jamaican, drink in the same pub over four acts and four centuries. They're still at it when the Irish, the Jews and the Bengalis arrive. No racial stereotype goes unmocked.

> IDA: Fucking Micks! Why—if one Mick wants to say
> something to another Mick—why can't he just say it?
> Why do they have to get pissed, beat each other up,
> and then write a song about it?
> LAURIE: Because Irish is an oral culture.

Richard was a stand-up before he started writing plays. He would go on to write *One Man, Two Guvnors,* which had nothing much on its agenda besides wanting to make people laugh. *England People Very Nice* got almost as many laughs, none of them subtle, but it was also historically informed, with a lot on its mind. The same two young actors, Michelle Terry and Sacha Dhawan, did a bravura job of being in love across the racial divide in each of its four acts, and carried much of the show's raw optimism about the tumultuous integration of wave after wave of refugees to Britain. The French get beaten up, their grandchildren beat up the Irish, who beat up the Jews, and most of them end up outgrowing Bethnal Green and moving to Essex to live in suburban tranquillity. But in the fourth and final act, Sacha as Bangladeshi Mister Mushi and Michelle as Irish-Jewish-English Deborah, who marry during the war, live long enough to see some of their grandchildren radicalised at the local mosque. The play asks whether the centuries-old pattern of persecution followed by integration is finally under threat from militant Islamism.

Nobody could accuse *England People Very Nice* of delicacy. Nobody did. It worked like a scurrilous cartoon, the action peppered with projected comic strips. Towards the end of the play, as its tone darkens, Mushi, a devout Muslim, listens in disgust to an animated caricature of a sermon lifted verbatim from the kind of garbage that Wahabi preachers spew out on the Internet.

> You Muslims living in the West, you care more about how often your bins are emptied, than how your women dress. If a farmer wants to judge a bull, he does not look at the bull, he has a look at what the cows are up to. And Allah will judge you!

Satire is in the eye of the beholder. To the *Daily Mail,* the National was still "HQ of the multiculturalism-is-compulsory brigade." For the *Guardian,* it was just as much an article of faith that the National Theatre should never deviate from the liberal consensus. Even a tonal deviation was enough to incite accusations of apostasy, and a history of immigration from the raucous viewpoint of the white working class was way beyond the pale. "Seven people from diverse backgrounds" were sent to the Olivier to record their dismay. Their diversity didn't extend to their way of looking at the world: they were all regular *Guardian* contributors.

England People Very Nice ridiculed racism and celebrated immigration, but acknowledged that it can be traumatic both for the newcomers and for the communities on the sharp end. Richard Bean's voice is simultaneously humane, mordant, hilarious, offensive, angry, and tolerant of any amount of deviation from polite conformity. His plays are torrents of theatrical energy. Despite my sympathy for the *Guardian*'s doctrinal pieties, I preferred to run a theatre that felt confident enough of itself to be able to poke them with a sharp stick.

And confident enough, occasionally, to forget about nuance, ambivalence and balance, and to stick the boot in. Polemic usually sits more comfortably in an 800-word column than in the theatre, but my admiration for the choreographer and director Lloyd Newson and his company DV8 Physical Theatre was unqualified, so when his focus turned to freedom of speech, censorship, homophobia and religious fundamentalism, I was happy to follow.

The National co-produced four of Lloyd's shows. All of them were vivid demonstrations of what first drew me to his work in the 1980s, when he started to break the barriers between dance, theatre and film to explore difficult subject matter. Lloyd is a living rebuke to the idea that great theatre is built on compromise. His ferocious visions reach the stage undiluted. He's fierce even about when his shows go up—as advertised, to the second—and what happens to latecomers—not admitted.

"Maybe we can go up five minutes late to allow stragglers time to get to their seats," I suggested as we discussed the terms of our first co-production.

"It's the audience's job to be there on time," insisted Lloyd, who, though funny and good-natured, isn't someone you mess with.

With considerable misgivings I told the front-of-house team what the rules were. One night Madonna, who is a fan of Lloyd's work, showed up ten minutes late. The awed house management descended on her and did their steely best to bar the door. But they were no match for the Queen of Pop, who faced them down, and walked into the auditorium to watch the rest of the show.

By the time Lloyd arrived with *To Be Straight With You* in 2007, the front-of-house team had found ways of sneaking latecomers into the back of the circle without him knowing about it. The show was unclassifiable: based on eighty-five verbatim interviews, and communicated through an extraordinary synthesis of dance, text and video, it was driven by personal fury at religious intolerance of homosexuality. It had all forms of fundamentalism in its sights, nothing more disturbing than the testimony of a skipping fifteen-year-old from Hull who, after telling his parents that he was gay, was cornered by his family in a back alley and stabbed. The joyous whirl of the boy's skipping rope gradually transcended the horror of his tale, until it climaxed in his escape to London and the ecstatic embrace of his new gay friends.

Lloyd was sufficiently unsettled by what he discovered about radical Islam that he returned to it in 2011 for his next show, *Can We Talk About This?* He collected material from those who had found, to their cost, that there were things they couldn't say. He revisited the stories, among many others, of the fatwa against Salman Rushdie, the murder of the Dutch film-maker Theo Van Gogh, and the demonisation in 1984 of the headmaster Ray Honeyford for writing an article in a right-wing periodical hostile to prevailing dogmas about multiculturalism and its effect on education. "This is Islamophobic shit!" shouted an enraged patron halfway through. He was a plant, but he spoke for a large portion of the unnerved liberal audience.

Militant fundamentalism found a different context in *Dara,* set in Mughal India and adapted by Tanya Ronder in 2014 from the original by Pakistani playwright Shahid Nadeem. It was no less uncomfortable than Lloyd Newson's shows, but its chief concern was the ecumenical Islam promoted by its hero, and shared by the thousands of predominantly young Muslims who came to see it.

> I am Muslim, but my humanness is shared with anyone and everyone. If we choose to love one special person, does it mean that they are the only person worth loving? "To you, your religion, to me, mine." "There is no obligation in religion"—straight from the Quran. We cannot force our religion upon others.

Dara was written from a Pakistani point of view about the Indian subcontinent. More often, we saw the rest of the world from our own perspective, and the double-edged sword of Western intervention was the inevitable focus of many of our playwrights. Matt Charman, a young writer with a priceless nose for a story, wrote the 2009 play *The Observer,* in which there arrives in an unnamed West African country an idealistic international election observer, the embodiment of liberal intrusion. In 2010's *Blood and Gifts* by J. T. Rogers, a CIA station chief goes to Pakistan in 1981 to fund a Pashtun rebel group in their resistance to the Soviet invasion of Afghanistan. Moira Buffini's vast *Welcome to Thebes* (also 2010) reworked Greek myth to imagine a shattered African nation, newly emerged from civil war, that seeks the aid not of the West but of its wealthy neighbour. The wealthier nation's eagerness to impose democracy across the border is entirely motivated by profit: its president can only see Thebes as a "vast economic development zone."

I failed to find or develop African plays about Africa, though Bill T. Jones brought from New York his musical biography of the Nigerian musician Fela Kuti. Most of the Olivier Theatre audience in 2010 for *Fela!* seemed to be Nigerian: Fela Kuti's music brought them almost instantly to their feet. It took the white minority a little longer to follow suit. They swayed politely while the Nigerians partied.

Contemporary voices from the rest of Europe were also underrepresented. I sometimes read translations of plays that had caused a sensation in their original language and found myself totally foxed. Often, that was the point: many European theatres are so heavily subsidised that their writers need only engage a tiny elite, so it can be left up to the director and the audience to crack the code. I thought I couldn't ask the National's audience to crack something I couldn't crack myself.

But two plays stood out. *Our Class* by Tadeusz Słobodzianek was an act of political defiance in his native Poland. In 1941, 1,600 Jews were massacred in the town of Jedwabne. Many Poles, including the resurgent right-wing nationalists who govern them, are deeply resistant to recent investigations that blame their slaughter not on the occupying Nazis but on the local community. *Our Class* tells the stories of ten members of the same school class, from 1925 to the present: anti-Semitism is a constant. Tadeusz, a great bear of a man, felt impoverished by the absence of the tenth of his fellow Poles who were Jewish. He thought their culture, wiped out during the war, was part of his heritage, and had been extinguished before he was born.

3 Winters by Tena Štivičić, a Croatian playwright who wrote in her own idiomatic English, was set in the same house in Zagreb in 1945,

1990 and 2011. The violent tide of history washes through the Kos family almost as fiercely as it does through Tadeusz Słobodzianek's Jedwabne. Four generations adapt from the remains of monarchy through fascism, communism, civil war and ultimately to the implacable demands of free-market capitalism. Like so many of the best plays, *3 Winters* was about a family, and in particular its women, who fight and fall in love as the world seethes on their doorstep.

∽

At the Wednesday-morning meeting, I was usually more agitated than my associates by the size of a playwright's canvas, always looking for shows that would fill the two larger theatres. But the crying need to know each other is rarely better satisfied than in seeing ourselves in other families, tearing ourselves apart. Trying to balance plays that look inward with plays that look outward at the world, I looked often to plays with a tight focus but large ambitions. One family can immerse an audience in the wider Balkan tragedy. A small Cottesloe play about a north London Jewish family might say as much about the Middle East as a big Olivier epic.

When I took Mike Leigh to lunch in 2002 and asked him whether he'd make a play for the National, he said that nobody from the National had bought him lunch before, so yes, he'd make us a play. A grilled Dover sole? That's all it took? Lunch and total secrecy: he'd create it over four months of improvisation with seven or eight actors. Everybody knows how Mike works, so this wasn't a problem.

"I've been thinking it may be time for me to make something about *what we have in common*," said Mike, "but don't tell anyone." His eyes sparkled with merry acknowledgement of our Manchester Jewish roots. Although Jewish subject matter is a staple of the New York theatre, the London Jewish audience has always seemed less eager to see itself on stage, a function perhaps of the anxiety of European immigrant communities not to draw attention to themselves. But I reckoned we would cope with seeing ourselves in a new Mike Leigh play. It was announced in 2005, to great excitement, as Mike hadn't made a play for twelve years. The announcement made a big song and dance out of giving nothing away about it, not even its title. Nothing was more than enough to sell out its first booking period.

Under normal circumstances, Mike would have called some of his regular collaborators, and met some new ones, and together they would have improvised their way towards a play. But to improvise a play about an observant Jewish family, Mike needed eight actors whose shared experience included growing up in a Jewish family; which meant that Toby Whale and his colleagues in the Casting Department had to call all the London agents and ask them which of their clients were Jewish. The Jewish agents could reel off the list without pausing to think. The reply of the non-Jewish majority was usually, "I've no idea, darling. How would I know?"

Most people still don't. But to find actors for the Mike Leigh play, the agents had to call their clients and ask if they were Jewish. Mike brought eight of them together, and four months later he had a play. I was allowed in to see its final run-through.

"Here's my Jewish play," wrote Mike in the introduction to *Two Thousand Years* when he eventually published it: his plays, though generated through improvisation, are scripted by him before they reach the theatre. "All my films and plays have in one way or another dealt with identity. Who are you? What are you? Who is the real you, and who the persona defined by other people's expectations and preconceptions?"

Dave, the grandfather, says, "You're born Jewish. You are as you are."

Tammy, the granddaughter, says, "It's not the whole of me—I feel Jewish, and I don't feel Jewish."

I wasn't the only Jew to identify with a family that feels Jewish, doesn't feel Jewish, eats bacon, agonises over Israeli action in Gaza, and reacts in bewilderment to Josh the son's sudden embrace of ultra-Orthodoxy. But non-Jews were equally moved by Mike's passionate response to much wider questions about Israel and Palestine, religion and social progress.

After the first preview, I was hovering outside the Cottesloe to get a sniff of how it had gone down with its first audience, when a young reporter with a notebook buttonholed me. "Did you see the show?" he asked.

I said warily that I did.

"I'm from the *Guardian*," said the reporter, "what did you think?"

I said it was one of the most brilliant things I'd ever seen in my life, that I was Jewish and I could testify to its incredible insight into Jewish identity, but that you didn't have to be Jewish to be knocked out by it.

"Thanks very much," said the reporter, "could I quote you, and what's your name?"

I plucked a name out of the air. "Nigel Shapps, I'm forty-two," I said, knocking a few years off my real age, not because I'm Jewish, but because I'm vain.

The following day the *Guardian* ran a story about Mike Leigh's return to the theatre. Nigel Shapps was quoted with exemplary accuracy, though his age wasn't mentioned, which was a pity. Mike was even more impressed by Nigel than he had been by the Dover sole. *Two Thousand Years* moved to the Lyttelton to accommodate the demand for tickets, and Mike came back six years later with *Grief,* a devastating play that burrowed under the skin of a 1950s suburban family. Lesley Manville's performance as a war widow so traumatised by grief that she destroys her own daughter was incomparably moving.

Plays about families gave us many of our most involving evenings. At the centre of Lucinda Coxon's *Happy Now?* in 2008 was Kitty, a woman who has it all: a great job running a charity, a husband, two perfect children, a gay best friend. It caused more winces of recognition than anything we ever produced: at Kitty's permanent exhaustion, at the scramble to pack the children off to school, at the solipsism of the friends whose marriage is falling apart, at the mountainous self-regard of her worthy husband as he changes career from lawyer to teacher so he can feel better about himself, at her mother's black belt in pushing her daughter's buttons.

Stephen Beresford gave up a successful acting career to write his first play, *The Last of the Haussmans,* in 2012, so he knows what an actor needs to build a character and land a line. Julie Walters played Judy, a refugee from the 1960s, who has totally messed up her daughter and son, not least by dragging them with her to India when they were children to live in an ashram. Now they join her at her dilapidated house on the south Devon coast.

> JUDY: It's all second homes here now. Fucking fascist pigs.
> They don't want me to drive down the value of their
> exclusive little boltholes . . . This is property. Do you
> see? It's the greatest agent of control ever devised by
> any government anywhere. Get people to care about
> their property and you don't even have to police the
> state. They do it for you. Residents' association?
> They're worse than the Stasi.

Most of this could have been delivered without irony thirty years earlier, when it still seemed possible that the theatre could be a call to arms, and that audiences would leave enraged enough to bring down an unjust system. The system stayed put. Now the call to arms is much fainter: understanding who we are, and where we live, is a full-time job. The tainted legacy of the 1960s generation was one of the play's subjects, Judy's children apparently wrecked by her fabulous self-indulgence, although the play didn't settle for easy mockery either of the nightmare mother or of her values.

Simon Stephens's *Harper Regan* in 2008 sent Lesley Sharp in the title role on an odyssey to Stockport, where she arrives too late to tell her father she loved him. She has a series of bruising encounters with lonely men and a desperate confrontation with her mother. Harper's anger burns as fiercely as anything in Tena Štivičić's or Stephen Beresford's plays, but:

> Harper can't speak with rage . . .
> Harper puts her fist to her mouth . . .
> Harper looks at her. She can't speak. She's shaking.

Simon makes theatrical poetry out of the emotional reticence of the north of England. Like his frequent director Marianne Elliott, he grew up in Stockport. I grew up only a few miles away, in the relative comfort of Didsbury, a middle-class Manchester suburb, but the stoicism and emotional reticence of Simon's protagonists didn't seem strange to me. Simon was a teacher before he started writing plays full-time: he knows the lives he writes about.

❧

Many artists make art about lives they once lived, but it is hard to avoid how little of their art reaches the worlds they were once part of. At the National, much of our subject matter came from exactly that part of our society that feels most alienated from those who come to watch it. And if there was a non-metropolitan bias to our new playwriting, it was because most of the playwrights were themselves rooted in the world outside the metropolis, and their sympathy for it coursed through their work. In 2006 David Eldridge put the whole of Romford Market on the Olivier stage in *Market Boy*, a riotous spectacular about his own sentimental education selling stilettos as a market monkey in the mid-1980s among Mrs. Thatcher's own people.

> Give them what they want. And they'll give you what you want. We were put on this earth to chase women, and women were put here to buy shoes.

Our four most commercially successful plays—*The History Boys, War Horse, The Curious Incident of the Dog in the Night-Time* and *One Man, Two Guvnors*—all gave London a wide berth.

On its stages, the theatre is profoundly engaged with as much of the wider community as its writers and actors know from personal experience, or can reach through acts of creative empathy. But there's a constant struggle to extend the audience beyond the couple in Lucinda Coxon's *Happy Now?* to the kids in Nadia Fall's *Home*. Even Lucinda's couple would be a stretch, to be honest: too tired, and who's going to babysit? They used to go to the theatre before the kids arrived, and they may come back once the kids are old enough to look after themselves, but at least they'll feel they belong when they do.

No playwright insists more eloquently that the arts should not be the exclusive property of a privileged elite than Lee Hall, so when *The Pitmen Painters* opened at Live Theatre, Newcastle upon Tyne, in 2008, I hurried up to see it. "We're bringing this in," I told the planning meeting on the following Wednesday morning, not even waiting to discuss it with them.

The Pitmen Painters tells a true story. In 1934, the Woodhorn Colliery miners in Ashington, Northumberland, want to take evening classes in economics, but can't find a tutor, so instead settle for lessons in art appreciation. Their tutor soon realises that showing them slides of old masters is getting them nowhere, so he lets them paint. Their fame spreads, but they continue to work down the mines. What transforms them is the actual making of art, not its mere presence. One of the miners describes what it was like to paint his first canvas:

> And when I stopped to look at what I'd done, suddenly I realised it was light—it was morning—time for work— I thought it'd been an hour or something—I'd been on the whole night. And I was shaking—literally shaking—'cos for the first time in me life I'd really achieved something.

In Max Roberts's staging, you saw their paintings, which spoke for themselves about the enrichment of ordinary lives through art. They found transcendence in the mundane reality of the pithead and the pub, in their whippets and ponies, in a pint of beer and a game of draughts.

Lee Hall's movie *Billy Elliot* traced the transformation through dance of a young boy from a mining village. Billy gets lucky because he stumbles on a ballet class. The pitmen painters get lucky because they can't find anyone to teach them economics. The play ends in 1947, with the post-war promise of art and education for everyone. "They're not ganna leave yer Shakespeare and yer Goethe just for the upper classes now," says one of the pitmen. Successive governments have betrayed them. Lee Hall, who comes from the same world as Billy Elliot and the Ashington Group, got lucky like them, found a local youth theatre, and went to Cambridge. Because he's a successful playwright and screenwriter, I suppose he's now part of the reviled metropolitan elite, but he has repeatedly made art out of his anger, on behalf of his own community, at the broken promise of universal access to the arts.

Lee's play suggests a way through the constant frustration that too many of our fellow citizens leave school without the introduction they deserve to the cultural riches that their taxes help pay for. Every cultural institution in the country is committed to helping schools not just to appreciate art, but like the pitmen painters, to take part in it. At the National, I inherited the Connections programme, which started in 1995 in direct response to what schools told us they wanted. Every year, ten short plays are commissioned from established writers like Howard Brenton, Moira Buffini, Lucinda Coxon and Lee Hall, to mention only a few of those who have been the subjects of this chapter. Up to five hundred school and youth theatre groups throughout the country choose one of the ten. Every group performs its production at festivals in over forty partner theatres. In 2016, 10,000 young people took part: a mammoth Ashington Group, rolling up their sleeves, getting their hands dirty. A handful of groups travel to London to perform at a week-long festival at the National itself. Watching even the least memorable of them, you can see how confident they become, how deeply they share their writers' commitment to the huge range of subject matter they've chosen to address. Like the Ashington Group, the kids return to their communities. But for once, the playwrights' involvement in the wider community has been returned by the community's involvement in the plays. When they perform at the National, the kids and their supporters in the audience may be more boisterous than the average crowd for a Chekhov matinee, but you can't help noticing that in all essentials, their engagement with the event is the same: empathetic, immersed in the lives of others, passionate, inclusive, liberal. You want the same for everyone. To our incalculable cost, a malfunctioning polity has left half of us behind not just materially, but in the provision of art and arts education.

James Graham was twenty-eight, not much older than the Connections kids, when in 2010 I saw his play *The Whisky Taster* at the Bush Theatre. I asked him what he might write for the National. He launched into an impassioned monologue. "I'd been increasingly obsessed with the hung parliament of 1974–9," he later wrote, "long before the general election of 2010 gave me a handy modern comparison." The 2010 general election delivered a hung parliament and a formal coalition between the Conservatives and Liberal Democrats. But the hung parliament of the mid-1970s? Seriously? I couldn't imagine why we'd want a play, thirty years later, about the stuttering economy, the strikes, the parliamentary machinations behind the short-lived pact between the Labour government and the Liberals. My memory of it was in grim monochrome, but James, who wasn't even born when it happened, pitched it to me in saturated colour.

"OK," I said, "when can we have it?"

This House arrived within months. James isn't a writer who hangs around. He spoke to MPs from all sides of the House of Commons and decided that the real drama was in the Whips' Office. His unlikely chief protagonists were the Labour deputy chief whip, Walter Harrison, and the Conservative deputy chief whip, Jack Weatherill. He built around them an enormous play about the business of politics: exactly the kind of play I promised the Monsterists I wanted for the bigger theatres. I fretted that its appeal might not extend to those who weren't around at the time, and chickened out of scheduling it in the Olivier. I told James it would be better to produce it in the Cottesloe, where there'd be less pressure to sell tickets, and where his whispered corridor conspiracies wouldn't need banging to the back of the house. He looked a little crestfallen, but hurried away to write another draft of the play in response to the notes we'd given him.

First in the queue when *This House* opened in 2012 were the politicians, most of them at best intermittent patrons of the performing arts. But who doesn't love seeing themselves on stage? And to their astonishment, here was a play that, far from putting them in the pillory for their failures, relished the grubby realities of their vocation. The Cottesloe run sold out within days, and *This House* moved smoothly into the Olivier, where it continued to sell out to the extent that a West End transfer was frustrated only by the preference of the owners of the single available theatre for a new musical by Andrew Lloyd Webber. The one person who seemed not to be surprised by the scale of its success was the playwright himself.

James had hung his pitch on the similarities between the Lib-Lab pact and the coalition government of 2010, which turned out to be beside the point. Behind its delight at the surreal wheeling and dealing of the two Whips' Offices was an awestruck belief in parliamentary process that recalled Michael Frayn's *Democracy*. Beyond that was an enormous sense of loss. Its politicians were from another age: they seemed to have real lives, rooted in real communities. Walter Harrison was an electrician and union official before he entered Parliament, Jack Weatherill an apprentice tailor before he took over the family firm. Both fought in the Second World War. Parliament is poorer for the current dominance of consultants, researchers and newspaper columnists: those whose only career has been politics. The play mourned the disappearance of political tribes that had lives outside politics, and for political enmity that was based on something more than individual vanity.

This House built to an act of simple human decency. As the vote of confidence that was to bring down the Callaghan government loomed, the Labour MP Alfred Broughton was on his deathbed and unable to vote. Jack Weatherill offered Walter Harrison his own abstention to compensate for the government's missing vote, a move that would have enraged his leader and ended his career. Harrison was so moved that he refused Weatherill's offer, and the government fell by a single vote. James Graham did more than reveal a friendship that reached across the party divide. He used it to insist that there are values—principle, decency, honesty—that transcend personal gain. *This House* finally made it to the West End in 2016, a few months after the country fell victim, in the EU referendum campaign and its aftermath, to the frivolous rivalries of a self-serving political elite for whom principle, decency and honesty were negotiable commodities.

❦

"A big, scabrous, state-of-the-nation satire. Working title: *Hacked,*" said Richard Bean. "What do you think?"

Among my replies were: "Of course, yes please. When can we have it? And by the time you've written it, they'll be done with the trial of Rebekah Brooks, won't they?"

Richard's friend and fellow dramatist Clive Coleman is also a journalist: he was covering the continuing legal proceedings around phone hacking at News International. Clive thought the hacking scandal showed how badly we had been kidding ourselves that integrity ran through our institutions—Parliament, the police, our fearless free press—like a stick of rock. In fact, we'd always known about the control the Murdoch press exercised over the political class. Now we knew about how close News International was to the Metropolitan Police: there was something increasingly ridiculous about the Met's red-faced outrage at anyone who dared question its refusal to act on the mountain of evidence against News International. The arrest in 2011 of Rebekah Brooks, its chief executive, at last promised to reveal how far the Murdoch press had sewn up politics, law enforcement and the country.

With substantial contributions from Clive, Richard wrapped up the play long before the legal system wrapped up the case. "Right," says Wilson, the editor of the *Free Press* to the assembled journos,

> we haven't had a decent scum story recently. Who are the scum!? The scum are Scousers, obviously—gyppos; the unemployed; druggies; MEPs; feminists; northerners; criminals; prisoners; teenage mums; asylum-seekers; illegal immigrants; legal immigrants; squatters; kiddie-fiddlers; cyclists; trade unionists; the IRA; and career women who rely on childcare. (*Beat.*) Any one of those is a scum story, any two of those is a double-scum story and a guaranteed hard-on.

During the play, Paige Britain, the news editor of the *Free Press,* ingratiates herself with its Irish proprietor, Paschal O'Leary, hacks the phone of famous cricketer Jasper Donald, has sex with the prime minister, hacks the queen's phone, takes Wilson's job as editor, hacks the phones of missing twelve-year-old twins and sets up their father for their murder. She's arrested, charged with conspiracy to intercept communications, convicted, sentenced to two years, and on her release, given her own chat show on O'Leary's American TV channel where her guests include Madonna, Vladimir Putin and the Pope.

Meanwhile, the trial of Rebekah Brooks and her co-defendants had been postponed, and didn't start until 28 October 2013, more than a year after Richard first proposed the play. We knew we couldn't schedule it until the trial was over, as even this, a satirical caricature of the case, would contravene the laws covering contempt of court. These would be mystifying to an American dramatist brought up on the First Amendment, but British law puts the assumption of innocence ahead of the protection of free speech, and forbids the publication of any material that could prejudice a trial. We suspected that it would take no more than a public announcement of our intention to produce the play to land us in hot water. So we postponed it for six months, left an unidentified gap in the programme, and within the National we referred to it only as the new Richard Bean. When it finally opens, we thought, maybe only a few months after the verdicts come in, it will at the very least amaze by its topicality.

As rehearsals approached, the trial dragged on. We consulted Andrew Caldecott QC, an expert in contempt of court. He confirmed that it would put us on the wrong side of the law to announce, let alone perform, the play while the trial continued. He reassured us that the contempt laws didn't extend to rehearsals: if we kept them secret we'd be OK. Richard Bean wondered whether he'd found the play funny. He advised us that it was very funny, but that of course we wouldn't be able to perform it if Rebekah Brooks was acquitted. This stopped us in our tracks. We have to perform it, I told him, as there's a huge gap in the schedule for it. He said we'd lay ourselves open to a massive libel claim.

"But the play doesn't in any way suggest that Paige Britain is in fact Rebekah Brooks," I said, "or that Paschal O'Leary is Rupert Murdoch, or that any of the sleazy journos in the play are direct representations of the allegedly sleazy journos at the *News of the World*. Nobody is saying that anyone hacked the queen's phone or had sex with the prime minister! We have no opinion about the guilt of any of the defendants—we're happy to leave that to the jury. It's satire!"

Andrew Caldecott confirmed that satire can be a defence in law, but his advice was not to risk it.

Walking back to the National from Andrew's chambers in the Temple, I said to Nick Starr that we were screwed. I couldn't seriously ask the National Theatre Board to support the production of a play that might never reach the stage. Maybe it was time to start thinking of an alternative.

We returned to Andrew's chambers a few days later to comb through the play for potentially actionable material. As the list got longer, my heart sank. In the draft we were discussing, Paige Britain is news editor of the *Free Press,* is promoted to editor and is the brains behind phone hacking on an industrial scale. Rebekah Brooks was a feature writer on the *News of the World,* was promoted to editor and her defence was that she knew nothing whatsoever about phone hacking. The problem was not that the play suggested there was industrial-scale phone hacking, or that there was an unhealthy relationship between sections of the press, sections of the Metropolitan Police, and sections of the political establishment. None of that was in dispute. The problem was who the play seemed to identify as guilty of breaking the law.

"So is Rebekah Brooks's defence," I asked, "that she was too stupid or too incompetent to know what was going on at her own paper?"

More or less, we all agreed.

"So what if instead of Paschal O'Leary promoting Paige Britain to editor, he promotes someone else who's too dim to know what's going on? If Paige Britain doesn't make it to editor, she can't be identified as Rebekah Brooks, can she? We'd have another editor, an innocent editor, and no suggestion that the editor has broken the law."

Richard sketched out who the alternative editor could be: she'd love horses, she'd have long wavy hair, she'd be married to a soap star, she'd be stupid, she'd be innocent of any wrongdoing. Andrew thought that would do it. We spent the rest of the conference making sure that none of Rebekah Brooks's co-defendants would be able to identify themselves in the play.

The trial, which had begun in October 2013, showed no sign of ending when rehearsals started on 28 April 2014. I told the cast that there were two versions of the play. In the one they had, Paige Britain, guilty as sin, becomes editor of the *Free Press.* In the second version, horse-loving Virginia White becomes editor, Paige Britain stays news editor, hacks and lies her way through the play, and poor, innocent Virginia is too dim to notice.

"You'd better learn both versions," I said to the actors. "If the jury convicts the defendants, we'll do the first version. If it acquits them, we'll do the second. Meanwhile, not a word."

If I knew anything about Rebekah Brooks, whom I had never met, it was that she was charming. We talked to many people whose paths she had crossed. They all testified to her magnetism. She could not be more fascinating than Billie Piper, who played Paige Britain. As much as any actor I've ever worked with, she carries with her the inexplicable electric charge that brings an audience helplessly to heel. She also has needle-sharp comic timing, so there was nothing she couldn't get away with. Her most memorable victim was Aaron Neil as Sir Sully Kassam, commissioner of the Metropolitan Police and proud standard-bearer of its diversity: Asian, gay and half-witted. He held regular press conferences to explain his force's indiscretions:

> Unfortunately, on my watch there have been disproportionately more Afro-Caribbean men shot and killed by armed officers. I'd like to be able to say that just as many white men had been shot accidentally, but unfortunately I can't. Working together with the communities, we will be putting that right in the coming year.

But nobody outside the National knew the play was happening, so we hadn't sold a single ticket, and the trial looked like it would run longer than *The Mousetrap.* We had a mole, of sorts: somebody knew an Old Bailey judge, and called him to ask what the word was on when the trial might end. Maybe the middle of June was the good news. The bad news was that the jury could take anything up to six weeks to consider its verdict.

"And by the way," said the Old Bailey judge, "don't even think of letting anyone know what you're up to."

I had to report to the National Theatre board that a play scheduled to have its first performance on 10 June might not open until August. We stood to lose several hundreds of thousands of pounds in box-office revenue. They took it on the chin.

On the day of what should have been the first performance, Mr. Justice Saunders was summing up in the trial of Rebekah Brooks. We performed the play, now called *Great Britain,* to about fifty friends and family. I made a speech to them before it started: "If you tell ANYONE about this, you'll be arrested and Mr. Justice Saunders WILL SEND YOU TO PRISON FOR CONTEMPT OF COURT." They sat in total silence throughout the play.

"Thanks for the speech," said Richard Bean.

The next day, the jury retired to consider its verdict. That night, another fifty friends and family pitched up. I toned down my speech, and they started to laugh. We stuck with the Paige Britain Guilty version because I thought it would be too confusing for the actors to keep two versions in their heads simultaneously. We played it eight times in secret to tiny invited audiences, and then it stopped to allow Sean O'Casey's *The Silver Tassie* back into the repertoire.

On 24 June, two weeks after it was supposed to have opened, my assistant Niamh Dilworth ran into my office and yelled that the jury was about to give its verdict. Two of the defendants were guilty but Rebekah Brooks and five other defendants were acquitted on all charges.

"That's a much better ending!" I cried. "Rehearsals start this afternoon for the Not Guilty Version! Start selling tickets!"

We decided to wait until the next morning to announce the play and put it on sale, so it wouldn't have to compete with news of the verdicts. At 9 a.m. on 25 June, Lucinda Morrison, head of press, convened my last, and most enjoyable, press conference as director of the

National Theatre. I told the assembled journalists that Richard Bean had written a play called *Great Britain,* that it would open on Monday night, that its first public performance would be its press night, and that I hoped they'd be there. I let Richard talk a little about what happened in the play before pulling the plug on him.

"You can't censor the playwright," said the omniscient show-business reporter Baz Bamigboye, who alone among the hacks had already got wind of the play.

"I get censored all the time," said Richard.

The entire run sold out within a few days, and when it finally opened, stupid, horse-loving Virginia White got one of the biggest laughs of the night when the cops arrived to arrest her and the rest of the staff of the *Free Press,* and she cried in panic, "What have we done?!" But maybe there was a faint air of disappointment that our foul-mouthed, scabrous satire didn't aim higher. Maybe it could never match the rabbit we pulled from the hat in announcing so quickly that we had a play about a trial that had put the whole establishment in the dock. Maybe the play could never quite rise to how keenly the public wanted the Murdoch press dismembered limb from limb, the Met pinned to a wall, the politicians reduced to rubble, and a sick society anatomised.

But *Great Britain* landed its punches, and like all the best satire, it knew what was decent and what wasn't, and it had a great time slinging mud at its many indecent targets. We announced that as soon as it closed at the National, it would move to the Theatre Royal Haymarket in the West End. It seemed like a no-brainer.

After her trial, Rebekah Brooks went to the U.S. to lie low. A year later she came back as CEO of News International, a development that was beyond even Richard Bean's satirical imagination.

"Phone hacking?" says Paige to the audience. "Give me a break, it's riding a bike without lights. None of you give a damn about us hacking a bunch of trouser-dropping, publicity-seeking celebrities, or royals. For Christ's sake, isn't that what you pay them for?"

Bullseye. By the time *Great Britain* transferred, nobody gave much of a damn about any of it anymore. The West End audience laughed, but they'd already moved on. They knew that the exposure at the Old Bailey of the corruption and criminality at the heart of the new establishment had barely dented its ascendancy. *Great Britain,* a very funny, very topical play, was ancient history by the end of the year.

❧

Committed to producing up to twenty shows every year, at least half of them new, we were bound to make mistakes at the Wednesday meeting. Sometimes we misjudged a play, and saw in it more than it turned out to offer. Sometimes we didn't do a good play proper justice. A poor evening of classical theatre is usually blamed on the director, justifiably. A poor new play is invariably blamed on the playwright. *Omertà* prevents me from naming the guilty directors of some fine plays that barely survived their ministrations. A couple of times, it was me.

But when it worked, I was never happier than in rehearsal with a living playwright. John Hodge's *Collaborators* in 2011 was the first play from the screenwriter of films like *Shallow Grave* and *Trainspotting,* so it was no surprise that it gripped like a vice. John had been commissioned to write a screenplay based on Simon Sebag Montefiore's *Young Stalin* and had been astonished to discover in a footnote that the great playwright and novelist Mikhail Bulgakov had once accepted a commission to write a hagiographic bio-play about young Stalin for the Moscow Art Theatre. John tried to persuade his producers that making a film about Bulgakov's play about Stalin would be an interesting way of making a film about Stalin. They weren't convinced, so he wrote a play instead, a lethal comic masterpiece about tyranny and the compromises art is forced to make with it. John knew about compromise: he'd worked in Hollywood.

"How do I know I can trust you?" Bulgakov asks the NKVD man who comes to commission the Stalin play.

"Sir, I think you've spent too long in the world of show business," says the NKVD man, affronted. "Here in the Secret Police, a man's word is his bond."

The brilliant central conceit has Stalin offer to write the play while Bulgakov runs the Soviet Union, until before he knows what he's doing, he's organising the Great Terror. John's portrait of Stalin—charming, seductive, impenetrable, terrifying—was meat and drink to Simon Russell Beale. He won the prizes, but knew that the play's real burden was carried by Alex Jennings as Bulgakov, whose desperate struggle to hang on to his integrity achieved tragic profundity. *Collaborators* peers into a vortex of fear, and invites the audience to laugh in nervous relief from the safety of the auditorium. This, it says, is what tyrants look like: a salutary corrective to the hysterical fearmongering in twenty-first-century politics that sees tyranny in the imperfect bureaucracies that were built to keep despots at bay.

John Hodge was part of a flood of playwrights new to the National in the last years of my directorship, when plays by women finally outnumbered plays by men. Lucy Prebble, who answered the phones for me and Nick Starr in 2003, came back at last as a playwright in 2012 with *The Effect,* an exceptionally moving play that asked the big existential questions: what is love, what makes us human, are we more than a set of physical responses to chemical stimuli? Like *Hamlet,* it asked what a man is, if his chief good and market of his time be but to sleep and feed.

Rona Munro's vast *James Plays,* a trilogy about the Scottish kings James I, James II and James III, also had Shakespearean ambition and were as much about the present as the past. Commissioned and co-produced by the National Theatre of Scotland, they opened at the Edinburgh Festival just before the referendum on Scottish independence in 2014, and were playing in the Olivier on the night the result was announced. They were funny, violent, informative, sexy, and staged with swashbuckling élan by Laurie Sansom. At the climax of *James III: The True Mirror,* Queen Margaret, the Danish wife of James III, rounds on the Scottish Parliament:

> You know the problem with you lot? You've got fuck all except attitude. You scream and shout about how you want things done and how things ought to be done and when the chance comes look at you! What are you frightened of?

Ten years after making heavy weather of the two *Henry IV* plays in the same theatre, I couldn't help thinking how much more fun I was having with Munro on Scotland than Shakespeare on England.

A temporary theatre rose next to the river in 2013: a bright red shed, designed by Steve Tompkins, whose mastery as a theatre architect at the start of the twenty-first century recalls Frank Matcham's at the start of the twentieth. It was home to plays that looked forward to a new National Theatre by Tanya Ronder, the TEAM, debbie tucker green, Frances Ya-Chu Cowhig, Polly Stenham, Nick Payne and Carrie Cracknell. My last first night, four days before I left the National, was Sam Holcroft's *Rules for Living,* a dizzying comedy about a family Christmas, the rules we write for ourselves, and the mechanisms we use for coping with them. It was her second play for the National. The first, *Edgar and Annabel,* was a weirdly funny Orwellian satire. I thought that there's probably nothing this writer can't do, and she'll still be writing plays for the National when it reaches its centenary.

❧

The day I left the National, seventy playwrights were under commission. More than thirty of them have since delivered plays, and many of those have already been produced. At the planning meeting, we strove to balance the work of young playwrights with plays from giants of the British theatre, like Tom Stoppard, Harold Pinter and Alan Bennett. There was never a shortage of the former. Most Wednesdays, I gloomily reported that I'd heard nothing from the giants.

Since *Rosencrantz and Guildenstern Are Dead* in 1967, Tom Stoppard had written a play for every decade of the National's existence. I kept asking him for another, but he only writes when he has something to say. I had to wait until my time was almost up before he sent me *The Hard Problem,* which had the uncompromising seriousness and grave beauty of one of Beethoven's Late Quartets. But it was full of jokes, and was about people young enough to be the grandchildren of the audience who saw the first production of *Rosencrantz and Guildenstern.* Tom is a magician, and has something of Prospero about him, but there was nothing valedictory about his play.

The hard problem is consciousness. Hilary, a young psychology student, is in bed with her young tutor, which in Tom's universe is a set-up for a scene that's sexy, funny, sad and passionately thoughtful.

HILARY: Explain consciousness.
Impatiently, Spike takes her finger and holds it to the flame of the candle for a moment before she snatches it away with a little gasp.
SPIKE: Flame—finger—brain; brain—finger—ouch.
Consciousness.
HILARY: Brilliant. Now do sorrow. (*Spike groans.*) You think you've done pain. If you wired me up you could track the signal, zip-zip. If you put my brain on a scanner you could locate the activity. Ping! Pain! Now do sorrow. How do I feel sorrow?
SPIKE: Do you feel sorrow?
HILARY: Yes.
SPIKE: I'm making you sad?
HILARY: Not everything is about you, Spike.

Tom returned to a theme that has preoccupied him throughout his career: the search for "some form of overall moral intelligence, otherwise we're just marking our own homework." Just as you thought you had the measure of *The Hard Problem,* it ambushed you with pain. When Hilary was a schoolgirl, she gave up a baby for adoption.

I missed her like half of me from the first day, and the worst thing was there was literally nothing I could give her, do for her, she'd just gone, and then I thought up something I could do, just to, just to be good, so that in return someone, God, I suppose, would look after her.

"Do you believe in God?" says her old school friend, Julia, after a pause.
"I have to," says Hilary. And then, as if to recommend Him to a puzzled audience of sceptics:

But I'll tell you what, though. Everyone should say a prayer every day, anyway, for who you love, just because it puts them in your diary.

"All directors want to warm my plays up and I want to cool them down," said Tom one day, about something I'd done that he thought sentimental. "We usually end up somewhere in between." I imagine that all his directors are as dumbfounded as I was by the layers of feeling that gradually emerge during rehearsal. When the Cottesloe Theatre reopened as the Dorfman in 2015, *The Hard Problem* was its first new play, and the last play I directed as director of the National. Forty-eight years after *Rosencrantz and Guildenstern* opened at the Old Vic, Tom shared the repertoire with Sam Holcroft, who is no older now than he was then.

✎

I was lucky to get a play from Tom. Shortly before Harold Pinter won the Nobel Prize in 2005, I was having dinner with the designer Bob Crowley in a restaurant not unlike the one he lampooned in *Celebration*; three years earlier I'd chickened out of saying that I couldn't share his enthusiasm for reviving a thirty-minute play that had only recently been produced at the Almeida. We saw Harold having dinner in the opposite corner. Bob waved to him: they'd worked together often. Maybe I should have been on my guard when Harold's wife, Antonia Fraser, made a hasty exit about twenty minutes later, but suddenly Harold was bearing down on me.

"You're a fucking liar," he shouted. The entire restaurant went silent. "You're a fucking liar, and you're a fucking shit." I had no idea what to say, so I said nothing.

"You told me you would revive *Celebration* at the National Theatre," said Harold, quieter now, but with Pinteresque menace. "You told me you'd put it in a double bill with *The Room*. You're a liar and a shit."

"I'm really sorry if I gave you that impression, Harold," I said meekly. "That wasn't my intention. I'm genuinely sorry."

"Don't fucking apologise to me," roared Harold, "I'm not interested in your fucking apology. You're a shit and a liar, and now I've fucking told you." And he left the restaurant.

Bob waited for all the other tables to stop looking at us. "Rite of passage," he said. "You can't call yourself director of the National Theatre until Harold Pinter has called you a shit."

Two years later, in 2007, I sent word to Harold that we'd like to do a new production of one of his early plays, *The Hothouse*. He couldn't have been more charming or enthusiastic. He was delighted we were doing it, delighted with the director Ian Rickson, delighted with the cast. A few days before its first preview, Ian told me that one of the cast was having unaccountable difficulties in learning it. Ian was worried he wouldn't make it. I'd worked with the actor, knew him to be reliable, and assured Ian that it would all be fine by the time he got in front of an audience.

At the first preview, the poor actor fell to pieces. During the first half he must have taken forty prompts. It was one of the most difficult nights I've ever spent in the theatre. At the interval, I met Harold and his party in a small room off the Lyttelton foyer. Nobody said a word until one of Harold's friends broke the ice.

"The actor playing Lush is very good," said Harold's friend, diverting attention from the actor who had fallen apart.

"What do you mean Lush is good?" said Harold, shaking with rage. "What about the play? Is the play no fucking good? What do you think of the fucking play?"

Harold's friend told him the play was a masterpiece, and the rest of the interval passed without incident. Nobody mentioned the actor who kept drying. During the second half, he dried even more.

After the show, I'd arranged to meet Harold and Ian Rickson for dinner. Harold lowered himself into his seat. There was a long, dreadful silence.

"He's a fucking fine actor," said Harold about the actor who had just ruined an otherwise excellent production. "It's a fucking hard job, acting. I've done it. Fucking hard. Tell him if he can't remember the line to make it up. He knows what he's doing. Tell him to make it up."

The following night, the actor, buoyed by Harold's vote of confidence, dried two or three times; the night after that he was word-perfect. He never dried again, and was as excellent as the rest of the production.

Harold Pinter was famously irascible and famously precise about each word, pause and punctuation mark in every one of the plays that together make up the most important body of work in post-war British theatre. But this is what happened at the first preview of *The Hothouse,* and it is my contribution to Pinter studies.

❧

"I spoke to Alan the other day," said George Fenton one evening in 2003 when he called to gossip. "He read me a joke from his new play." George is a composer, but like Harold Pinter, he started as an actor. He was in Alan Bennett's first play *Forty Years On,* and remains one of his best friends.

"Which new play?" I asked, trying to sound casual. "And by the way what was the joke?"

"I can't remember," said George, "but it made me laugh."

A couple of days later I arrived home to find a large brown envelope on the doormat. Attached to an apologetic note, saying he had no idea whether it was any good, was Alan's new play. Handwritten in block capitals on the front was: HECTOR'S BOYS or THE HISTORY BOYS.

5

A Way of Looking at Things

ALAN BENNETT

Richard Eyre set me up with Alan Bennett in 1990, after I suggested that *The Wind in the Willows,* Kenneth Grahame's Edwardian classic, would make a good Christmas show in the Olivier. We had dinner in Camden, north London, where we both live. As blind dates go it went OK—he said he was up for adapting the book—but we didn't get on particularly well. I was nervous of saying something stupid so there were long silences; Alan later complained that I had no small talk. He worried about the caravan, the barge, the train, the journeys underground to the houses of Rat, Badger and Mole. I told him if he wrote what he saw, I'd try to stage it. That's been our deal ever since, though there are fewer silences these days.

His first drafts are always a challenge. He works on a collection of long defunct portable typewriters, so he cuts and pastes, literally, a collage of abysmally typed scenes with barely decipherable hand-written additions. A heroic typist later makes it legible, then I write my notes in the margins. I try to talk him through the notes, but he quickly gets antsy. He's resistant to any conceptual or thematic enquiries.

"What do you think it's about, Alan?"

"It's about the madness of George III."

I've learned to be practical, concrete and succinct. *More of this. This goes on too long. This has been said before: do we need it? Scene not clear enough. King's recovery too laid-back, make more of it.* Many of these notes later found their way almost verbatim into *The Habit of Art,* his play within a play about W. H. Auden and Benjamin Britten, in exchanges between the actors and the onstage playwright.

> FITZ *(to Author)*: The reason why I'm forgetting this is
>   because I feel I've said it before.
> AUTHOR: You have said it before.
> FITZ: So do we need it?

"Yes," snaps the Stage Manager, Alan holding back from putting directly into the playwright's mouth what he must have often wanted to say to me himself.

The Wind in the Willows was full of things we didn't strictly need: I hadn't anticipated that Alan would find in it a subversive psycho-drama about the variously repressed lusts of a quartet of Edwardian bachelors.

> RAT: Do you like old Badger?
> MOLE: Oh yes.
> RAT: Not too fierce for you?
> MOLE: Fierce? I thought he was very kind.
> RAT: He is kind.
> MOLE: And understanding.
> RAT: Of course that comes with age, you see he's much older
>   than you or me.
> MOLE: He didn't seem old to me.
> RAT: Oh, he is . . .

Neither Rat nor Badger, in furious competition for the affections of the oblivious Mole, ever let on that they'd like to do more than warm his little toes; but an audience that came to celebrate the delights of a riverbank picnic was seduced into a kind of complicity with woodland creatures predatory less in tooth and claw than in pyjamas. Meanwhile, the staging took every possible advantage of the Olivier's drum revolve, which was having one of its intermittent periods in the sun.

The designer Mark Thompson, like a Victorian conjuror, produced a real train, a real car, a real barge, and the underground houses really were underground. Their inhabitants opened trapdoors in the stage as the drum corkscrewed up to reveal staircases winding down into cosy front parlours, which were eyed greedily by the weasels, stoats and ferrets who had a sideline as property speculators.

Their proposed redevelopment of Toad Hall as executive apartments and office accommodation is thwarted when Toad, Rat, Badger and Mole expel the occupying forces of wild wooders after a heroic battle. Toad looks for other ways to open his home to a wider public.

"Who knows," he muses, "Toad Hall might one day have its very own arts festival."

His riverbank neighbours, content in their Edwardian idyll, aren't enthusiastic.

Alan has equivocated about the Arcadian past since 1968, when the headmaster in *Forty Years On* laments the crowd that has found the door to the secret garden: "Now they will tear up the flowers by the roots, strip the borders and strew them with paper and broken bottles." Even in *The Wind in the Willows,* you can see the playwright wrestling with the big theme he announced in the closing lines of *Forty Years On*:

To let. A valuable site at the crossroads of the world. At present on offer to European clients. Outlying portions of the estate already disposed of to sitting tenants. Of some historical and period interest. Some alterations and improvements necessary.

Several of the best jokes in *The Wind in the Willows* emerged in rehearsal. Most playwrights genuinely admire actors for their ability to take dialogue that looks heavy on the page and make it fly. Alan is one of the few who occasionally allows actors to write lines for him: if an idea works, he'll take it. The converse is an absolute confidence about what matters. He and I rarely argue, partly because I know when it's not worth arguing with him. He'll leave me to cut a play if it's too long: he's not keen on putting a line through his own dialogue, even when he knows it's necessary. But if I cut something he knows to be good he draws another kind of line, and the cut material goes back in.

⌒♫)

I rarely know whether Alan is at work on a play until he pushes the first draft through my letter box. *The Madness of George III* arrived in the spring of 1991, when I was still one of Richard Eyre's associate directors at the National. It was based on fact. In 1788, George III apparently went mad. The diaries of his doctors and courtiers describe his symptoms in startling detail. The prime minister, William Pitt the Younger, increasingly alarmed by the king's incapacity, brought in a special "mad doctor" from Lincolnshire, one Dr. Willis, who reduced the king to meek acquiescence. The Prince of Wales, meanwhile, allied himself with the parliamentary opposition, who tried to push through a Regency bill. But in the spring of 1789, in the nick of time, the king seemed to come to his senses, so the Regency bill failed.

The play brings to life with forensic wit a forgotten constitutional crisis, but it was clear as I read it that it needed a titanic performance at its centre. In a huge stroke of luck, I'd just seen Nigel Hawthorne play the bereaved C. S. Lewis in *Shadowlands*. I'd always admired Nigel as a comic actor of consummate skill, as commanding on stage as he was in *Yes, Minister,* but I can't remember ever being more surprised by grief in a theatre. The surprise must have been evident at dinner after the show, as Nigel couldn't quite disguise how pissed off he was that I was so taken aback. He was fifty before he achieved the recognition he deserved, and he never quite forgave the rest of us for being so slow. Maybe I would have imagined him as the king who bullies his son, badgers his prime minister and shouts at his doctors, but if I hadn't seen *Shadowlands,* I'd have had no idea how completely he would expose himself when the king descends into babbling incontinence.

The first draft, though often moving and funny, came and went. It was enormously long, and the parliamentary manoeuvring was exhausting. And it didn't entirely justify the playwright's insistence that it was about the madness of George III. It ended with a long,

discursive scene in front of St. Paul's where the king's doctors squab-
bled about which of them was responsible for his recovery. They were
joined by a doctor in modern dress: Dr. Richard Hunter, one of the
two authors of the book that first suggested that the king was in fact
suffering from porphyria, a physical illness that attacks the nervous
system and has all the symptoms of madness. Then the politicians
came on, then the king, all arguing about the king's body and the body
politic, until the king shut them all up and delivered the message:

> The real lesson, if I may say so, is that what makes an illness
> perilous is celebrity. Or, as in my case, royalty ... I tell you,
> dear people, if you're poorly it's safer to be poor and ordinary.

As we started to rehearse, it became clear that the scene, apart from
being too long, was beside the point. Nigel's performance was so
powerful that the king's suffering was enough in itself, and the celebration of his recovery was the only possible finale. Nigel started
writing me letters on the train on his way to work: "I'm writing this
for you to look at sometime during the day as I don't want to take
up more rehearsal time discussing THE END ... How can the king,
how can I as an actor after taking the audience through a highly emotional and naturalistic evening, play the scene Alan is expecting? It's
not a history lesson. People can read all that up for themselves!"

Alan's endings often take time to emerge. Dr. Hunter soon
morphed into Dr. Ida Macalpine, who made a brief appearance in the
penultimate scene with her book to tell the king's pages, and the audience, what was really wrong. Halfway through the run, Dr. Macalpine
was herself shown the door. All that remained of her diagnosis was
a programme note. The play ended with the king, and Nigel, trium-
phant, though Alan was fond enough of his original ending to include
it wistfully in his introduction to the play when it was published.

Nigel demanded total engagement from everyone around him: he
wanted his fellow actors to give as good as they got, and he wanted
me to challenge him never to fall back on his matchless technique
to conceal an absence of true feeling. He barely needed a monitor.
I watched a performance every three or four weeks, less often than

some directors watch their shows, and I'd often notice that Nigel had stopped doing something that always worked. "It was getting stale," he'd say. "I wasn't believing it anymore. Next time you come, I'll have found it again."

The play was a good deal more exercised by fact than most history plays, even in the scene, much the audience's favourite, that Alan wrote in response to the concern that we weren't making enough of the king's recovery. Dr. Willis has allowed a reading of *King Lear*. "I'd no idea what it was about," he says to the Lord Chancellor, Thurlow, who comes to visit just as they reach the reconciliation scene between Lear and Cordelia. The king dragoons Thurlow into playing Cordelia:

THURLOW: O my dear father! Restoration hang
    Thy medicine on my lips, and let this kiss
    Repair those violent harms that my two sisters
    Have in thy reverence made.
KING: Well, kiss me, man. Come on, come on. It's
    Shakespeare. (*Thurlow goes for the King's hand.*) No, no.
    Here, man. Here. (*Gives him his cheek.*) Push off now . . .
THURLOW: Your Majesty seems more yourself.
KING: Do I? Yes, I do. I have always been myself, even
    when I was ill. Only now I seem myself. That's the
    important thing. I have remembered how to seem.
    What, what?

Several of the scene's central conceits are true: George III loved Shakespeare, he identified with King Lear, and his courtiers knew he was on the mend when his verbal tics, particularly the "what, whats," returned—they'd disappeared during his illness. Alan is fastidious about this kind of thing. He's a historian by training, and he hates to depart from historical truth. Later, when we made the movie, it took weeks to persuade him to improve history a little and bring the king hurtling by coach from Kew to the doors of the Palace of Westminster in the nick of time, forestalling the Regency debate by a whisker. "We need a chase, Alan, we need action."

I've never stopped pressing the claims of narrative tension, urging Alan to channel more of what he wants to say into dramatic action. He has cooperated only up to a point, and he's been right to resist. His plots are simple, almost non-existent, vehicles less for suspense than for the revelation of character: he exploits his audience's trust to enlarge their sympathies.

A king falls ill, and gets better. Benjamin Britten visits W. H. Auden, but doesn't ask him to write the libretto for *Death in Venice*. An old lady parks her van outside the playwright's own north London house and stays for fourteen years, until one day she dies.

In *The Lady in the Van*, Maggie Smith launched Miss Shepherd from her yellow van like a grimy guided missile, and while the audience might not have wanted her as a house guest, in 1999 they couldn't get enough of her as the main attraction. One of Alan's most valuable gifts, not least to those who produce his plays, is his knack for creating whopping great parts that major actors want to play: there's nothing that the wider theatre audience wants to see more. I tried often, sometimes successfully, to persuade emerging playwrights that they could do worse than to build what they want to say around a big part for a big actor. Nurtured in black boxes, where they need to talk to only a handful of aficionados for a few short weeks, the new playwrights have many more opportunities to have their plays produced than Alan's generation. But they miss out on having to think about what it might be like with nine hundred people in the house, which is second nature to Alan, Michael Frayn, Tom Stoppard, even Harold Pinter. Before the 1970s, when the small studio theatres started to proliferate, if you wanted your play done in London, you had to think about writing for the West End.

❧

Now I'm home one evening in 2003, and I've just finished reading *Hector's Boys*.

Eight stellar history pupils at a Sheffield grammar school prepare to take the Oxford and Cambridge entrance examinations. They're all around eighteen, and they have three teachers. Mrs. Lintott favours "plainly stated and properly organised facts." Irwin is a recent graduate for whom history is less a matter of conviction than performance: "The wrong end of the stick is the right one. A question has a front door and a back door. Go in the back, or better still, the side." Hector, whose subject is English Literature, teaches General Studies, eggs on the boys to perform scenes from 1940s movies and quotes Larkin, Auden and Housman: "All knowledge is precious whether or not it serves the slightest human use." He also gives them lifts home on the back of his motorbike, when he tries to reach behind for a quick squeeze. The groping is more pathetic than predatory (and once Richard Griffiths has agreed to play Hector it becomes an anatomical impossibility for him to be any kind of nuisance to his pillion passenger). But the headmaster's wife claims to have spotted him one day "fiddling" outside the charity shop, and the headmaster seizes the opportunity to force him into early retirement. The most self-possessed of the boys, Dakin, is having a fling with the headmaster's secretary, so he knows enough about the headmaster's own indiscretions to be able to blackmail him into giving Hector his job back. All eight boys get into Oxbridge. Hector is killed in a motorbike accident.

I know the first draft is good, and I know it's funny. I think that the government's obsession with school league tables makes it pertinent, even urgent. Only three or four of the boys are in focus—most of them don't even have names—and I can't yet tell what Hector thinks or feels about much except literature and the purpose of education. I worry that the play may be a dazzling series of History and English lessons, of interest mainly to those who are turned on by the Dissolution of the Monasteries and the First World War poets.

"It's terrific, but it's esoteric," I tell the planning meeting at the National the following Wednesday. "Seventy or eighty performances, max."

Everybody prefers the alternative title, so when I see Alan, I persuade him to call it *The History Boys*. He's genuinely unsure whether it's any good. He tells me that the germ of the play was my own appearance on Michael Berkeley's Radio 3 programme, *Private Pas-*

sions, an upmarket *Desert Island Discs.* One of my choices was Rodgers and Hart's "Bewitched," sung by Ella Fitzgerald. Alan hadn't heard it in full before, and he was particularly taken with the lyrics:

> I'll sing to him
> Each spring to him
> And worship the trousers that cling to him,
> Bewitched, bothered and bewildered am I.

I once told Alan about my career as a boy treble at Manchester Grammar School, sometimes in the boys' choir with the Hallé Orchestra under Sir John Barbirolli, never sure whether it was kosher to sing the liturgical repertoire. In one of those mysterious acts of association that writers are prone to, Alan imagined a Jewish boy with an unbroken treble voice singing "Bewitched" to another boy. And here is unhappy, gay, Jewish Posner singing "Bewitched" to the beautiful Dakin.

But he isn't who I was: I didn't sing out about what I wanted, and for a long time I looked for it only in books. E. M. Forster's *Maurice* was published posthumously when I was fifteen. I hovered outside Willshaw's bookshop in the centre of Manchester, then darted inside and bought it as furtively as if it had been *Homo Hunks,* from whom I'd have run in terror had I any idea they existed. I was thrilled by suburban Maurice's surrender to Scudder the under-gamekeeper, presumably even rougher trade than Lady Chatterley's gamekeeper, though it was hard to tell, as Forster, unlike D. H. Lawrence, didn't give much away about what they got up to between the sheets. But though I was envious of Maurice, when at last I allowed myself off the leash long enough to be lured off the straight and narrow by boys less timid than me, I was covered in shame and confusion.

Still, Posner speaks to me. He's on the wrong side of the pass door, beating at the reinforced glass to be let into the party. It's an existential condition that Alan returns to again and again in his plays. "A sense of not sharing, of being out of it," says Hector, later in the play. "A holding back. Not being in the swim." And no matter how gregarious my job, this always cuts me to the quick. It's why I love his work.

But I need to talk to Alan about Posner singing "Bewitched" to Dakin, because although it's an outstanding scene, I have a problem with Posner's unbroken voice.

"He's eighteen. How can his voice not be broken?" I ask.

"My voice broke very late," says Alan.

"How late?" I ask.

"Sixteen," says Alan.

"Eighteen is another matter," I say, "and in any case, how do we cast it? We'll have to cast a thirteen-year-old, because that's the only way we'll find someone with an unbroken voice, and all the other boys will be professional actors in their early twenties, so it won't make any sense."

"It makes no sense that a woman burns her husband's precious manuscript and then shoots herself in the head," says Alan with an air of finality, and as this is the first time I've ever known him to compare himself to Ibsen, I decide to drop it.

I sometimes think that he deliberately buries clues in his first drafts. The director has to sniff out the good stuff, like a pig hunting truffles. "Whatever the state of Posner's voice, how lonely is he? How unhappy? Why isn't Hector more upset by losing his job? He seems to sail through the play without ever engaging emotionally with anyone else, or even himself. How good a teacher is he, or is he only a classroom entertainer?"

Alan stops me before I say too much: he never likes me to labour the point, and it's always a good idea to leave him to go off in his own direction if he's agreeing with the general drift.

"Any ideas about casting?" I ask.

"I thought about Frances de la Tour for Mrs. Lintott," he says.

I can immediately hear her say every line, though I've barely met her. In fact, the only time she's ever talked to me was at the National Theatre company meeting when I was introduced as the new director. Frankie, as I wouldn't have dared to call her then, was in a play in the Cottesloe. She stood up and asked if she could say a few words. "I have no idea who you are," she said, "but on behalf of the entire profession, welcome."

At the same moment, Alan and I realise that Hector should be

Richard Griffiths, who has the wit and grace to persuade an audience to forgive him for his fumbling interferences on the motorbike. Richard comes to see me in my office, and sits gloomily on the sofa.

"I can't turn it down," he says.

I wonder why he's so unhappy about it.

"It'll bankrupt me," he says. "I can't live off the kind of money this place pays."

I assure him he'll be on knights and dames rate, the National's special top salary. But this is a fraction of what he gets in the movies, and much less than what any leading actor can earn in television, so it doesn't cheer him up. An hour later, after several entertaining stories about the plays he's been in and the pittance he's been paid for them, he accepts the part and trudges miserably out of the office.

The headmaster is easy: Clive Merrison took over Dr. Willis in *The Madness of George III* and we know how well he can do humourless monomania. And we meet Stephen Campbell Moore who plays the young teacher Irwin with unexpected sympathy, and seems steely enough not to let Richard Griffiths' Hector walk all over him.

A few weeks later, we read the second draft at the National Theatre Studio. Dominic Cooper has asked to play Dakin. "I think you may be too old, to be honest," I say to him. He points out mildly that he's playing a twelve-year-old in *His Dark Materials,* so he's reading Dakin.

Other members of the cast of *His Dark Materials* join the class. Ben Whishaw is Scripps, Russell Tovey is Boy 2 (most of them are still nameless) and Samuel Barnett is Posner. "All the unbroken-voice actors are busy," I lie to Alan.

The reading is patchy. I'm excited, because the second draft has some sensational things in it. There's a new scene at the end of Act I: just after Hector loses his job, he returns to the classroom to find Posner waiting for a private lesson. They read through a short poem by Thomas Hardy, "Drummer Hodge," and in talking about it they seem to answer the questions I asked about them in the first draft. How does Hector feel about being fired? Devastated. How good a teacher is he? Superb. How lonely is Posner? Very. Why does Hector seem so emotionally distant? Because he's even lonelier than Posner.

Alan is depressed, as he always is by a first reading, but I have a whiff of how it might be after a few weeks' rehearsal. I start to think that seventy performances won't be enough. I ask Alan what he thought of the actors playing the history boys, but warn him not to like Ben Whishaw too much as he's got another job playing Hamlet. Alan likes Dominic, and he thinks Russell Tovey should be Rudge, the dull, sporty boy played very well at the reading by Jamie Parker, who has let slip that he plays the piano so we've moved him on to Scripps. Alan also likes Sam Barnett, but insists that as his voice is broken, he's not suitable for Posner.

"But he sings like an angel!" I say. "And we can't cast some twelve-year-old with an unbroken voice. *It would look ridiculous.*"

Alan asks the casting director, Toby Whale, to arrange auditions for some child actors with unbroken voices. "Or maybe it could be a woman who looks like an eighteen-year-old boy," he offers, trying to help. Toby looks at his shoes.

"Tell Sam Barnett to sit tight," I growl at him when Alan leaves. "Don't let him accept another job."

We need actors to play Boys 1, 2, 3 and 4, and to stamp them with enough individuality to provoke the playwright into finding names for them. Toby brings in a lot more actors in their early twenties and we keep telling Alan that the thirteen-year-olds are on their way. We particularly like two Mancunians, Andrew Knott and Sacha Dhawan. Andrew reminds me of the boys I was at school with. Sacha tells us he's going to read a poem he's written himself.

"Did this guy train?" I whisper to Toby. "Has nobody told him that's a bad idea?"

"He's not trained, and he actually is eighteen, so give him a break," mutters Toby. The poem is rather good, and Sacha reads it with such conviction that we can't imagine turning him down. Samuel Anderson is cool, which is a tone of voice we haven't found yet, so we want him too.

Late in the day, the door flies open and in barrels a fat guy who never stops talking. He's either super-confident or super-nervous, but either way he's very funny. "What have you done most recently?" I ask.

"A sitcom called *Fat Friends,*" he says, and cackles in delight, like the Wicked Witch of the West. He's called James Corden, and we decide he'll be great as Boy 4, who eventually gets a name—Timms—and a lot more lines, some of which he writes for himself.

"What about Posner?" asks Alan.

"We've run out of time. I'm casting Sam Barnett," I say firmly. Alan says nothing.

A few months later, in his introduction to the published edition of the play, he concedes that as broken-voiced Posner, "the heir to the character I never quite wrote," Sam Barnett is perfect.

❧

A life in the theatre is a solution to any number of psychological challenges, and acting in the school play at Manchester Grammar, I was seduced by a camaraderie that seemed less fraught with emotional hazard than I was used to at home. We changed for the play in the masters' common room, our costumes laid out on smoke-stained armchairs around a coal fire. We'd stick on false beards or strap ourselves into overstuffed bras, and settle into the armchairs, loftily passing judgement on the director. A handful of English teachers directed in turn, and each one had his fierce partisans. I was for Brian Phythian, a teacher with all Hector's passion and charisma, and none of his faults. He ran the Dramatic Society, and I wouldn't be in the theatre today if I hadn't found myself at his rehearsals. Forty years later, I'm still drawn to the circle around the fire, to its familial security and its clarity of purpose. And in the safety of the rehearsal room, I still confront all the stuff that threatens to be too painful in the world outside.

Sitting in Bob Crowley's studio, talking about the designs for *The History Boys,* I'm thinking about Brian Phythian, my own sixth-form classroom, and the echoing corridors of my own grammar school, and I can remember them without the journey to Manchester. "Though we wouldn't have lined up to sing a Gracie Fields number before we went off for our Oxbridge interviews," I say to Bob. "So it's hardly social realism." But we both think that the aphoristic wit of Alan's dialogue needs grounding in scruffy actuality. We fiddle around in the Lyttelton model box with some grey card walls; we put them on tracks, at right angles to each other. After a couple of hours, we've worked out how to get from classroom to staff room to headmaster's study to corridor to changing room and back again. It's the quickest we've ever worked: it usually takes months.

Sam Anderson, Stephen Campbell Moore, James Corden, Sacha Dhawan, Andy Knott and Jamie Parker show up for the first day of school tense and nervous. Sam Barnett, Dominic Cooper and Russell Tovey have been through *His Dark Materials* and know their way around, so they arrive smug, like the second form. Richard Griffiths sidles up to James. "Don't look so frightened," he says, "the time to get scared is when they give out the payslips."

Then we read through the play. "Here's the deal," I say at the end. "There's a lot in this play that I didn't get till I looked it up. There's a lot of history I didn't know and a lot of poetry I didn't recognise. Can we all agree that there is no question so stupid that you can't ask it?"

We start each day with Alan teaching Auden, Larkin and Walt Whitman, and me teaching Shakespeare and Wilfred Owen. Richard, who is ferociously well read, takes all of us down forgotten literary byways, which are much funnier than *Leaves of Grass.* I can't remember ever enjoying myself more. And although the company is even shorter of women than *Henry V*—there's only Frankie, her understudy and the stage managers—the rehearsal-room testosterone count is low. Nobody's playing football. Jamie and Sam Barnett sing songs from the shows at the piano. Russell and Dom puzzle out "The Whitsun Weddings." James shares recipes. And I'm surprised how easily I play Dad, a role I didn't think I coveted, but now seems to work fine. Maybe it's the subject matter of the play that civilises, even feminises, a roomful of young actors who, if they'd been in *Henry V,* would have been as belligerent as the English army. Or maybe I've got lucky with these guys, who go on to spend two frictionless years together, and remain close ten years later.

They learn that Alan is a stylist as demanding as Oscar Wilde: the history boys are often far wittier and more articulate than even the cleverest Oxbridge entrant. Dakin mulls over his ordeals on the back of Hector's motorbike. "Lecher though one is, or aspires to be, it occurs to me that the lot of woman cannot be easy, who must suffer such inexpert male fumblings virtually on a daily basis." It's closer to Jack Worthing than the daily banter of a Sheffield teenager, and although it needs to be rooted in concrete reality, it also needs no less breath control or intellectual élan than Restoration comedy. I encourage all the history boys to pull back on their instinctive naturalism, and think in paragraphs. They watch Richard, hear him wind his way through every long, coiling sentence and arrive faultlessly at its destination. By the fourth week, Dom tosses off the aspirant-lecher speech with the same insouciance he brings to his campaign to have sex with the headmaster's secretary: "Apropos Passchendaele, can I bring you up to speed on Fiona?"

Richard, Frankie and Clive Merrison all know how funny the play is. The others have to take a lot of it on trust. The French scene is their Waterloo: in one of his lessons, Hector, for no good reason, possibly to make them more rounded human beings, has them improvise a brothel scene in French. Eventually I'm reduced to speaking their lines very slowly into the voice recorders on their phones, so they can parrot them back. Posner is the madame, Dakin the client.

POSNER: Bonjour, monsieur.
DAKIN: Bonjour, chérie.
POSNER: Entrez, s'il vous plait. Voilà votre lit et voici votre prostituée.
HECTOR: Oh. Ici on appelle un chat un chat.

Dom, as the client, has his trousers off, and James, as the prostitute, is going through the menu ("Pour dix francs je peux vous montrer ma prodigieuse poitrine"), when the headmaster walks into the classroom. Hector makes him speak French ("L'anglais, c'est interdit"), but the headmaster's vocabulary is limited ("Pourquoi cet garçon . . . Dakin, isn't it? . . . est sans ses . . . trousers?"). Hector smoothly explains that Dakin is a wounded soldier, "un mutilé de guerre," in a field hospital at Ypres. The class ditches the brothel scene and moans in agony. By the fifth week of rehearsal, most of them are on top of the French, but they're dreading playing it to an audience, as they assume everyone will be as mystified as they are.

As I sit in the Lyttelton waiting for the first preview I remember what it's like when an audience decides a play isn't doing it for them, and there's not much you can do backstage after the show beyond trying to keep everybody's spirits up. More often, I've sat in preview audiences who don't quite know what they think, in which case you must do what you can to make the show more persuasive. But from the moment Richard first strides on in his motorbike gear, this audience decides that *The History Boys* is the play they've been waiting to see.

About five minutes in, Frankie and Richard are discussing the universities they went to. "Durham was very good for history," says Frankie, bone dry, "it's where I had my first pizza. Other things, too, of course, but it's the pizza that stands out." The audience roars as if it's the first funny line they've ever heard in a theatre.

A couple of minutes later, it's the French lesson, and they explode. Clive Merrison and Steve Campbell Moore are waiting in the wings for their entrance. "Jesus," says Clive, "we're going to kill this stone dead." But there's nothing that an English audience likes more than someone caught with his trousers down, so when the headmaster comes on and sees Dakin in his underpants, they go nuclear.

Soon the laughs start coming for lines that aren't even funny. "You're very young, sir," says Sacha as Akthar to Steve as Irwin, during one of Irwin's lessons. "This isn't your gap year, is it, sir?" Who knew? Certainly not Sacha, whose first professional play this is, so his mum and dad are here to see him hit the back of the net.

During the first half, most of the cast get to speak directly to the audience, but it's ten minutes into Act 2 before Frankie, after a vexing confrontation with the headmaster, turns front. "I have not hitherto been allotted an inner voice," she says after a lethally timed pause, landing perhaps the biggest laugh of the evening, "my role a patient and not unamused sufferance of the predilections and preoccupations of men."

Frankie is less surprised by the response than I am. "I'm talking to them about my whole career, darling," she tells me later. "The woman never gets the inner voice. They realise that." Which is why they cheer when she asks the class: "Can you, for a moment, imagine how dispiriting it is to teach five centuries of masculine ineptitude?" Alan writes a part for her in all his subsequent plays.

"How do you define history, Mr. Rudge?" Frankie asks quick-witted Russell playing slow-witted Rudge in a mock interview.

"How do I define history?" repeats Russell. "It's just one fucking thing after another."

Another perfectly timed laugh, and the audience has developed an appetite for the play's considerable substance so they recognise another contribution to one of its central debates. But they are blind-sided by Thomas Hardy and "Drummer Hodge." After the disastrous interview with the headmaster that leads to him losing his job, Hector finds Posner waiting alone in the classroom.

"What have we learned this week?" asks Hector, and Posner speaks by and from the heart:

> They throw in Drummer Hodge, to rest
> Uncoffined—just as found:
> His landmark is a kopje-crest
> That breaks the veldt around;
> And foreign constellations west
> Each night above his mound.
>
> Young Hodge the Drummer never knew—
> Fresh from his Wessex home—
> The meaning of the broad Karoo,
> The Bush, the dusty loam,
> And why uprose to nightly view
> Strange stars amid the gloam.
>
> Yet portion of that unknown plain
> Will Hodge for ever be;
> His homely Northern breast and brain
> Grow to some Southern tree,
> And strange-eyed constellations reign
> His stars eternally.

By the end of Sam's recitation, the silence in the auditorium is tangible, thick with concentration. How does the death of poor Hodge speak so keenly across the decades about a heartsick student and a ruined old man? "Any thoughts?" asks Hector. "Anything about his name?"

And at last, Hector puts aside foolish things, and opens the door to literature. "The important thing," he says, "is that he *has* a name," and he tells Posner about the Zulu and Boer wars:

> the first campaigns when soldiers ... or common soldiers ... were commemorated, the names of the dead recorded and inscribed on war memorials ... So, thrown into a common grave though he may be, he is still Hodge the drummer. Lost boy though he is on the other side of the world, he still has a name.

There are three lost boys on stage, Hodge, Posner and Hector, and it seems as if Hardy has written about all of them.

"'Uncoffined' is a typical Hardy usage," continues Hector. "A compound adjective, formed by putting 'un-' in front of the noun. Or verb, of course. Un-kissed. Un-rejoicing. Un-confessed. Un-embraced." Richard and Sam sit either side of a classroom table, unrejoicing, unembraced, and they have pulled the audience in so close that they need do no more than think and feel. They have stopped acting. Richard continues:

> The best moments in reading are when you come across something—a thought, a feeling, a way of looking at things—which you had thought special and particular to you. Now here it is, set down by someone else, a person you have never met, someone even who is long dead. And it is as if a hand has come out and taken yours.

For a moment, it seems as if Sam might take Richard's hand. He reaches out in a gesture so tentative that in any other scene, in any other play, nobody would notice. Tonight, nine hundred people share

Alan's "way of looking at things," and they hold their breath; but Hector is locked in a world where the only possible fellowship is with dead poets, so the moment passes, though not before Richard, Sam, Alan and Thomas Hardy have embraced the Lyttelton audience in a fellowship of the lonely. It's one of the reasons they come to the theatre, to know what the Banished Duke in *As You Like It* tells Orlando: "Thou seest we are not all alone unhappy."

(Alan later gets a letter from Hardy's biographer Claire Tomalin, who points out that Hector gets "Drummer Hodge" wrong. Hodge was the generic name for common labourers, a little like Joe Bloggs, and Hardy uses it not to individualise Hodge but as an ironic commentary on the way soldiers like him are tossed into common graves, the forgotten casualties of war. Alan comes clean about his mistake in the *London Review of Books,* though I think that I'd have said to Claire Tomalin: well spotted, of course Hector gets it wrong, that was the whole idea. By misreading the poem, he allows us a glimpse of his soul.)

At the end of *The History Boys,* the eight boys sit in a line and Mrs. Lintott talks us through their futures, most of them "pillars of a community that no longer has much use for pillars." Dakin is happy enough as an international tax lawyer. Timms has put together a chain of dry-cleaners and takes drugs at the weekend. Rudge builds affordable homes for first-time buyers. Seven of the eight of them are just about OK, and they aren't complaining, but their energy is gone: it's as if they've grown another skin, and they are keeping their secrets, suppressing their disappointments. They have grown up, and it's not as great as they thought it was going to be. They stare blankly at us and we know them to be us, and we're relieved to be them because otherwise we'd be Posner, who hasn't grown up, so life has defeated him.

Earlier in the play Sam hit the comedy bullseye with:

> I'm a Jew.
> I'm small.
> I'm homosexual.
> And I live in Sheffield.
> I'm fucked.

But Posner really is fucked. He never needed E. M. Forster to tell him who he was, but his self-awareness hasn't saved him. His life hasn't gone well, the way many lives don't, and even the luckiest of us know how close we've been to the abyss. Defeated, disappointed and generally fucked as we all feel ourselves at least sometimes to be, we can only be grateful to the fucked who people Alan's plays.

The first preview of *The History Boys* is the most euphoric night I will ever spend at the National. By the time the official opening arrives a week later, we all feel unstoppable. An hour before the show goes up, someone smokes a secret cigarette in the Lyttelton flies, and the sprinklers go off. The stage is drenched and the lighting system goes down. By seven, when we're due to start, water is still dripping heavily from the flies. We ask the audience to wait in the foyer, and give everyone a free drink. The lights go back on, but the program that controls them from cue to cue has lost its memory. Mark Henderson, the lighting designer, agrees to relight the show as it happens. At seven thirty we give the audience a second drink while the stage crew finishes the salvage operation, and at eight we let them in. I come on to explain the delay, and tell them the entire cast has been mopping the stage for the last two hours, which is an outrageous lie, but as they've all had a couple of drinks too many, they buy it. And the image of Richard Griffiths on his hands and knees with a towel does no harm to the way they receive the play.

Two and a half years later in New York, the eight history boys and three teachers commemorate the dead Hector for the last time at a Sunday matinee on Broadway. In the final seconds, Hector's ghost returns to haunt them, and I know the words Richard speaks will haunt all of us too, because they remind us of what we've all learned from each other, and of why we decided to spend our lives in the theatre in the first place.

> Pass the parcel.
> That's sometimes all you can do.
> Take it, feel it, and pass it on.
> Not for me, not for you, but for someone, somewhere,
>   one day.

Pass it on, boys.
That's the game I wanted you to learn.
Pass it on.

꒰∾꒱

Alan first mentioned *The Habit of Art* on a flight to New York: we were on our way to catch up with *The History Boys* company. He imagined a meeting in Oxford between W. H. Auden and Benjamin Britten about the opera *Death in Venice*. Before Britten arrives, the young Humphrey Carpenter, who would later go on to write fine biographies of both, arrives in Auden's rooms at Christ Church hoping to interview him. Auden is expecting a rent boy.

AUDEN: Take off your trousers.
CARPENTER: What for?
AUDEN: What do you think? Come along, it's half past.
CARPENTER: What am I being asked to do?
AUDEN: You aren't being asked to do anything. You're being paid. This is a transaction. I am going to suck you off.
CARPENTER: But I'm with the BBC.
AUDEN: Really? Well, that can't be helped. Ideally I would have preferred someone who was more a son of the soil, but it takes all sorts.

After he's cleared up who's who, Auden says to Stuart, the real rent boy, "You are a rent boy. I am a poet. Over the wall lives the Dean of Christ Church. We all have our parts to play." And all of them are worth the playwright's attention, Auden might have added.

In the play about the rehearsal of the play about Auden and Britten, the author was Elliot Levey, whose nimble wit always endears him to his colleagues. He channelled the resentments of every angry young playwright he'd ever seen in a rehearsal room. He was nothing like Alan, but Alan kept telling me how much he liked him, so maybe the suppressed fury of his performance struck a chord.

The best scene in the play was a confrontation between Britten and Auden about sexuality and art, literature and music, creativity and inspiration, self-restraint and letting it all hang out, old age and persistence. Both composer and poet have the habit of art. They keep going.

"Still hanging on then?" said Linda at the stage door when Alan turned up for the first day of rehearsals for his next play, *People*. And still practising the habit of art. Word leaked out before *People* opened that it was an attack on the National Trust, which it wasn't, but it was set in a single room in a large and derelict country house in the middle of Yorkshire, occupied by two old ladies: Lady Dorothy Stacpoole and her companion, Iris. The National Trust turns up in the person of Lumsden.

> LUMSDEN: Forgive me if I enthuse, but I see this house as a
>   metaphor. Tell a child the story of England and it is all
>   here.
> DOROTHY: Yes. I would be deceiving you, Mr. Lumsden, if I
>   said I had not heard such twaddle before.
>   I particularly abhor metaphor.
>   Metaphor is fraud.
>   England with all its faults.
>   A country house with all its shortcomings.
>   The one is not the other . . . however much the Trust
>   would like us to think so. I will not collaborate in your
>   conceit of country. It is a pretend England.

Alan has always denied he deals in metaphor: "It's about the madness of George III." But never averse to having his cake and eating it, he has Dorothy rent out the house as a location for hard porn, before succumbing to the Trust and handing it over. *People* was the consummation of Alan's creative relationship with Frances de la Tour, who played Dorothy, and a sardonic return to the secret garden in *Forty Years On,* though it didn't seem to share the headmaster's nostalgia for what it was like before the crowds found the key to the door. Much better to make porn in the garden than yearn for it to be something that it never was.

While we were working on *People,* Alan showed me a short radio play called *Cocktail Sticks,* and wondered whether there was anything we could do with it. It was straightforwardly autobiographical, a portrait of his parents. In a small masterpiece of self-reproach, it charted the distance that gradually opened as he outgrew them. I said we'd be happy to do something with it.

Most actors can do Alan. Alex Jennings caught not just his voice and mannerisms, but his wry melancholy and boundless empathy.

"He's uncanny," said Maggie Smith about Alex when she came to see it. She also said how peculiar it was that for such a shy man, Alan was so ready to put himself centre stage.

"Can you remember why we never made the movie of *The Lady in the Van* in 1999?" I asked Alan.

"I didn't think Maggie wanted to do it," said Alan.

"I bet she did," I said, "and even if she didn't then, I bet she'd do it now, if Alex played you. You know how much she loves him. And you, of course."

Which is how we decided to make the movie of *The Lady in the Van.* But I couldn't have made *The Lady in the Van* if I hadn't made *The Madness of King George,* and I couldn't have made *The Madness of King George* if Alan hadn't insisted whoever made it had to employ me as its director and Nigel Hawthorne as the king. In that, as in everything else we've done together since Richard Eyre introduced us, Alan Bennett has been the best luck I've had.

6

Knowing Nothing

MOVIES

Samuel Goldwyn Junior was the opposite of everything you'd ever heard about the brazen original. Sam was soft-spoken, cultured and self-effacing. He was more interested in the ideas and talents of other people than anyone I have ever met in the movie business. He was also a passionate Anglophile, which may have partly explained his determination in 1994, long before I started to think about running the National Theatre, to finance *The Madness of George III*. It didn't occur to him that the king could be played by anyone other than Nigel Hawthorne, and he was sanguine about putting me behind the camera.

"It's easy," he said. "Tell the director of photography how you see it. He'll do the rest. You won't have a problem."

I knew only one director of photography, Andrew Dunn, whose former girlfriend had been in a play I'd directed.

"He's good," said Sam. "Ask him. And who will design it?"

"It should look like *Barry Lyndon*," I said, aiming high. Ken Adam, designer of *Dr. Strangelove* and all the early James Bond movies, had won an Oscar for it.

"So ask Ken Adam," said Sam.

"Ken Adam won't be interested in working with me. He works with Kubrick."

"What's the worst he can say? No?" said Sam, a question I've asked many directors since.

I tracked Ken down to a hotel in New York and turned up in his room with the screenplay. "Alan Bennett?" said Ken. "I'd very much like to do it."

"I know nothing about making movies," I said apologetically.

"Don't worry," said Ken, "I probably know enough to get us started."

"You only direct your first film once," said Andrew Dunn. "Next time, you'll know too much. You'll be worrying about where they're going to put the honeywagons. Ask for everything that occurs to you. Don't let anyone tell you it's impossible."

I knew so little that I didn't know that a honeywagon is a trailer full of toilets. I didn't know that it's generally a bad idea for a film unit to be constantly on the move, dragging the honeywagons in its wake, so it's as well to stay in each location for as long as possible and find several different uses for it.

Ken Adam wasn't interested in impossible. He had watched the Reichstag fire, fled Berlin with his family in 1934, joined the RAF and flown long-range bombing missions over Germany, the country of his birth. He designed the war room for *Dr. Strangelove* and Fort Knox for *Goldfinger.* He insisted on exactly the right grand house for every scene, and he seemed to know all their owners. "I'll just knock on the door and see if Johnny Arundel is at home." The honeywagons were never off the road.

Ken, Andrew and the editor Tariq Anwar were my film school. Tariq sternly took me through each day's rushes and showed me where I'd gone wrong. The most depressing difference between rehearsing a scene for a play and shooting one for a movie is the moment in the shower the following morning when you realise how you should have been doing it all along. You can go back to the rehearsal room and fix a play. You're lumbered with what you shot for eternity.

One of Alan's stage directions, later cut, asked for the mad king to be followed by the petrified court like something from Eisenstein's *Ivan the Terrible.* Even Ken Adam was daunted by that, though he'd have done fine on an Eisenstein set. Knowing nothing, but surrounded by people who knew a lot, I made a better movie than I ever did when I knew more.

Sam Goldwyn knew how to sell it, too. "Outside England, nobody knows who George III was," he said. Americans know him only as King George, the Tyrant, unfit to be the ruler of a free people. So we gave the film a new title: *The Madness of King George*. Someone reported that Sam had changed it because he was a vulgar Hollywood mogul who didn't want the dumb American audience to think that *The Madness of George III* was the sequel to *The Madness of George 1* and *The Madness of George 2*.

"It's a great story," said Sam, and made no attempt to deny it. The TV networks picked it up, and it was all over the evening news. The movie sold tickets. It was nominated for four Oscars. The night before the ceremony, Sam gave a dinner at the Beverly Hills house he inherited from his father. The first Sam Goldwyn remortgaged the house every time he wanted to make a new movie. "And when the movie made money, he paid off the mortgage, and threw a party," said Sam. He was urbane and elegant, but he was his father's son. I still wonder whether he planted the sequel story himself.

Some years later at an official function, a young RAF officer, an equerry at Buckingham Palace, asked me whether I was the *Madness of King George* chap. I said that I was.

"Absolute godsend!" he said. "How did you know?"

How did I know what?

"When I got this job, I knew nothing about it, nothing about what was expected, so I asked them about the etiquette, the bowing and nodding and backing out of the room and so forth; was there a handbook, was there someone who could teach me? And they said: rent the DVD of *The Madness of King George* and watch it like a hawk—it's all there. So I did, terrific film, marvellous acting and so on, and all the etiquette absolutely tremendous. How did you know?"

"We made it up," I said.

"You're joking?" said the equerry, stricken.

"It's kind of what we do in the movies—make things up."

Actually, I'd taken quite a lot of care when we did the play to find out about the bowing and scraping, but nobody looks for documentary reality in stage ceremonial, so it acquired a life of its own. And nobody comes to the theatre looking for an instruction manual. I'm always amazed by the assumption that film shows you the thing itself.

⟨∽ᵍ⟩

After *The Madness of King George,* boxfuls of scripts arrived. "You should move to Hollywood. You'll be surrounded with love," said one Hollywood producer with terrifying sincerity. The script that set my pulse racing was Arthur Miller's own screenplay for *The Crucible,* which was sent by Twentieth Century Fox, where Sam Goldwyn's right-hand man Tom Rothman had just moved. Tom is as cultured and shrewd as Sam, but much, much louder. He's still my best friend in Hollywood.

I visited Arthur Miller in his apartment on the Upper East Side of New York. He was dubious. Over the years, directors had come and gone and *The Crucible* had never been made. He asked what I wanted to do with the language. I didn't want to do anything with the language: why would I want to mess with his flinty Puritan prose? He thawed a little. The last director who'd made a pitch for it had told him he'd need to contemporise the archaic dialogue for the multiplex audience.

I knew nothing then about how or why Hollywood movies got the go-ahead. *The Crucible* would never have been made in 1995 if Daniel Day-Lewis hadn't said he'd play John Proctor. He read it, we met to discuss it, he said he'd do it. The phone rang all day with congratulations from agents and executives. It seemed so easy.

Arthur asked me to spend a few days with him in his house in Connecticut. *The Crucible* flashed green on the screen of an IBM computer in the hut where he'd written since the early 1950s. I told him how I saw the film, and he tapped away at the keyboard. It was like giving Shakespeare notes on *Macbeth.* He asked me about casting. I told him that Paul Scofield wanted to play Danforth, the deputy governor who presides over the witch trials. I could have said nothing that would have better pleased him: his respect for the leading actors of the British theatre was limitless.

He knew none of the young Americans who wanted to play seventeen-year-old Abigail Williams, "a strikingly beautiful girl . . .

with an endless capacity for dissembling." She is the principal accuser in the witch trials, and it gradually emerges that she and John Proctor have been lovers; Proctor's shame surges through the story.

"How do you see her?" I asked Arthur.

"The thing nobody remembers about Marilyn," said Arthur, "was that she wasn't just beautiful. She was an extraordinary life force. A life force."

He answered a question about Abigail Williams by talking about Marilyn Monroe, whom I hadn't mentioned. He met Marilyn for the first time in Hollywood in 1951. Though he later wrote that they had yet to start a sexual relationship, when he returned to his first wife and two children on the East Coast, "the thought of putting Marilyn out of my life was unbearable." Back home, he wrote *The Crucible* in 1952, a courageous act of resistance to Senator Joseph McCarthy's Communist witch-hunts, but it was impossible not to suspect that he shared John Proctor's emotional turbulence as he wrote it. Abigail Williams and a dozen other teenage girls are caught dancing naked in the forest; they protect themselves by accusing blameless villagers of consorting with the Devil. But as the witch-hunt spirals out of control, the spine of the play is Proctor's adultery and the terrible wasteland of his marriage, and its most moving scene is his reconciliation with his wife, Elizabeth, just before he goes to the gallows. "Suspicion kissed you when I did," says Elizabeth. "I never knew how I should say my love. It were a cold house I kept!"

Winona Ryder played Abigail and Joan Allen played Elizabeth. We built Salem Village on Hog Island, in the mouth of the Essex River on the North Shore of Massachusetts, a few miles from Puritan Salem. Andrew Dunn and Tariq Anwar came over from London. Daniel arrived several weeks early to help build John Proctor's house and farm John Proctor's land. He lived John Proctor's life, took into his bloodstream the daily rhythms of a Puritan farmer, changed his musculature. His total immersion in the parts he plays is famous: he needs to persuade himself, when the camera rolls, that he isn't acting. Though telling someone else's story and speaking someone else's lines, he does everything he can to corner himself into total spontaneity. He starts by taking on his character's identity, and he sticks with it through long days on the set. Shot after shot, take after take, a film actor must be ready to deliver a few perfect seconds at the crew's convenience. Maybe he's acting for a total of only a few minutes during the day, but every time the director calls "Action!" he has to be in the zone. Some actors go blank between takes, others are noisily hyperactive.

Out of Daniel's complete absorption come performances that stand comparison with the best in the history of cinema. Off set, he's gentle and mischievous. Even on set, he must sometimes have been Daniel, as I have a photo of him sitting on a bench outside John Proctor's house, drinking a can of Coke and laughing, which wouldn't have cut much ice with the Puritans of Massachusetts.

Daniel was in awe of Paul Scofield, whom he'd never met. He expected a magus, but when Paul arrived three weeks before the shoot to rehearse their scenes, they seemed to be on different planets. Daniel would have preferred not to rehearse at all: he held the script at arm's length, as if it was a radioactive reminder that on the day he'd be telling a preordained story rather than living an unplanned life. He muttered through it, committing to nothing, leaving all the work of bringing it to life for when we shot it. Paul sounded the text for its music. He started with the vowels. He carefully placed every word in the two-octave span of his amazing voice, as if he was singing opera. They seemed bemused by each other. But when the camera rolled, they were in exactly the same place. They'd arrived there separately, but they were in perfect sympathy: open, combustible and spontaneous.

Paul wasn't much interested in talking about acting or about the part, though he told me that what attracted him to Danforth was the realisation that his extreme zealotry was the dark side of the faith of Thomas More, whose glowing integrity had won him his Oscar in *A Man for All Seasons*. "St. Thomas was an enthusiastic burner of Protestants," he reminded us, with relish. Otherwise, he was happy to know what was required. Faster, slower, louder, where do I stand? Once, between takes, I started some elaborate analysis of a scene's subtle irony. He stopped me: "Do you mean more comedy?" I said yes, and retreated behind the camera.

On a film set, a director should be succinct and precise. There is no call for the kind of open-ended discussion that makes a theatre rehearsal room so hospitable to verbosity. It need take only a moment to communicate with actors—like Paul and Daniel, like Maggie Smith or Nigel Hawthorne—whose gift is absolute, who sometimes stand amazed at themselves, uncertain where it comes from. Paul could summon terrors, real terrors, but between takes he was larky. He would swirl his costume and say, "I love this cloak."

The film is strongest when it's closest to the play, inside the Proctors' cold house, in the meeting house where Danforth interrogates the girls who cry witch. When Abigail Williams senses that her case is falling apart, she looks up to the rafters and says she sees a yellow bird spreading its wings: witchcraft! Her hysteria infects the other girls, the judges believe them, and the witches are sentenced to death. I had a whole island at my command, perched on the edge of a continent. I let the yellow bird chase the girls out of the meeting house into the ocean, the entire village in pursuit. "It's a movie!" I told myself. And it looked great, a vivid image of collective hysteria. But it slackened the scene's merciless narrative grip: we'd have done better to stay inside.

The film's emotional climax is something else I pulled onto the edge of the New World. When we came to shoot the final scene for Elizabeth and John Proctor, in a small prison cell on the Massachusetts coast, a violent nor'easter was blowing. So I had them taken outside, and they made peace with each other as the tempest raged around them, and the ocean lashed the shore. The storm was so loud that we had to re-voice the entire scene, but Joan Allen and Daniel Day-Lewis found the same grace in the sound studio as they had in the freezing cold of the day, and it's the best thing in the movie.

The Crucible was a flop at the box office: maybe it was too solemn, and at the same time I was too anxious to prove my cinematic credentials with stampedes into the ocean and other unnecessary hyperactivity. But it was an exciting shoot. Living for three months through the New England fall, I thought for the first and only time that I preferred making movies to directing plays.

While I was working on *The Crucible,* the playwright Wendy Was-
serstein introduced me to the Hollywood producer Larry Mark.
Wendy had written a screenplay for him based on a novel by Stephen
McCauley, *The Object of My Affection.* Her plays were major events in
New York, though London never warmed to her sassy, insecure East
Coast women, who juggled their hard-won independence with their
need to be loved. She had a gargantuan talent for friendship, but she
was lonely and she wrote about it. Like her heroines, she used laughter to keep the demons at bay.

We worked together on four or five different screenplays, while
I slowly realised that if your last movie lost money, you aren't sur-
rounded by love anymore, so none of them was made. But Larry
Mark knew where the hoops were and how to jump through them, so
two years after *The Crucible,* in 1997, Wendy and I made *The Object of
My Affection.* By that time, the screenplay had taken big liberties with
Stephen McCauley's book, but he never complained: novelists have
low expectations of the movie business.

The central idea was Stephen's, but Wendy made it her own: Jennifer Aniston lets her gay best friend Paul Rudd move in with her
when he leaves his boyfriend. Her own boyfriend is starting to drive
her mad, and when she gets pregnant she decides to keep the baby
but end the relationship. She asks Paul to raise the baby with her. He
wants to be a father, so he agrees. As she slowly falls in love with Paul,
he falls in love with another man. He leaves her, and breaks her heart.

Around the central couple Wendy wrote pungent dialogue for
actors like Alan Alda, Allison Janney and Nigel Hawthorne. The
money for the movie came with Jennifer, who is exceptionally skilled,
funny and poignant. She and Paul had transparent rapport. Twenty
years later, there's nothing wrong with one part of the film's premise:
that a lonely, intelligent woman might crave the companionship of
a gay man, and fall in love with him. But these days, a gay American
who wants to be a father can marry his boyfriend and have children.
There's a scene where Paul looks through a chain-link fence into a
playground where a young father is playing baseball with his seven-

year-old son, as if locked out of paradise. It's mawkish but heartfelt: I identified with it, and Paul played it with touching sincerity. But the future belonged to the gay activists who were agitating for the societal change that has left the movie behind.

There was an honest melancholy to the first cut: falling in love's a bitch, sex gets in the way, Jennifer and Paul know they'll never love their partners as much as they love each other. But at test screenings, the audience wanted everybody to be happy, so the studio did too. We reshot the last scene, and the movie was a modest success at the box office, years after Larry Mark first commissioned it and a tribute to his Hollywood resilience.

One afternoon, two years after we made *The Object of My Affection,* Wendy called me.

"I'm about to deliver a baby," she said.

"Whose?" I asked, assuming she was in a maternity ward with a pregnant friend, or maybe researching a new play.

"Mine," she said, and squealed with laughter.

She rationed her secrets among her friends. I'd seen her many times during her pregnancy but noticed nothing, though I knew she was having IVF: we once returned early from a writing trip to Martha's Vineyard so she could have treatment. She never told me who the donor was, and I never asked. Her daughter Lucy Jane was born three months premature. In her most celebrated play, *The Heidi Chronicles,* her alter ego Heidi Holland never compromises, stays single, feels "stranded," and in the last scene overcomes her loneliness by adopting a baby. For the next six years, Wendy lived with Lucy Jane the life she wrote for Heidi, but she was keeping another secret. Everybody could tell something was wrong, but believed her when she said she had Bell's palsy. In fact, she had lymphoma. She died in January 2006, leaving her vast circle bereft.

Arthur Miller remembered that Marilyn wasn't merely beautiful: she was a life force. Wendy thought herself unbeautiful, and loved herself a fraction as much as others loved her. She would have found the comparison with Marilyn ludicrous, but it's what comes to mind.

⁊∾৩

By the end of the 1990s I realised I had neither Larry Mark's resilience nor the vocation for the American film business. My calling is for the theatre, where nobody ever threatens to surround you with love. And I'm not sure what I bring to the party beyond a proprietorial interest in Alan Bennett's work, so I kept my head down until, in 2005, I could claim ownership of it again.

As soon as *The History Boys* opened, film companies made offers, some of them keen to make "a contribution to the casting process." Alan and I wanted the same four teachers and eight boys, and nobody to mess with the script. We share an agent in Anthony Jones, whom we both value for his readiness to dispense with the assumption that a client needs a constant deluge of flattery. What I need is never to be treated as if I'm needy. Alan swears that Anthony calls him mainly to tell him of the achievements of his competitors: "Good morning. I thought it might interest you to know that Harold Pinter has just won the Nobel Prize."

He also knows how to find the money for the films his clients want to make. "If you want to make *The History Boys* without interference," he told us, "make it for less than £2 million." Everybody worked for much less than their market rate, and took a cut of the profits, which were considerable partly because we'd spent so little in the first place. The same trick worked even better on *The Lady in the Van*.

I thought there was no point in trying too hard to have the History Boys run through Sheffield like the possessed girls in *The Crucible* ran into the Atlantic Ocean. We didn't have the budget, and more to the point, the material worked because it was set in an enclosed world, though we did manage a field trip to Fountains Abbey. We spent five of the six weeks it took us to shoot it back at school. The film has a lot of what made *The History Boys* so captivating on stage. But you'd never know, if you hadn't seen the play, that the French scene went nuclear or that the audience stopped breathing in the "Drummer Hodge" scene, though Richard and Sam were just as truthful for the camera as they had been in the show.

The play is still alive in countless new productions, many of them in schools and colleges. And when somebody sent me a pirated camcorder video of a performance by the original cast on Broadway, and I remembered the depth of the silence and the spontaneity of the laughter, I also remembered why I work in the theatre.

⟨∿⟩

I first went to Alan's house, where the lady in the van lived, in the autumn of 1989, a few months after she died. After I moved to Camden Town in the early 1980s, I used to take the detour around Gloucester Crescent on my way to the High Street, mainly to try to work out which creative titan lived where. The crescent was home to any number of writers, film and theatre directors, publishers, journalists and artists; and although I discovered that Alan lived at 23, I had no idea what the yellow van was about, though I wondered whether the derelict old lady who appeared to live in it was his mother.

I didn't think to ask about her when I finally arrived in the study; nor did most of the people who visited the house when she was in the drive. I only realised what I'd missed when Alan finally wrote about her in the *London Review of Books*. Her fame spread in 1999 when Maggie Smith played her on stage. Now, in 2014, Alan was offering for the film the real house in the real street where it all happened.

He insists that there was nothing remarkable, and certainly nothing kind, about what strikes everyone else as fifteen years of lunatic self-sacrifice. He invited Miss Shepherd to park her van in his drive for a month or two, "just till you sort yourself out," and she stayed until she died of old age. Many of the residents of Gloucester Crescent have been there for decades, and shuddered in horror when the van made its ghostly reappearance. The view from the study window helped me understand how Alan survived. I'd sat with him there often enough over the years, but it was only when the van was in situ that I started to get some sense of it as it must have been to the writer who sat at the desk, looking at it. For the part of him that never left the study, the chaos was there not to be suffered, but to be recorded.

So although the movie showed how it actually was, where it actually happened, it isn't literally the thing itself.

This really happened:

(AB *approaches the van.*)

AB: Miss Shepherd. In future I would prefer it if you didn't use my lavatory. There are lavatories at the bottom of the High Street. Use those.

MISS SHEPHERD: They smell. I'm by nature a very clean person. I have a testimonial for a Clean Room, awarded me some years ago, and my aunt, herself spotless, said I was the cleanest of my mother's children (AB *gives up, and goes*)—particularly in the unseen places.

But this, which followed it, didn't:

(AB *catches Alan Bennett's eye as he passes the study door.*)

It's a movie as much about how a writer writes, and why he chooses what to write about, as it is about his subject. Alan splits himself into two: "the self who does the writing and the self who does the living." Alex Jennings played both of them, adding two more incisive performances to the twelve we'd already worked on together.

It's also about what a writer does to what happens in front of his nose to turn it into a story worth telling. Always scrupulous about any departure from the historical record, Alan wrote into the screenplay not just his reluctant recognition that his best subject was living on his doorstep, but his struggle to tell her story without occasionally inventing it, and his discovery that "you don't put yourself into what you write—you find yourself there." So it seemed only fair that after her death, he let Miss Shepherd return from the grave to write her own ending.

MISS SHEPHERD: This thing you're trying to write, you could pump it up a bit . . . Why do you just let me die? I'd like to go up into heaven. An ascension, possibly. A transfiguration.

Her Assumption was the first piece of CGI I ever directed, shot on a big sound stage at Shepperton Studios. "It's like making a proper film at last," said one of the crew, after six weeks squashed into Alan's tiny study. But I'd never been happier on a movie set than I was in 23 Gloucester Crescent, shooting a film about the writer whose plays have been such an important part of my life.

Maggie crawled non-stop in and out of the van, ran up and down the crescent and occasionally complained about her hip. She was in pain, but I hardened my heart: we were on a tight schedule, and I thought if I started apologising, I'd never stop. "I've no time for sorry," I muttered, like Miss Shepherd. I did finally feel guilty when she had to have the hip replaced, a few months after we finished.

We found small parts for the entire cast of *The History Boys.* Maggie eyed them suspiciously from the van. "Here comes another member of the family. I feel very left out."

There is nothing Maggie can't do. At more than one point in the film, she even suggests that she is simultaneously playing what happened and what the writer would have preferred to happen. She is demanding above all of herself, always at her best when the scene asks most of her. Towards the end of *The Lady in the Van,* Miss Shepherd walks into a church hall to filch some free cake. A young pianist starts to play Schubert for the assembled senior citizens. Miss Shepherd's first instinct is to flee: she's avoided music like a curse since she was forced as a young woman to give up her career as a professional pianist. But she turns back.

"Why would she stay? She hates music," said Maggie.

"It's a turning point," I offered, "or is it something about the way the young pianist plays? Does it remind her of the way she used to play?"

"It's very peculiar. It makes no sense. She'd leave the room. Why does she stay?" This kind of thing could go on for several minutes, a necessary build-up. "I don't understand why she listens."

"She just does. We're ready to go."

As the camera slowly pushes in on her, you can see in Miss Shepherd's rheumy eyes her entire vanished youth, a future thrown down the drain. But Maggie never believes you when you tell her she's good.

We were in Camden Town, so life imitated art. I arrived early one Monday morning to find the Art Department evacuating the van of its contents. It had been left in the drive over the weekend, and a couple of drunks had set up temporary home in it. Miss Shepherd's apparently filthy furnishings were now genuinely filthy. "Don't tell Maggie! Don't tell Maggie!" they cried as they took the dirty mattresses away to be deep-cleaned, then made fake-filthy all over again. But they were never filthy enough for her: between takes she looked for food to smear on them. She was delighted when I eventually told her.

The week before we started she went to Oxford, to look through the archive that Alan gifted to the Bodleian Library. It includes the collected writings of Miss Shepherd. Her religious pamphlets, scrawled notes and shopping lists were carefully preserved by her landlord and now share the shelves with the First Folio, the Gutenberg Bible and the original conducting score of Handel's *Messiah*. Through Maggie she achieved a whole new level of posthumous fame.

PART THREE

Old Things

7

A Reason to Do It

SHAKESPEARE

"It was obvious why you did *Henry V,* just after the Iraq War," said a member of the audience at a Q&A before a performance of *Henry IV Part 1* in 2005. "What about *Henry IV*? Was there a reason to do it? Or was it just that Michael Gambon was available to play Falstaff?"

"There is no wrong time to do these plays," I replied sententiously. "They will always speak to us." I might just as well have quoted Ben Jonson: "He was not of an age, but for all time."

Shakespeare was of an age, of course: he wrote for a specific audience at a specific time. And as his plays have hardly ever been off the stage since he wrote them, they are also (so far) for all time. But so much has been said about him that it's easy to find yourself saying it again. King Lear is an Everest of a part. *Twelfth Night* is suffused with autumnal melancholy. The *Henry IV* plays are an incomparable panorama of England. There's a whole parade of clichés about Shakespeare's plays that imply there's nothing new to say about them. But the reason to do them is always to discover them as if for the first time, and to confront the competing claims of then and now.

Awed by *Henry IV,* I never got much further than the incomparable panorama of England. Only in the last few decades have professional historians caught up with the way Shakespeare interweaves high politics with the concerns of ordinary people. In a Rochester inn yard, a carrier blames the death of his friend on inflation: "Poor fellow never joy'd since the price of oats rose, it was the death of him." In Gloucestershire, two neighbours talk about student tuition fees: "I dare say my cousin William is become a good scholar. He is at Oxford still, is he not?" says the first. "Indeed, sir, to my cost," moans the second.

The two plays are as interested in the tavern as the court, and they layer the medieval past with the Elizabethan present. The Boar's Head and its patrons are lifted from the London pubs that their first audience drank in, two hundred years after the reign of Henry IV. The monarchs and politicians that they gossip about come from the pages of the historian Holinshed, but the Prince of Wales has his eyes firmly fixed on the future. "Past and to come seems best; things present worst," says the Archbishop of York: a familiar enough sentiment. There is nothing specifically medieval about a frustrated prince struggling to escape the burden of his birth by knocking around the streets of London with a bunch of troublemakers. The tensions between Prince Hal and Henry IV, the mother of all father–son relationships, are universal. A father treats his son with contempt; the son has to deal with it. What's new—or rather, what's old—about that?

But loving the *Henry IV* plays too much, I felt more constrained by them than I did by *Henry V*. I was wary of bringing too much of the present to them. I wasn't convinced that a narrative about civil war in England, the consequences of regicide, and the stricken conscience of the usurper would make much sense if the plays were presented, as they were in the 1590s, in a modern context. I thought in 2005 that they were driven by a specifically Tudor terror of a return to the bloody chaos of the Wars of the Roses. Writing now, in 2016, that terror feels much closer. Town and country are divided, and so are North and South, Scotland and England. There is nothing remote about Hotspur's rage, on behalf of the neglected North, at "the jeering and disdained contempt" of the proud king. Falstaff, milking Gloucestershire for money and "continual laughter," is the incarnation of London's contempt for Middle England. I overestimated the stability of our body politic and I wish I could have another go at tapping into folk memories of civil strife.

And I underestimated the tremendous freewheeling energy of the plays. They move from the king to Francis the pot boy; from the cynical Falstaff to Owen Glendower who claims, with the utmost seriousness, that he can raise spirits from the vasty deep. There are wild juxtapositions not just of location and class, ancient and modern, but of ways of looking at the world, ways of making theatre. The plays have more faith in the expressive possibilities of the stage than I did. I smoothed too many of their jagged edges. I could have sharpened the contrast between the vaudevillian tavern scenes, the sobriety of the English court, the bucolic detail of the Gloucestershire orchard, the cinematic bravura of the battles.

About Michael Gambon, my questioner in the Olivier Theatre was right. I directed seven of Shakespeare's plays at the National between 2003 and 2015: *Henry V, Henry IV Part 1, Henry IV Part 2, Much Ado About Nothing, Hamlet, Timon of Athens* and *Othello.* All of them started to make sense to me because I could imagine particular actors bringing them alive.

Michael is so irresistible to his audience that he wasted no time on Falstaff's geniality. He softened nothing that makes "that old white-bearded Satan" satanic. Simply by being Gambon, he reconciled two schools of literary criticism: the academic idolaters of Falstaff, for whom he represents in his wit and appetite a justification for any amount of extracurricular drunkenness and lechery, and those who recoil at his serial immorality.

When Gambon spoke to the audience, he worked on the assumption that they were all wannabe Falstaffs. Soliloquies and asides need a clearly defined relationship between character and audience, and more often than not rely on the assumption that the audience is filled with apprentices. The maid in a Restoration comedy, when she turns front and comments on the action, speaks to a host of maids less expert than she is. Richard III speaks to student tyrants, with whom he shares the insights of the master. Hamlet assumes in his audience a philosophical thirst that requires them to make the same journey as his own. In each case, the actor must be clear whom he's speaking to, and what he wants of them. Gambon did not doubt that his seedy old drinking buddies out front would have as few qualms as he did about recruiting the worst dross he could find and sending them into the cannon's mouth.

> I have led my ragamuffins where they are pepper'd; there's not three of my hundred and fifty left alive, and they are for the town's end to beg during life.

A hundred and forty-seven dead, three left to beg for the rest of their lives, and the wages of the dead to be collected by Falstaff in perpetuity if he can get away with it. Job done. And still on the lookout for any opportunity, however grubby: *Henry IV Part 1* ended with Gambon looting the corpses that still littered the battlefield. Michael's innate carelessness about his own *amour propre* dissolved the line between Gambon and Falstaff. At an early preview, they dug each other out of trouble without a whiff of shame.

> The better part of discretion is valour, in the which better part I have sav'd my life. (*Pause.*) No, that's not right. The better part of valour is discretion. That'll do.

Matthew Macfadyen was no more judgemental of Prince Hal than Michael was of Falstaff. The prince declares his hand within minutes of his first entrance, promising to throw off his loose behaviour at his own convenience, looking forward to his glittering reformation and the applause which he knows will greet it. Matthew solicited no sympathy, nor expected censure. In their superb disregard for their audiences' opinions, he and Gambon were in total harmony. Their objectivity was a reflection of the way the plays are written: it's never easy to know what Shakespeare himself thinks, but in these plays the authorial point of view is as good as absent and he seems to work almost as a documentarian.

Hal, Falstaff, the king: the plays, like most of Shakespeare's history plays, have little time for women. Despite being written when the most successful and powerful of all English women was on the throne, they marginalise women more even than they have been marginalised by history. There is no mention of Hal's mother; he refers to his stepmother once, without respect; Hotspur, Northumberland and Mortimer have wives who together take up only a few minutes' stage time; there's a hostess and a whore, and that's about it. What kind of incomparable panorama of England leaves out half of its population? And what kind of production makes no amends for what may be an acknowledgement of historical reality, but feels hard to defend in the context of the age-old insistence that Shakespeare is for all time?

I no longer think it's good enough to insist only that Shakespeare held the mirror up to his own world. To perform his plays is to invite universal participation in them. He demanded of his own audience a suspension of disbelief: piece out our imperfections with your thoughts, and before we get to all our other imperfections, those boys wearing dresses? They're women.

I think we can make the same demands on ourselves. If we claim him as our national playwright, we could start by allowing in the entire nation. Nobody now seriously thinks that skin colour should preclude actors from taking part in the performance of Shakespeare's plays, any more than I should be precluded from directing them because I am a third-generation Jewish immigrant. They belong to all of us: to Adrian Lester as Henry V and David Harewood as Hotspur as much as to (Irish) Michael Gambon as Falstaff. Audiences had no problem with any of them, and will soon have no problem with equal representation of women in the companies who perform his plays. Over the last few years, experiments with gender-blind casting have shown great confidence in the audience's acceptance of the invitation to join an imaginative conspiracy, which is one way of describing an evening in the theatre. Had I included more women in the *Henry IV* company, I would have forced myself to be less anodyne. I would have had to create a stage world where women were part of the political power structure, or a world less confined by the literal representation of power.

Still, the production had its strengths, particularly in its articulation of the great dying fall of *Part 2*. "A pox of this gout! Or a gout of this pox! For one or the other plays the rogue with my great toe," says

Falstaff to his cronies in the audience, and the girl he puts on his knee tells him it's time "to patch up thine old body for heaven." They're all obsessed with decay and mortality. "Is it not strange that desire should so many years outlive performance?" asks Poins as he watches gouty, poxy Falstaff trying to get it on.

"Jesu, Jesu, the mad days that I have spent!" boasts ancient Justice Shallow to his fellow Justice, Silence. "And to see how many of my old acquaintance are dead!"

"We shall all follow, cousin," says Silence.

Shallow was John Wood, with whom I had once done *King Lear* at the RSC. He was revered and even feared by his fellow actors for his fierce intelligence. Fifteen years after *Lear,* and struggling with ill health, he applied his forensic wit to another old man, but this one, instead of raging against an unjust cosmos, seemed to tiptoe to the edge of the grave, dare himself to look in, and creep away in disbelief. As John and Michael Gambon recalled their misspent youth, Michael's eyes turned watery with regret. John asked after Jane Nightwork, a prostitute they both knew. "Doth she hold her own well?"

"Old, old, Master Shallow," said Michael, seeing himself in her wrinkled face.

"Nay, she must be old, she cannot choose but be old, certain she's old," said John, and although he didn't actually say "but I'm not old, I can choose not to be old, I will never be old," that's what you saw: an old man in denial of the relentless passage of time, and in denial too of the fact that he didn't make enough of it while he had it. "Jesus, the days that we have seen!" he said, trying to persuade Michael that they were cut from the same cloth.

"We have heard the chimes at midnight, Master Shallow," said Michael, though you knew as he said it that whether Shallow was there or not when the chimes struck was a matter of indifference to him.

"That we have, that we have, that we have, in faith, Sir John, we have," said John. He hadn't, which was why he had to say he had so often.

John was sometimes so wracked with coughing in the wings that we worried he wouldn't make it onto the stage. With iron will, he suppressed the illness that killed him six years later, and was always there for his entrance. Deluded, shallow Shallow—a man with less iron in his soul than anyone else in England—was the last part he played in the theatre.

~~❧~~

I first met John when I had lunch with him at an indifferent restaurant on 58th Street in New York in 1987 to persuade him to play Prospero in *The Tempest* at the RSC, where I worked briefly before Richard Eyre brought me to the National. I was overawed: John had been part of my Shakespearean education. His Brutus in the RSC's 1972 *Julius Caesar* was the most exciting performance I'd ever seen, a man whose integrity was undercut by his own delight in it, his intellect the source of his self-destructive pride. John's intellect and imagination were supported by a voice of extraordinary expressive range that enabled him to communicate whatever he was thinking to the back of even the largest house.

Imagination and intellect in an actor are nothing without the technique to allow an audience, or a camera, access to them. John had spent a decade in America trying to persuade himself that he was as technically equipped in front of a camera as he was in front of an audience. Maybe the energy that fuelled his stage performances were a handicap in the movies. The camera likes to discover what an actor thinks or feels. Actors more accustomed to reaching out to an audience in a theatre sometimes mistake the need not to demonstrate to the camera for a need to do less, or even do nothing. In fact, the camera ruthlessly exposes nothing for what it is: nothing. Film acting requires every bit as much imagination and variety as stage acting. John's film performances are much better than he thought they were, and he never did too little to be compelling, but it was on stage that he was at his most fascinating. He was happy to return to Shakespeare.

As Prospero, his long, thin frame quivered with a furious hunger for control. His voice wasn't serene or beautiful, and beauty is in any event beside the point. A stage voice is not an end in itself, but I have watched actors construct in rehearsal subtle performances that are ultimately stymied by voices too weak or flat to convey what stays hidden beneath the surface. John's voice was a direct emanation of Prospero's rough magic. His memorial service in 2011 ended with it, recorded live at the Royal Shakespeare Theatre in 1988.

> Graves at my command
> Have wak'd their sleepers, op'd, and let 'em forth
> By my so potent art.

Graves opened and the dead rose in the yawning chasm of the vowels: *graves, wak'd, op'd, forth, art.* These days, nobody has as many stops on the baroque organ as John had, or even wants them. One of the many admiring actors who had come to remember him said with regret that it would be impossible to imagine doing it like that now. With the company of actors who came regularly to the National to perform Shakespeare, I evolved a way of dealing with the text that valued supple naturalism above all. But I miss John's wild music.

I miss too his lack of sentimentality and his volatility, which went some way towards justifying the abstraction of the two productions we did together in Stratford. As King Lear, his wrath when his eldest daughter Goneril demanded a reduction in the number of his followers was terrifying: "Detested kite, thou liest." The rage of all the Lears I had ever seen swelled from this accusation to a crescendo of raw hatred. But John, sweeping his men out of Goneril's house, suddenly turned back to her, possessed by love for her, unable as a father to leave his eldest daughter without embracing her passionately. And in the heat of his embrace, on the verge of asking her to forgive him, love and hate became indivisible, and he found himself cursing her.

> Hear, Nature, hear, dear goddess, hear!
> Suspend thy purpose, if thou didst intend
> To make this creature fruitful.
> Into her womb convey sterility,
> Dry up in her the organs of increase,

And from her derogate body never spring
A babe to honour her!

He hated her because he loved her; he cursed her with sterility because he couldn't bear to leave her. Like so many of the insights I have witnessed in rehearsal, this seemed to come unbidden: I have no idea whether John had planned it. But it was rooted in our bleak shared vision of the play: in the moral universe of *King Lear,* every impulse towards good is mocked by its opposite.

There is no right answer to the question Lear asks his three daughters: "Which of you shall we say doth love us most?" The truth, which is what Cordelia tells him, is probably the worst answer of all:

> I love your Majesty
> According to my bond; no more nor less.

Ethical absolutes collapse under the weight of lived experience. Gloucester blames the gods:

> As flies to wanton boys are we to th' gods,
> They kill us for their sport.

But it isn't the gods who do the killing in *King Lear.* The wanton boys are men and women, and so are the flies. When John got fed up of his tiny, rubbery Fool, he swatted her, picked her up by the scruff of her neck and put her on a hook on the back of a door, where she hung limply until he needed her again. It was no surprise to hear at the end of the play that somewhere along the line, unremarked and ignored, she'd died, hanged, without even being given a death scene.

Cordelia's murder is the last of the play's cruelties, but her reconciliation with her father is almost as troubling as the violence that severs them. The play looks at the love between parent and child and finds it contains the seeds of its own destruction. Lear's downfall is that he treats his three daughters almost literally as his flesh and blood: he expects them to be as obedient to his will as his own body. His two elder daughters would rather destroy him completely than bend to his will; his youngest flirts briefly with autonomy, but when she returns to rescue him, he wants to spend the rest of his life in a prison cell with her, singing like birds in a cage, and can hardly wait to have her all to himself again:

> Have I caught thee?
> He that parts us shall bring a brand from heaven,
> And fire us hence like foxes.

He has learned nothing and there is little to relieve his self-absorption: he's caught her and he isn't going to let her go. It doesn't occur to him that she might have feelings of her own about being incarcerated with him. Not for the last time, I looked for grace in Shakespeare and found it undermined by his ruthless honesty.

I suspect I short-changed anybody who came looking for magnificence. The romantic critical tradition may be dead, but the attachment of audiences to it dies hard, possibly because it has morphed into the formula behind the Hollywood blockbuster. Most superheroes would have no trouble answering to Hazlitt's description of Lear's mind:

> a tall ship driven about by the winds, buffeted by the furious waves, but that still rides above the storm, having its anchor fixed in the bottom of the sea; or it is like the sharp rock circled by the eddying whirlpool that foams and beats against it, or like the solid promontory pushed from its basis by the force of an earthquake.

But the protagonists of *King Lear* are less buffeted by the furious waves than adrift in a senseless moral wilderness. Although there was an undeniable thrill in hearing John's great voice defy the elements, there was no escaping the absurdity of his defiance.

❧

John Wood was the reason I did *King Lear* and *The Tempest,* and he was reason enough, but both productions suffered from a lack of specificity in their stage worlds. These days, I could not stage *King Lear* without making clearer choices about Lear's kingdom, and about the systems that underpin his power as a king as well as a father. And I'd want to know a lot more about the poor, naked wretches whose lives he finally starts to think about when he's forced to join them.

Shakespeare never conceives of his characters shorn of the physical reality of the world around them. In 2009, I directed Racine's *Phèdre,* which does exactly that. The French neoclassical theatre, in self-conscious imitation of the Greek, reduces suffering to its essentials. Phèdre's every waking thought is consumed by the need to take her stepson into her bed, and the subsequent need to conceal it from her husband. The intensity of the tragic experience requires a single-minded focus on the central action alone. Nothing else matters in Racine's Greece.

In Shakespeare's Egypt, there's time for every kind of diversion. Halfway through *Antony and Cleopatra,* Cleopatra asks for music, "moody food of us that trade in love." Then she changes her mind, and decides to play billiards instead. But the woman she wants to play with has a sore arm, and suggests that she'd be better off playing with her eunuch. All Shakespeare's plays are steeped in the mess of life, and by the time I staged *Hamlet* in 2010, they seemed to me not to respond well to the kind of staging that aims to abstract them back to their essentials.

Most British shows start in a set designer's studio. Directors in the rest of Europe develop their ideas about a play with a dramaturg, whose job is to be the intellectual conscience of a production. We are furtive enough about our intellectual foundations to be embarrassed even by the dramaturg's job title: hardly any British theatres have one. When I direct Shakespeare, I smuggle in Peter Holland, now professor in Shakespeare Studies at Notre Dame University, who taught me when I was at Cambridge. With him I talk about the play, as I used to talk in his room in Trinity Hall; but with the designer I start to talk about how to do it.

Vicki Mortimer, who designed *Hamlet,* works in a tiny, freezing studio in an old factory on the Wandsworth Road, with high, cracked windows. She's never designed a West End musical: if she had, she'd have premises as warm as those of three of my other frequent collaborators, Bob Crowley, Tim Hatley and Mark Thompson, whose studios are as elegant as their sets. But the process is the same, whatever the surroundings. We read the play to each other: I cast myself in the best parts. We talk about what it means, and how we imagine it taking shape. We collect photos and paintings. The designer starts to sketch, then to build a rough 1:50 model of the set in white card. There can be twenty different models before we settle on the one that makes it to the beautiful 1:25 final version.

There are one or two highly strung, combative theatre designers: I occasionally came across them as director of the National. As a director of plays, I've worked only with the serene majority. Vicki, imperturbable even during the chaos of a technical rehearsal, can take a play quietly apart as the wind rattles the windows of her studio.

Although I wanted a *Hamlet* saturated in the indignities and ambiguities of the real world, I was taken with the idea that Elsinore is less a concrete image of the world than a series of theatrical images: thematically expressive rather than suggestive of a real centre of power. I remembered a *Hamlet* where the stage walls themselves dissolved at the touch, the director and designer responding to the play's febrile uncertainty about the solidity of objective reality, unfolding it through a series of theatrical coups. I went to Berlin to see the famous 2008 *Hamlet* directed by Thomas Ostermeier. Hamlet was a fat-suited clown, rapping, ad-libbing, organising an audience singalong. The show started in the rain, with a dumbshow of old Hamlet's funeral. Hamlet stared into the grave for what seemed like an age, then fell in. As he clambered out, he started to eat the mud: a savage and dangerous plunge into what the play has to say about madness, decay and death. Mud, it must be said, is something of a constant in contemporary German theatre. The text was heavily cut, rearranged and rewritten, and was played by six actors, Gertrude and Ophelia doubling up, so the consequence of Hamlet's misogyny was to erase the distinction between his mother and his lover. It was sensational.

One way of connecting Shakespeare to the audience is to treat the stage with a poetic freedom analogous to Shakespeare's verse at its most exploratory. Many of the plays sink under the weight of too literal a response to the world they purport to represent. Whatever my reservations about the cool abstraction of my RSC *Tempest,* at least it wasn't *Treasure Island* without the parrot. In many of his romantic comedies, Shakespeare plays with the idea that the experience of love remakes reality. Think about *A Midsummer Night's Dream* or *Twelfth Night,* and you're very quickly imagining on stage a high-fantastical world shaped by fancy.

And yet: the world of *Twelfth Night* is also a world of late-Tudor gentility, a world with a strict domestic hierarchy where fancy is undermined by cakes, ale and box hedges. A director, pulled between the solid reality of Shakespeare's world and the poetic freedom of his imagination, must balance the theatrical virtues of each and discover the point of maximum personal conviction. With Vicki building and rebuilding the *Hamlet* world in white card, I thought I could better help an audience hear Hamlet's internal debate about theatricality and truth, and experience his struggles with his idea of himself, if it experienced with him the world that has brought him to his crisis. I wanted to root him in a coherent world more than I wanted to create a theatrical commentary on it.

So Vicki binned mountains of cardboard, and we moved on to asking ourselves what and when was Hamlet's world. Staging *King Lear,* I thought there was no right time, no wrong time, tried to blend past and present, found some timeless middle way. Timeless, I think now, means insipid. It means that those behind the production haven't thought hard enough about the play, or that they're scared of committing to a partial vision of it. Any vision of the play is bound to be partial. To aspire to anything else is folly or arrogance.

Hamlet was certainly conceived as a contemporary state-of-the-nation play about Elizabethan England: a surveillance state, a totalitarian monarchy with a highly developed spy network. Elizabeth I exerted control through an internal security system that must have impinged on everyone who watched its first performance. At Elsinore, you can't reveal yourself without risking your life. Everything is observed, everything is suspect, no social gesture is trustworthy. Polonius the spymaster sends one of his staff to spy even on his son, Laertes; he forces his daughter Ophelia to spy on her lover,

Hamlet; and meanwhile Hamlet's oldest friends, Rosencrantz and Guildenstern, are hired by the king to spy on Hamlet.

Shakespeare's audience knew exactly what the play was talking about. Many of Shakespeare's colleagues at some time or another found themselves behind bars for saying the wrong thing in front of the wrong person at the wrong time. There's an unimpeachable argument for creating on stage a vivid image of the late-Elizabethan world that gave birth to the play. But that, I said to Vicki, would rob the National's audience of something that Shakespeare's audience took for granted. Hamlet does not ask us to marvel at a strange world, but to recognise our own.

Few of us in Britain today can pretend that we know what it's like to live in a security state, but I wanted to create on stage a world that would be immediately and viscerally recognisable as a world where you put your life in danger by saying the wrong thing. In all Shakespeare's great tragedies, the personal and the political reflect each other: the internal and social lives of the tragic hero are inextricably linked. Hamlet is paralysed as much by the barrier the state puts in the way of anyone knowing anyone else, as he is by his desperate search to know what's going on inside himself. As Elsinore slowly took shape in white card on a model of the Olivier stage, it started to resemble a post-Soviet Central European dictatorship: a baroque palace, now the centre of a modern security state, kitted out with the hardware of the security state, and inhabited by the kind of people who know what it's like to live in terror of their neighbours.

☙

"Who's there?" is the terror-struck first line of the play, though the sentry who shouts it is terrified not of his neighbour but of the ghost he saw on the battlements of Elsinore the previous night. The second sentry turns the question back on the first: "Nay answer me! Stand and unfold yourself!"

In other words: never mind who's there, show me who you are. It turns out to be what Hamlet wants from everyone around him. It is what he wants from himself. He spends the whole play struggling with himself, trying to unfold himself to himself. He tries in vain to persuade those around him—his mother, his girlfriend, his friends, the ghost of his father—to reveal themselves fully to him. For those involved in the performance of Shakespeare's plays, "unfold yourself!" is how to act them.

It is never true of a play that all the answers are available in the text. It isn't how plays work. Novels can give you everything you need to know, but plays are only dimly detectable until they are performed. It is primarily through the imagination, craft and personality of the actor that you encounter Hamlet, Gertrude or the gravedigger. Even Shakespeare's great parts ask more questions than they answer, and require an actor to fill in fascinating gaps left quite deliberately. His smaller parts, however striking, often leave to the actor almost all the work of creating a character with a real biography.

Rory Kinnear was playing Sir Fopling Flutter in *The Man of Mode* when I realised I'd found an actor whose intellect measured up to Hamlet's, without whom I would never have dreamed of doing the play. In George Etherege's Restoration comedy, Rory sang, played the piano, and made short work of Sir Fopling's contorted syntax, but his outrageous ostentation could not conceal his bone-deep insecurity and loneliness. A couple of weeks into the run, I asked him to call by my office, and before he'd had a chance to settle on the black leather sofa, I asked him to play first Hamlet, and then Iago, and whether he'd mind warming up by playing Vindice in *The Revenger's Tragedy*.

I have often found myself enjoying an actor in rehearsal so much that I start to imagine other plays we can do together. But Sir Fopling Flutter is monumentally stupid; Hamlet and Iago aren't. So when I heard myself persuading Rory to play them, I took myself by surprise almost as much as him. I'd learned to beware the baleful look with which he greeted glib or lazy ideas. He looked mournfully at me now, as if Hamlet and Iago were two more of them, his suspicion a reminder of the melancholy and introspection he'd found even in the most ridiculous fop in the repertoire. Eventually the look evaporated, and he said yes. As he left the office he may have been thinking of the time he spent at the National as a small boy, hanging out in his dad's dressing room: Roy Kinnear, the great comic actor, died when Rory was ten.

Simon Russell Beale, another practised Shakespearean, once said that acting is three-dimensional literary criticism. I'm not sure I agree with him. The literary critic reveals the text and the circumstances that gave birth to it. The actor reveals the play, for which the text is only the starting point. Rory uncovered things that Shakespeare left out of *Hamlet,* things that would have made the play last as long as *War and Peace* if he'd put them in, like what really went on between Hamlet and Ophelia before the play starts. That things *have* gone on is plain from the pile of letters she returns to him. "I did love you once," he says, though he never says why he's stopped loving her; and I've seen it done so sardonically that it's impossible to believe. And a couple of lines later, he says, "I loved you not." Which doesn't make it any easier to know whether he did, though it's a familiar contradiction: lovers, like Lear and his daughters, can love and not love simultaneously. In any event, it feels like there's a missing scene near the start of the play for Hamlet and Ophelia that allows you to experience how they are with each other before things start to go wrong. You don't see them together until he's apparently mad.

But a good Hamlet will unavoidably reveal himself as much as he reveals Hamlet, and it is in the combination of the two that the text comes alive. Rory believed "I did love you once," so we believed him, but he trusted Ophelia as little as he trusted anyone else at Elsinore, as little as he trusted himself. In five words, he told you what could have taken Tolstoy four chapters. What he didn't tell you, of course, was what Ophelia felt about him. She's manipulated by her father and by the king, forced to return Hamlet's love letters to him, abused by Hamlet and neglected by Shakespeare: her only soliloquy is almost entirely about Hamlet, revealing little about herself beyond her dejection. But although Ruth Negga had less to work with than Rory, she revealed a hard core of integrity in Ophelia, and her madness was less the result of shock at her father's death than the intolerable tension between what she was and the role she was forced to play.

Shakespeare's plays require an actor always to consider what is not in them as much as what is. And, approached without preconceptions, they also turn out to be not completely trustworthy about what's actually there. Actors can never entirely trust what their characters say about themselves to other characters, nor what other characters say about them. Although Hamlet is painfully honest about himself, he contradicts himself about whether he loved Ophelia because he carries within him both love and its absence. Stage tradition has it that he adored his father, and there's evidence for it in his brief eulogy to him:

> He was a man, take him for all in all;
> I shall not look upon his like again.

But one of the most striking things about the scene between Hamlet and his father's ghost is that the ghost utters not one affectionate word towards his son. The old king is consumed entirely with his own situation, which is understandable enough. He has only recently been murdered by his brother and is now compelled to watch from Purgatory as the same brother beds his wife, under which circumstances we might all find ourselves obsessed by thoughts of revenge. But the absence of anything recognisable as a bond between father and son led us to examine the whole nature of their relationship. The old king was a brutal warrior: there's admiring talk of all the smiting he did when he was alive. Hamlet is a thirty-year-old graduate student who has been absent from his father's court for many years. They have little in common, and it is the gulf between them, we thought, more than the bond between them, that consumes Hamlet, and is one of the things that makes it impossible for him to take immediate action in response to the ghost's demands for revenge.

Sometimes, in rehearsal, you notice that the text doesn't necessarily support what you assume to be centuries of performance practice. In the scene between Hamlet and his mother Gertrude, at the height of their impassioned argument with each other, the ghost reappears to remind Hamlet not to forget what he's been told to do. "Alas, he's mad," says his mother, as Hamlet struggles to control himself. "Whereon do you look?" she asks, apparently unable to see what Hamlet sees.

But when you think about it, you're forced to wonder why Gertrude can't see the ghost. Everybody else who comes across him sees him perfectly clearly. Horatio sees him. The sentries on the battlements see him. Which led us to ask whether it's possible that Gertrude *does* see the ghost, but can't bring herself to admit to Hamlet that she can see him, so she lies. And once whoever is playing Gertrude has decided that she's lying, she must ask herself why she's lying, and whether she's a habitual liar. There are good answers to both questions. She's lying because, even if she wasn't complicit in the murder of her husband, she knows exactly what happened, and like most of the rest of the court, she knows she has married the murderer. Maybe, like the Gertrude in John Updike's novel *Gertrude and Claudius,* she betrayed her husband with Claudius long before the murder. Maybe her whole story in the play is underpinned by a consuming guilt about what she has done, or at least has allowed to happen, which was why Clare Higgins's Gertrude covered up her horror at the sight of her husband's ghost, and continued to talk to her son as if she had seen nothing. For those who knew the play, it was an opportunity to watch it as if they'd never seen it before. Although there were a few, inevitably, who had seen it before, as Clare turned out not to be the first Gertrude to see the ghost. There are few ideas about Shakespeare that someone hasn't already had, though it's always worth having them again as there is nothing more vivid on stage than a scene played with the conviction that comes from its participants' own sense of discovery.

Clare Higgins decided Gertrude was a liar several months before we started rehearsals, when a group of us—including Clare, Rory, Vicki and Peter Holland—spent a week reading through the play as part of the long and gripping journey towards understanding it and deciding how to do it. Clare was baffled by Gertrude's famous description to Laertes of his sister Ophelia's suicide.

> There is a willow grows aslant a brook
> That shows his hoar leaves in the glassy stream.
> There with fantastic garlands did she come
> Of crow-flowers, nettles, daisies and long purples
> That liberal shepherds give a grosser name,
> But our cold maids do dead men's fingers call them.

It's a famous set-piece, lush and picturesque, completely unlike anything else in the play and a fantastically inappropriate way of telling a brother his sister has just killed herself. Clare had already started to run with the idea that Gertrude lies about the ghost. Maybe, we thought, she's also lying about Ophelia's suicide. She's sweetening the pill, pretending it was an accident (though that doesn't wash with the priest who buries her), to spare Laertes the full horror. There is nothing pretty about Shakespeare's other suicides: Othello, Cassius, Antony, Lady Macbeth, even Romeo and Juliet are spared nothing. But Gertrude claims that Ophelia died after she fell in the weeping brook while trying to hang a garland on the branch of a tree.

> Her clothes spread wide,
> And mermaid-like awhile they bore her up;
> Which time she chanted snatches of old tunes,
> As one incapable of her own distress,
> Or like a creature native and endued
> Unto that element. But long it could not be
> Till that her garments, heavy with their drink,
> Pulled the poor wretch from her melodious lay
> To muddy death.

There's a much-reproduced painting by the Pre-Raphaelite John Everett Millais in Tate Britain which in its serene voluptuousness is both a precise illustration of what Gertrude says, and total garbage. It certainly isn't Shakespearean: it's as far from elbow-deep in the real world as it's possible to be. It can't be true.

Which is where we left it until we came to rehearse it, by which time we were groping towards a more complete idea of Gertrude's complicity in the assassination of her first husband. "Gertrude's lying because Ophelia was murdered," I shouted one day. "Claudius had her killed: in her madness, she was capable of saying anything! She knew Hamlet had killed her father. She might have known all sorts of things about her father's work as spymaster. She had to go!" And that's what we did: she was abducted by two of Claudius's men, and dragged offstage. In a regime so tainted by murder and betrayal, it seemed to make perfect sense. When my father, a retired barrister, saw the production, he said that Gertrude wouldn't have lasted a second in the witness box. "You say that after she fell into the brook, her clothes bore her up awhile. Can you perhaps tell the court why you didn't call for help? Or try to rescue her before her garments pulled her down to muddy death?"

My most mind-expanding insights into Shakespeare have come from actors in the rehearsal room, without the long preamble with which directors usually preface even the most banal of suggestions. As a tribe, we can barely ask an actor to move to the left without writing an essay about it, but actors get on with it. One day, without warning, David Calder, who played Polonius, approached the end of his speech of advice to Laertes and flinched. He seemed to dry. And then, under the heavy weight of what felt like deep personal shame, he said:

> This above all: to thine own self be true,
> And it will follow, as the night the day,
> Thou canst not then be false to any man.

From the heart, like many, or even most, fathers, he wants his son not to make his own mistakes. Mired in a corrupt court, he, like everyone else, is incapable of dealing truthfully with others, and of being true to himself. And David Calder's Polonius knew it.

It would be just as plausible to present the Polonius of tradition, a man incapable of self-knowledge, puffed up with self-regard. But David remade three lines worn thin by their relentless repetition, out of context, often by public liars. And suddenly, we knew that Polonius had helped Claudius assassinate the old king, and was tortured by his own treachery.

Here was the real Shakespeare: an actor who provides for other actors myriad ways of telling his stories and of being his characters. His intuitive openness to interpretation is sometimes mistaken for unfathomable complexity. His relish for ambiguity is taken as a challenge to those who would pin him down. But they are consequences of his calling: he writes plays.

No actor is more open to contradiction than Rory, or more capable of the wild mood swings that are a function of Hamlet's infirmity. "What is your cause of distemper?" asks his unreliable friend Rosencrantz, in the way you might ask a friend why he's so depressed. Neither Rory nor I were keen to attempt a diagnosis. There is nothing to be gained by deciding that Hamlet suffers from bipolarity or clinical depression or anything else that, if only the right medication was available, would spare him the trouble of being in the play. To present Hamlet as a case study is to reduce him. Rory, like the best Shakespeareans, subsumed himself into the role, and allowed himself to be surprised by what happened to him.

When Hamlet comes back to Denmark after Claudius's abortive attempt to have him exiled to England and murdered, he has changed in a way he never tries to explain. He's been forced into action, sent Rosencrantz and Guildenstern spitefully to their doom, rescued by pirates, but he seems, finally, to have discovered an inner peace. He stops soliloquising: whatever it is that he's found is impervious to his customary self-analysis. Horatio tries to stop him from the reckless folly of duelling with Laertes, but Hamlet will have none of it.

> Not a whit. We defy augury. There's a special providence in the fall of a sparrow. If it be now, 'tis not to come. If it be not to come, it will be now. If it be now, yet it will come. The readiness is all. Since no man knows aught of what he leaves, what is't to leave betimes? Let be.

The most profound change to his inner life has happened offstage, where the observed of all observers was not available for observation. "Let be," he says, as if he's finally relinquishing control, content to leave his fate to a special providence.

And yet, when he's dying, what seems to possess him is the need to control the story that gets told after his death. Three separate times he urges Horatio to tell it right:

> report me and my cause aright
To the unsatisfied . . .

If thou didst ever hold me in thy heart,
Absent thee from felicity awhile,
And in this harsh world draw thy breath in pain,
To tell my story . . .
So tell him [Fortinbras], with the occurrents, more
    and less,
Which have solicited—the rest is silence.

He's preoccupied by his posthumous reputation even at the moment
of his death. It seems less like letting be than a desperate struggle
with what he's learned about truth: that it's relative, that everyone
in Elsinore has their own version of it, that in the end "to be" is to
be immersed in oneself alone. When Horatio tries to tell Hamlet's
story to Fortinbras, he barely scratches the surface: he was his best
friend, but he has no real idea what his story really was. And Fortinbras couldn't care less, because it suits him to cast Hamlet in his own
conqueror's story, giving him a soldier's burial with "soldiers' music
and the rites of war." In 2010, Fortinbras organised it for the cameras: a cliché of contemporary Shakespeare but an unavoidable truth
about contemporary power. Hamlet's funeral will be nothing to do
with Hamlet. The man who had "that within that passeth show" is
now part of someone else's show, someone else's truth.

"Were you not worried that by setting the play in a paranoid
modern surveillance state you would rob it of grandeur? If Hamlet
is no longer a prince, where's his nobility?" Here again, at a pre-show
Q & A, was the atavistic desire of the Shakespeare audience for
magnificence, nobility, transcendence. But I cannot believe there is
anything inherently magnificent these days in royalty. Its currency is
debased, and contemporary dramatists are more likely to look to it
for titillation than for tragedy. There is magnificence in Hamlet, but
it is less in his position at court than in his mind. There is heroism in
the way he thinks about himself and his place in the world. There is
elation in the experience of his brutal honesty with himself, grandeur
in his direct communion with the audience, and nobility in his determination never to say "love me" but "understand me."

The paranoid surveillance state is nothing new, but the particular world we created for *Hamlet* was undreamed of when Shakespeare wrote it. Among the reasons to do the classical repertoire are both the discovery that things never change and the discovery that things change completely. The staging of the classics always involves walking the tightrope between now and then. It is one of the many marks of Shakespeare's dominance that, in his plays, then seems so much closer to now than it does in much of the repertoire that has been written over the four centuries since he died.

8

The Original Production

STAGING THE CLASSICS

Three weeks into rehearsals for Oscar Wilde's *The Importance of Being Earnest* in the West End, Maggie Smith suggested I might like to come with her to Sir John Gielgud's house for lunch. "He did the original production," said Maggie, "so he may be able to tell us where we're going wrong." Although she was right that I'd like to have lunch with Sir John, the original production was directed in 1895, before he was born, by the actor-manager George Alexander, who also played Jack Worthing. But in February 1993, I was past caring about that: I was fumbling the funniest play in the English language, it was refusing to take wing, and I'd have taken help from the theatre cat.

Sir John lived with his Hungarian partner, Martin Hensler, in an exquisite eighteenth-century house in Buckinghamshire with ornamental gardens, an aviary and an ornate rococo interior. He greeted us at the door, delighted to see Maggie, whom he obviously adored.

"I can't imagine why you're wasting your time with Lady Bracknell," he said to her, "it's a supporting role."

She howled with laughter, which pleased him, though he wasn't joking. He was still livid with Dame Edith Evans for stealing the show when he made the mistake of casting her as Lady Bracknell opposite his own Jack Worthing in his famous 1939 production.

"Jack Worthing is the leading part," he continued over lunch. "Alexander played Jack Worthing. He commissioned the play for himself. The first Lady Bracknell was Rose Leclercq. She wasn't a commanding actress." I thought it wasn't a good idea to ask Maggie to be less commanding.

"I first played Jack Worthing in 1930, directed by Nigel Playfair," said Gielgud. "Lady Bracknell was my aunt, Mabel Terry-Lewis. She had no sense of humour, so she was surprised the audience found her lines so funny, but she knew the play wasn't about her. Then in 1939, I directed it myself and cast Edith. My production was better than Playfair's, but Edith distorted it. We played it on and off right through the war. In 1940 Jack Hawkins played Algernon, Gwen Ffrangcon-Davies played Gwendolen, Peggy Ashcroft played Cecily, Margaret Rutherford played Prism. But all the audience cared about was Edith. The king and queen came to see it in 1946. Still Edith."

I asked why his production was better than Playfair's.

"It balanced the real and the artificial," said Gielgud. "Playfair's production was like a revue. You need to base the fantasy in reality, act it with deadly seriousness, be aware only inwardly of the fun. You need to know where to breathe, of course."

Sir John quoted Jack Worthing from memory. Every phrase was perfectly poised, every breath like music.

"John has just done an episode of *Inspector Morse*," said Martin to Maggie. "We found out what John Thaw gets paid for playing Morse. I mean, it's unbelievable. John didn't get half as much. I was furious with his agent. What do they pay you for a film these days?"

Sir John seemed uninterested in money, so he left Martin to interrogate Maggie. He smiled at me benignly, and it suddenly occurred to me to ask him whether he'd known George Alexander.

"He died when I was quite young, maybe fourteen," said Sir John, "but I met him several times. My great-aunt Ellen Terry knew him well. We all thought very poorly of him because of the disgraceful way he treated poor Wilde when he came out of jail. And I knew Lord Alfred Douglas. He came to see me in my dressing room after my opening night in 1939. He was an old man by then. I asked him about the first opening night in 1895. All he claimed to remember was that he'd written most of the best lines himself."

We were prevented from hearing about the original production only by the Terry family's disdain for George Alexander and by the delusional vanity of the ancient Bosie. Otherwise, I thought as I sat at John Gielgud's lunch table, I'm two degrees of separation from Oscar Wilde, I'm eating lunch with someone who knew his lover, his director, his actors, and when he quoted Jack Worthing to me, he was almost certainly saying the lines the way Oscar wanted them said. *The Importance of Being Earnest* "must originally have been thought funny because it tilted so brilliantly at contemporary society. The people who laughed at it were, many of them, laughing at themselves," Gielgud wrote in his book *Stage Directions*. "Today we laugh at the very idea that such types could ever have existed." So for Sir John, the tightrope between now and then had to be walked back towards the past.

And perhaps Wilde's hermetically sealed world is impervious to the negotiations with contemporary sensibility that old plays normally require. What *The Importance of Being Earnest* needs most of all is actors who know how to land every line. So perhaps what it asks of a director is nothing more than a sure hand in casting, and meticulous attention to phrasing, timing and the arrangement of the furniture. If directors don't know where best to put the door to Algernon's flat in Half Moon Street so as to deliver Lady Bracknell's first entrance with maximum sizzle (and that, at least, I got right), their sensitivity to the play's gay subtext is surplus to requirements.

Maggie was sceptical about anything that hindered the real work, which was to bring life to the play from moment to moment. She'd worked with Sir John, she knew how to play Wilde, and she saw off the shade of wicked old Dame Edith by playing Lady Bracknell as if nobody had ever played her before. She barely gave voice to the handbag. She didn't need to: she merely mouthed it, and before the audience had realised what it had missed, she'd moved them into the cloakroom at Victoria Station, onto the Brighton line, and stopped the show with "The line is immaterial." Lady Bracknell was still the main event.

⁘

Wilde may be a special case. Much of the canon of Anglo-Irish comedy of manners grows more remote by the year, and needs mediation, though the prerequisites are always the same. An actor must think, breathe and feel through long, sinuous paragraphs. You have to reconcile this with the ever-evolving demand to be *real* and *natural,* knowing that what seemed real ten years ago seems stagey today and what seemed natural a hundred years ago now seems ridiculous. And all this as you let them see who you are, see the workings of your heart, your world and the part you play in it. The job is the same whether you're Mrs. Lintott in *The History Boys* in 2004:

> I'm reluctant at this stage in the game to expose you to new ideas, but having taught you all history on a strictly non-gender-orientated basis I just wonder whether it occurs to any of you how dispiriting this can be?

Or Lady Bracknell in 1895:

> Mr. Worthing, I confess I feel somewhat bewildered by what you have just told me. To be born, or at any rate bred, in a handbag, whether it had handles or not, seems to me to display a contempt for the ordinary decencies of family life that reminds one of the worst excesses of the French Revolution. And I presume you know what that unfortunate movement led to?

Or Dorimant in *The Man of Mode* in 1676:

> She means insensibly to insinuate a discourse of me, and artificially raise her jealousy to such a height, that transported with the first motions of her passion, she shall fly upon me with all the fury imaginable as soon as ever I enter; the quarrel being thus happily begun, I am to play my part, confess and justify all my roguery, swear her impertinence and ill humour makes her intolerable, tax her with the next fop that comes into my head, and in a huff march away.

None of these people speak the way people spoke, even then. The actor's job is to make the audience believe they did, but the whole pack of cards comes tumbling down if you do that by trying to speak the way people speak now.

One of the director's jobs is to create a stage world where dialogue written in the high style seems inevitable and spontaneous. Alan Bennett's world is easy enough. The world of Restoration comedy has grown more remote during my theatregoing lifetime. As a teenager with little more experience of the theatre than what I'd seen at the Manchester Library Theatre, nothing was more alive to me than a man in a full-bottomed wig or a woman with a fan. Restoration comedy was rarely off the stages of the repertory theatres, guaranteed to pull the crowds. *The First Churchills* was big on television, Charles II was as familiar as Elizabeth I, the contrived syntax of Etherege and William Wycherley was as easy as Oscar Wilde, and the only thing funnier than a fop was a cuckold.

Even by 1986, when I was an associate director of the Royal Exchange Theatre, Manchester, the plays seemed to have grown stranger, the streets of Restoration London less ordinary, the rules of Restoration theatre no longer part of shared theatrical experience. But Ian McDiarmid, a fellow associate director of the Exchange, suggested to me that we could do Wycherley's *The Country Wife* together, with Ian as the cuckold Pinchwife. It's the funniest of the Restoration comedies, and the saddest, and I charged headlong into the obvious common ground between the materialistic, hedonistic 1670s and the loadsamoney excess of the 1980s. Gary Oldman was the rake, Horner, who puts it around that he's been castrated after contracting the pox in France, so that the husbands trust him with their wives. Gary has since made a career in American movies by pushing into dark corners, and asking the kind of questions he asked about Horner: what kind of man is so driven to fuck everything that moves that he's prepared to tell the town he's a eunuch? It was one of the most single-minded performances I've ever seen, relentlessly sexy, almost psychotic. It was also very funny, and it worked because Gary was in total control of Wycherley's convoluted syntax. He devoured the text. Offstage, he could quote most of *Hamlet* by heart.

When I did *The Man of Mode* at the National in 2007, I still thought that I could bring an audience closer to Etherege's world by linking it to our own. But in the intervening years, the Restoration had slipped even further from the collective grasp. There is nothing remote about the fierce cynicism of the dramatists, nor their satirical relish for towns they excoriate. But the texture of their world, their ruthless celebration of the pursuit of pleasure after the privations of Cromwell's Commonwealth, their indulgence of the viciousness of the dominant male, and the complexity of their language: these become ever weirder. And I had lost some of the operatic extravagance, the easy flamboyance that kept *The Country Wife* airborne. On the Olivier stage, London felt too much like London, and the audience sat there wondering why they were all speaking funny.

I'd done better the previous year with *The Alchemist,* which might have been made for modern London. Written in 1610, sixty-six years before *The Man of Mode,* Ben Jonson's English may be harder to grasp; but it's easier to spend time with chancers parting fools from their money than with rakes parting women from their self-respect. Spectacularly well plotted, *The Alchemist* is about a scam: three con artists take up residence in a house in Blackfriars and persuade a procession of marks that they can turn base metal into gold. Like all the most enjoyable satirists, Jonson simultaneously occupies the moral high ground and wallows gleefully with the pigs in the trough. His three swindlers—Subtle, Face and Doll Common—are virtuoso performers: they switch costume and character as often as a burlesque drag queen. Alex Jennings, Simon Russell Beale and Lesley Manville ran dizzying rings around the suckers who arrived at the house hoping to get rich or get laid: Doll has a sideline in the sex trade. The suckers included Ian Richardson as Sir Epicure Mammon, who needs money to pay for his weakness for fine dining.

> I myself will have
> The beards of barbels served instead of salads;
> Oiled mushrooms; and the swelling unctuous paps
> Of a fat pregnant sow, newly cut off,
> Dressed with an exquisite and poignant sauce.

In rehearsal with Shakespeare, you feel spiritually enlarged. You flatter yourself that through the intimacy of your contact with his plays, you are better equipped to know yourself and to understand the world around you. There is nothing in *The Alchemist* to feed your self-regard. The mysteries of the human heart are not on its agenda. But if you gather actors as inventive as its central trio of hustlers, you're delighted to roll in the mud with them. I'd been watching Ian Richardson since I was a small child. On tour in Manchester as Master Ford in *The Merry Wives of Windsor* in the late 1960s, listening to Falstaff promise to bed his wife, he turned pink with shock, purple with rage, green with jealousy, then white with horror, a whole rainbow of emotion, and I have been hooked on Shakespeare ever since. He took an almost debauched pleasure in Sir Epicure's grotesque fantasies, and equal delight in the profligate skills of Alex, Simon and Lesley.

Ben Jonson was even pricklier than Harold Pinter. He once murdered an actor, which Harold would have thought a bridge too far, and got himself off on a technicality. When he finally went to jail, it was for having a go at the way James I sold knighthoods, in a play called *Eastward Ho!* Despite the warmth of his tribute to Shakespeare in the First Folio, he found much of what Shakespeare wrote ridiculous. He sneered at his Latin, his Greek, his geography and his stupid plots: there is nothing in Shakespeare to compare with the perfection of Jonson's plotting in *The Alchemist*. But it is through Shakespeare that generations of audiences have learned what they want from an evening in the theatre. And because the way they hear the English language has been conditioned by Shakespeare, they're often left floundering by Jonson's obscurities.

When Face threatens to blow the whistle on Subtle, he tells him he's going to:

> Write thee up bawd in Paul's; have all thy tricks
> Of coz'ning with a hollow coal, dust, scrapings,
> Searching for things lost, with a sieve and shears,
> Erecting figures in your row of houses,
> And taking in of shadows with a glass,

Told in red letters; and a face cut for thee
Worse than Gamaliel Ratsey's.

All this within the first five minutes of the play. "Hang on in there," I told the audience at a pre-show talk one evening. "It gets easier. Even with Shakespeare, the first five minutes are always a problem. I sit there thinking that I have no idea what these people are talking about and I'm supposed to be the director of the National Theatre. But you'll tune into *The Alchemist* eventually. So don't give up!"

But you're forced to ask yourself what kind of classical theatre is so hitched to the text that someone has to stand up before the show and tell the audience not to worry if they don't get it. And by the way, who the hell is Gamaliel Ratsey?

He was a highwayman, hanged in 1605, and the delight of imagining the laugh he'd have got at the Globe in 1610 can be left to anyone with the time to read the footnotes, so you cut him. If you read through the rest of the speech slowly it's actually not too difficult, but there's no chance the audience is going to grasp it spoken at full speed in the heat of an argument, even if it's spoken by Simon Russell Beale. So you cut that too: the play is much too long anyway. But there's no getting around its many difficulties, so you're forced to ask yourself whether you should bite the bullet and translate Ben Jonson.

Ten years on, I wish we'd gone further. We untangled some of the worst knots, and replaced words that had disappeared, like "slops," with words that meant the same thing, like "trousers." "The first recorded use of the word trousers was in 1603 so we're fine!" I cried in triumph, after looking it up. But in the end, trousers are funny, slops aren't, and authenticity is for the academy. Jonson's English is going the same way as Chaucer's: a pleasure to read, but not performable in the original. At some point in the future, the same will start to be true of Shakespeare.

Those who had the patience to tune into it loved *The Alchemist* as much as I did, but some didn't, and several complaints about the inaudibility of the actors landed on my desk. They may not have been perfectly comprehensible, but they were audible enough. Most of the complaints were signed in spidery handwriting and compared the shortcomings of modern actors to the splendid clarity of the stars of their youth. I always apologised, and occasionally added that in the National's archive there were letters of complaint to Sir Laurence Olivier from older patrons of the Old Vic about the very generation of actors my correspondents remembered with such admiration.

Only now, released from the shackles of leadership, do I feel able to suggest that one's hearing deteriorates with age. If actors shout loud enough to be heard by the hardest of hearing, they will inevitably compromise the truthfulness of their performances. There's a balance to be struck between absolute honesty and absolute audibility, and a version of the truth that includes a thousand people every night but stops short of deafening the majority who aren't deaf. The induction hearing loops provided in nearly every theatre in the country are very good, though I learned never to mention them in my letters of apology, as if I did there'd usually be an explosion of rage by return of post.

❧

"We can always do *Arms and the Man*," I said, whenever the weekly planning meeting threatened to run out of ideas. Nobody could think of anything they'd less like to see, so the ideas started to flow. George Bernard Shaw was a useful symbol of the self-satisfied West End, his plays advertised by roguish photographic vignettes of beloved stars of yesteryear. But by the time we started to plan 2007, I knew that the audience for the Travelex £10 Season was up for anything, and that it was my unfortunate responsibility to give them Shaw. I recognised his importance, even if I dreaded having to sit through endless performances. I sat down to read him for the first time in decades and started what I thought would be a long slog through *Saint Joan*. "You should read this. I promise you'll want to do it," I said to Marianne Elliott afterwards. She'd just joined the National as an associate director and wondered why I was trying to press on her something from the collected works of the perpetrator of *Arms and the Man*.

But she read *Saint Joan*, and her production of it was a great event, voted favourite Travelex show in an audience poll. Anne-Marie Duff played Joan: slight and vulnerable, she swept before her the French army, and the Olivier audience, with her incandescent self-belief. With a spasm of guilt, I started to feel the lure of Shaw. You can't tell which side he's on: Joan burns with the unquenchable flame of conscience, while the authorities defend the wider community from the dangerous anarchy of the unfettered individual. "What will it be when every girl thinks herself a Joan, and every man a Mahomet?" There are women who think they are Joan, and men who take instructions from Mahomet, all over the world now. Marianne did not address them directly, nor the authorities who struggle to contain them, but Shaw's play from 1923 saw them as clearly as we do who live with them, and with greater insight.

"You should read *Major Barbara* next," suggested Philip Pullman, who after *His Dark Materials* had joined the National's board. Hayden Phillips, Chris Hogg's shrewd successor as chair, levitated with excitement. After a distinguished career as a Civil Service mandarin, Hayden could never quite conceal his desire to start over as an actor. Theatre boards aren't supposed to get involved in what they call the art, but it was hard to resist Philip's advocacy or Hayden's enthusiasm. I read *Major Barbara*.

"Maybe you should play Andrew Undershaft," I said the next day to Simon Russell Beale, who was as sceptical about Shaw as I was. "Maybe I should direct it. It will do us good. We'll find out how much we can make ourselves like Shaw."

Simon read the play. "I never play alpha males," he said. "Are you sure?"

Andrew Undershaft is certainly alpha: a successful arms manufacturer who returns to his estranged family and discovers that his daughter Barbara is a major in the Salvation Army. He challenges her to visit his factory, and in exchange visits her shelter. He rips the veil of hypocrisy off the business of saving souls: Barbara's mission is dependent on those it despises, the whisky distillers and arms dealers whose money it solicits. For Undershaft, the only real crime is poverty, and the Salvation Army cons the poor with dreams of heaven.

From *Saint Joan* we had learned how little credence to give the old charge that Shaw was without passion. His people throb with the visceral excitement of argument. If an actor commits to it body and soul, argument becomes as passionate as a declaration of love. We still cut a third of it: Shaw is so entranced by the sound of his own voice that he can't get enough of it. For a modern audience, enough is more than enough. But what remains has the kind of muscularity that makes it a dream to play in the Olivier, which is more hospitable to fiery rhetoric than to delicate restraint. Plays conceived by Shaw for performance behind a small Victorian proscenium arch turn out to be ideally suited to a big public arena. "Do you call poverty a crime?" asks Barbara's fiancé, and Undershaft replies:

> The worst of crimes. All the other crimes are virtues beside it. Poverty blights whole cities; spreads horrible pestilences; strikes dead the very souls of all who come within sight, sound or smell of it. What you call crime is nothing: a murder here and a theft there, a blow now and a curse then; what do they matter? They are only the accidents and illnesses of life: there are not fifty genuine professional criminals in London. But there are millions of poor people, abject people, dirty people, ill-fed, ill-clothed people.

Even this is pruned, and it continues for at least as long again. But in performance it's thrilling. And Simon never minded how long it went on for. "I love long speeches," he said.

Another of the charges against Shaw is harder to dismiss: that though his plays may be passionate in argument, they avoid emotion, rather as he ran away from emotional turbulence in his life. On the page, it's often hard to point to any deep level of engagement with the characters he creates. But as soon as you get his plays into rehearsal, you realise how pregnant with emotion are the situations he creates. In *Major Barbara,* a man returns to his family after an absence of twenty-five years and his daughter meets her father for the first time in her life.

In the dialogue he writes for them, Shaw couldn't care less about how either of them feels. He's much more interested in their conflicting beliefs. But the text, of course, is only half the story. The relationship between Undershaft and Hayley Atwell as Barbara grew from what they didn't say to each other far more than from what they actually said. Simon was moved beyond words by his first sight of his daughter. Hayley tried to convert him because she felt his unhappiness not in what he said but in what he couldn't say, in the fact that he couldn't even bring himself to touch her. Much of the best acting springs from need. "I want!" screams the actor, often inwardly. With Shaw, it is necessarily inward, because he rarely writes emotional need into what his characters say.

Less defensible than his readiness to leave his actors to do the emotional heavy lifting is that Shaw can never resist undercutting them if he can see an opening for a lame wisecrack. You can spend a morning building an emotional life around a scene only for it to collapse under the weight of his humour. "Take us seriously, you facetious prick!" I yelled at him one day, but he was too busy moving on to the next insufferable one-liner:

> Like all young men, you greatly exaggerate the difference between one young woman and another.

"Cut!" we all cried. But we had to admit that he almost single-handedly reintroduced serious theatre to London after more than a century of sentimental melodrama and trivial comedy, and he knew that his late-Victorian audience would have rejected his plays if he hadn't sugared the pill with jokes.

Shaw's glib dishonesty was the dark underbelly of what makes his plays crackle with energy. He was an apologist for Stalin and, briefly, for Hitler, but his intellectual terrorism now, as then, is a challenge to the complacency of the *bien pensants* who come to the theatre.

> When you vote, you only change the names of the Cabinet. When you shoot, you pull down governments, inaugurate new epochs, abolish old orders and set up new . . . NOTHING IS EVER DONE IN THIS WORLD UNTIL MEN ARE PREPARED TO KILL ONE ANOTHER IF IT IS NOT DONE.

In 2008, I couldn't ask the crowd in the Olivier to pretend that it was watching the original production and knew nothing of where the world's Undershafts had led us since 1905. Shaw asks for his final act to take place in the yard of the munitions factory with an idyllic view of the model town it sustains, which loads the dice far too heavily in Undershaft's favour. So we pulled it inside a surreal warehouse, packed with row upon row of enormous missiles, and underscored it with a constant ostinato of distant explosions. The wicked eloquence of the arms dealer still gave the disasters of the twentieth century a run for their money.

Simon and I finished up as Shaw's grudging admirers and the National produced two more of his plays before I finished. From being my bête noire, he virtually became my house dramatist. *The Doctor's Dilemma* in 2012 and *Man and Superman* in 2015 were as packed out as *Saint Joan* and *Major Barbara* had been. *Man and Superman* was lit up by Ralph Fiennes as John Tanner, some of whose ideas about sexual politics are now as offensive as Undershaft's about peacekeeping; but Ralph's mind worked at such seductive speed that he landed them as persuasively as if they'd been the work of Gloria Steinem.

❧

Ralph Fiennes's charisma is unique, and has sustained a brilliant career on stage and screen, but he is not alone in his speed of thought, his vocal penetration and his ability to work through the text to an underlying emotional truth. They are the necessary equipment of any actor who wants to communicate the great body of classical theatre written in English. Those of us who direct it are indebted to the continuing excellence of British drama schools. Despite big changes to the profession for which they prepare their students, the great drama schools remain committed to the classical tradition. Their graduates, who saddle themselves with vast debts to finance their training, will never make a living in the theatre substantial enough to pay them off. They must be equipped to act in front of the camera, where if they're lucky they can earn enough to raise a family and subsidise a theatre career. Film and television put a premium on the kind of naturalism that won't get an actor very far with George Bernard Shaw, let alone

George Etherege. Fifty years ago, when Restoration comedy was still a rep staple, it was worth taking the trouble to devote whole courses to it, and to send actors into the world with special expertise in snapping open a fan. It would be hard to argue for that now, but young actors still enter the profession ready not just for film, but also for the highly wrought artifice of a complex text. The best of them never stop learning to reconcile their desire to be real with the demand made by the great playwrights of the past to be articulate. The young ones sit quietly in rehearsal and watch Ian Richardson and Maggie Smith, who watched Ralph Richardson and Edith Evans.

Directors differ in the way they bring together actors and text. Some start with the text, some end with it. Some take the text apart around a table, find out what it means, why it's being said, how to say it spontaneously, what surrounds it. Others create a world, maybe through improvisation; then they encourage actors to build characters within it, and finally lead them back to the text in the last few days of rehearsal. I've seen both approaches work, and admire colleagues at both ends of the spectrum. Although I place myself at the end that starts with the text, I'm not, like some directors, obsessed with it to the degree that I won't let actors get on their feet to play a scene until they've picked it to pieces. As they start to get under its skin, I like them to inhabit it physically. I don't like a rehearsal studio to feel like a seminar room.

On the tiny handful of occasions at the National when a company of actors came close to mutiny, it was always because the director refused to move on to the business of doing the play: "We've been sitting around talking about it for *weeks*." Or, just as frustrating: "Why are we improvising? Why are we playing games? When will somebody tell us where to come on, when to sit down, and how to say the lines?" Most actors buy into rehearsal games only up to a point. Secretly, they like being told what to do, if only to be able to resist it.

The rigours of classical text continue into the twentieth century. The actors in the National's production of Terence Rattigan's 1939 play *After the Dance,* its first in London for seventy years, were thoroughly in command of dialogue as brittle as anything in *The Man of Mode.* But they earthed their hard-drinking throwbacks to the roaring twenties in melancholy exhaustion, and an appalled recognition of their own irrelevance in the face of the global catastrophe that is about to engulf them. James Joyce's 1915 *Exiles* isn't *Finnegans Wake,* but it still isn't easy. Joyce fans flew in from all over the world in 2006, like ardent connoisseurs of avant-garde jazz. The linguistic extravagance of the Irish repertoire is maybe closer to the way the Irish still speak than Rattigan and Noël Coward are to the grunting incoherence of the English. Irish actors are rarely fazed by complex text, and have been as central to the English classical tradition as Irish playwrights like Congreve, Farquhar, Sheridan, Wilde, Shaw and Beckett. The Scottish cast of Ena Lamont Stewart's 1947 *Men Should Weep,* set in a Glasgow tenement, met the English audience halfway in their delivery of the Glasgow dialect. Its wild music was easier to tune into than Ben Jonson.

> Christ Almighty! A we've done wrong is tae be born intae poverty! Whit dae they think this kind o life dis tae a man? Whiles it turns ye intae a wild animal. Whiles ye're a human question mark, aye askin why? Why? Why? There's nae answer. Ye end up a bent back and a heid hanging in shame for whit ye canna help.

Errol John found music just as potent in a Port of Spain backyard, and in the Trinidian English they speak there, in his 1957 *Moon on a Rainbow Shawl.* And for the Louisiana Sicilian community in *The Rose Tattoo,* Tennessee Williams wrote dialogue in 1950 that seems to come from the same world as Italian opera.

❧

The Rose Tattoo was a personal triumph for Zoë Wanamaker, and was cast and prepared by the director Steven Pimlott, who died after rehearsing it for a little more than a week in February 2007. He had been diagnosed with cancer the previous summer, and when he went into remission, it seemed an urgent necessity to stage one of the twentieth century's most life-affirming plays.

We started talking about the theatre at Manchester Grammar

School, though it may be more accurate to say that I started listening to him, as when I arrived at the school he was already a dazzling talker. In the Dramatic Society, his Gertrude and Mother Courage were the stuff of legend. In 1968 we were both in *Oh What a Lovely War!* Steven was the undisputed highlight, delivering the recruiting song "I'll Make a Man of You" with outrageous laid-back allure in an off-the-shoulder satin evening gown. There was an outing a few months later to see the recently released Richard Attenborough film. We gave it a reluctant thumbs up, though there was universal dismay at Maggie Smith's failure to measure up to Pimlott. We both played in the school orchestra and in the local youth orchestra: Steven was a marvellous oboist, I was a dodgy flautist. When I went to Cambridge, he was my entrée into undergraduate theatre. I acted in his shows, he in mine, and I played his servant, which seemed right, in Molière's *Le Bourgeois Gentilhomme.*

His friends struggled to keep up with his enthusiasms, which acknowledged no boundaries between high art and low, and were a massive influence on my own. He could be inflamed by Mozart, Agatha Christie, Shakespeare, Gilbert and Sullivan, French classical drama, Blackpool Pleasure Beach, and while it wouldn't be true to say that, like Shakespeare's Banished Duke, he could see good in everything—he was magnificently dismissive of what he didn't like— there was nobody more catholic in his taste, or more generous. He was completely at ease outside the English tradition. He was fluent in French and German: he met his German wife when he directed her in a French opera in Krefeld. And he was impressive in Italian and Russian. He knew and felt their cultures from within, and in his productions of continental classics, he was often more a poet than a narrator, as much a mystic as an analyst. It was how he approached the English repertoire, too, alert always to those things in heaven and earth that were undreamt of by many of his British contemporaries.

Tennessee Williams was right up his street: he responded viscerally to Williams's emotional rawness, his poetic extravagance, his sympathy with those clinging on by their fingernails. We assumed he would be able to see it through, though we agreed that if anything happened, I'd be his backup. So we worked together for the first time in nearly thirty years, but I never properly told him how much I owed him.

⌒∽∂

I would have liked to see Steven take on the European repertoire at the National. He was keen to direct *The Misanthrope*. As it was, I drew a total blank on Molière, and from the great canon of French classical theatre managed one Racine and one Marivaux, which was not enough. In my defence, the French repertoire is notoriously hard to translate, though outside the English-speaking theatre, translation is often synonymous with adaptation and liberation, so difficult old texts can be pulled wherever a director wants them to go.

British audiences don't expect a facsimile of the original production, but they won't go with a director beyond the point where they lose sight of the playwright. They want a production to tell them what kind of play they've come to see, which still leaves a director with a vast amount of room for manoeuvre, but they usually smell a rat if the play is nothing more than a vehicle for the director's imagination. They prefer the director's imagination to reveal the play, rather than the other way around.

This leaves too much room in the British theatre for the kind of production that does no more than apply a coat of gloss to a play and leave it to fend for itself. I'd far rather see a director go out on a limb than to draw an intellectual blank. And you can count on an audience to know enough about *Hedda Gabler* to take on the chin an argumentative production. But if you're inviting them to a play they're unlikely to have seen before, like Ibsen's monster epic *Emperor and Galilean,* which had never been staged in English before Jonathan Kent's production in 2011, they want access to Ibsen more than to its director.

Before biting the bullet, we read through the whole thing in turgid Victorian blank verse over a long day at the NT Studio: in A.D. 361, the Holy Roman Emperor Julian the Apostate tried to abolish Christianity as the religion of state and restore worship of the ancient gods. In the middle of the afternoon, with hours still to go, a soldier had to warn the emperor about the enemy's vanguard.

"The elephants are in the van!" shouted the soldier.

"I still want to do it," cried Jonathan, after the hysteria had died down. His riotous enthusiasm sustained the Almeida when he ran it, and is now a gift to the many theatres who queue up to work with him. His staging of *Emperor and Galilean* embraced the modernity of what Ibsen had to say about fundamentalism and totalitarianism, and at the same time gave its audience as lucid an account as possible of a play that it had never seen and would never see again.

Howard Davies was the director all actors wanted most to work with, and he made a series of productions of Russian classics that were wholly original not because he came at them from an unexpected angle but because moment by moment they were invested with complex, unpredictable truth. He worked with the Australian dramatist Andrew Upton, whose versions acknowledged the impossibility of creating an English mirror-image of the Russian originals, so he found independent life in them, based on but not bound by literal translations. When Gorky wrote *Philistines* in 1902, "naturalism was an experimental, even radical form of theatre," wrote Andrew. He and Howard restored naturalism to its radical roots.

Bulgakov's *The White Guard* is set in Kiev during the civil war that followed the Russian Revolution. The city is occupied by the Germans, under attack from Ukrainian nationalists, and preparing for the imminent arrival of the Bolsheviks. At the centre of a play that swings from high farce to grotesque horror then tragic elegy is an irresistible family of tsarists. Stalin couldn't get enough of them: he returned to see *The White Guard* over and over at the Moscow Art Theatre.

"The story's so good," said Howard at a planning meeting in 2010, before he went into rehearsal. "Youngish group, one woman, living like students in an apartment. They look after a young schoolboy relative. They argue about war, politics, get drunk, chase the girl to no effect. Then set off to put the world to rights. War turns out to be vile and shocking—farcical, absurd, cruel and pointless. Metaphor for life. The woman's brother dies a heroic death, his younger brother goes mad with distress. The schoolboy has his heart broken. They all meet up again in the apartment, older, wiser, damaged. It's Christmas. They try to celebrate but fall silent as the bells ring out.

And because there's no lead character, everyone will identify with whomever they want to, or have a point of entry through whichever experience chimes most truly or painfully. What's not to like?"

He took for granted that one of his jobs was to communicate the play's politics and historical context to an audience unfamiliar with them. His productions crackled with intellectual energy. But the way he described the play—not in terms of his concept, but of its humanity—was unpretentious and straightforward, a foundation for the wild and contradictory passions he and his actors unlocked in it. His death in 2016 robbed the British theatre of a large part of its conscience.

Deborah Warner is one of only a small handful of British directors since Peter Brook whose reputation means much outside the English-speaking world. Most of us are written off as hopeless reactionaries, though our playwrights are admired. There may be a connection between the primacy of British playwrights and the determination of British directors to put the plays rather than themselves centre stage, but if there is, it gets us no credit in the citadels of the European avant-garde. Deborah's production of Brecht's Mother Courage had in Fiona Shaw an artist whose thrilling command of a mighty part matched the vast following she brings with her to the theatre. She's always a hot ticket, though neither she nor Deborah could persuade me to love Beckett's Happy Days, despite their vivid work on it. I recognise its greatness, but it suffocates me: I'm less resilient than Winnie, its protagonist, who stays cheerful even when buried up to her neck. As director of the National, I suppressed my misgivings about Beckett. A bishop who had doubts about the existence of God would have been less fearful of exposure as a heretic.

❧

In one zone of the repertoire, the audience would go wherever the director wanted to take them. The out-and-out strangeness of the Greek tragedies is part of their continuing grip on the public imagination. Another part is the staggering immediacy of their 2,500-year-old passions. Even in London, the audience for the Greek plays expects radical solutions to their alien theology, their vanished cultural milieu, their remote theatrical conventions. Nobody comes to the theatre expecting to know what it was like to watch Sophocles in Athens in 450 B.C. They expect directors and actors to make major negotiations with the ancient world on their behalf, to find contemporary correlatives to the outlandish theatrical universe of the originals. Actors often do their best work with the Greeks, their imaginations released by terror.

No director responded with more intensity or authority to them than Katie Mitchell in her productions of two plays by Euripides: *Iphigenia at Aulis* and *Women of Troy.* She rejected the public, demonstrative element in the plays that made the Olivier their natural home: both filled the entire width of the Lyttelton proscenium arch. For *Iphigenia,* there was an immense requisitioned mansion, swarming with the marooned Greek army; in *Women of Troy,* the captured Trojan women waited for their brutal dispersal in a warehouse with huge iron doors. None of the action was shared with the audience. We were invited to peer as appalled observers as if through a transparent fourth wall. Katie's actors, disciples as much as colleagues, never played to the audience: their immersion in their hermetically sealed world was total. She led them beyond the frontiers of naturalism. It is assumed that the masked Chorus sang and danced its part in ancient Athens; Katie filled the plays with eerie bursts of song and dance. The Women of Troy danced jazz standards as if to ward off their inevitable end. There was a chorus of "All Things Bright and Beautiful" to give religious legitimacy to the sacrifice of Iphigenia. We were spared none of the pitiless barbarity of war, its moral anarchy, the desperation and dignity of the women who are caught up in it: everything that makes Euripides speak across the millennia.

Katie took her shows for small children—*The Cat in the Hat, Beauty and the Beast, Hansel and Gretel*—as seriously as she took Greek tragedy. Busloads of five-year-olds were ferried into the rehearsal room to watch run-throughs, interrogated about what they thought of them, their notes rigorously incorporated into the shows. She uses the stage to reflect the sheer strangeness of human experience, but I grew to dread her first previews.

"What do you think, boss?" she always asked.

Though disarmed by being called boss—she was alone in that—
the reply more and more often was: "I can't see and I can't hear." I
had nothing but admiration for a sensibility that is far outside the
British mainstream. I recognised the integrity of her absolute insistence on allowing the audience access to the experience rather than
making them part of it, of directing her actors to play only for each
other and never for the house, on lighting her hyperreal spaces strictly
in accordance with real onstage light sources regardless of whether
they revealed the action to the audience. But audibility and visibility
are negotiable only up to a point. I found it increasingly difficult to
defend her shows, and she did nothing at the National during my
last two years. She works with consistent success in Germany, where
audiences are readier to go wherever the director takes them, and
happier to accept the director's method of travel.

9

The Age and Body of the Time

MORE SHAKESPEARE

In a world consumed by greed, Timon of Athens, plutocrat and philanthropist, is a man whose estimation of his own worth is entirely financial. After he runs out of money, he faces a catastrophic credit crunch. Those he thought to be his friends—a bunch of unscrupulous bankers, politicians and their disgusting hangers-on in the arts world—desert him. He turns on them, and flees to a wasteland outside the city. There, digging for food, he finds gold. He spends the rest of the play spewing invective against the parasites who are now queuing up to befriend him again, his misanthropy eventually consuming him. He leaves the stage to die of self-disgust.

Timon of Athens is often rediscovered in the wake of a financial crisis, but in 2012, as Greece imploded under the weight of its debts, I resisted the temptation to build a production entirely around the title. The play has nothing to say about Athens. Its original targets were the aristocratic big-shots and Scottish bankers who were the new game in town after the accession of James I, but it would have taken a theatrical imagination less opportunistic than mine not to recognise in it a satirical image of fat-cat twenty-first-century London. And in the poet and painter who crawl around Timon, touching him for his money, desperate for his patronage, slagging him off as soon as his back is turned, I saw a hideous reflection of my own circle.

The first scene in the 2012 production in the Olivier is a reception at a grand art gallery endowed by Timon. It observes to the letter many of the First Folio's unusually detailed stage directions—"*Enter Lord Timon, addressing himself courteously to every suitor*"—as they devour champagne and canapés in front of El Greco's *Christ Driving the Money Changers from the Temple*. The irony of the setting would be overwrought if it wasn't the sober truth. The El Greco is in the National Gallery, where I have drunk champagne in front of masterpieces of religious art that mocked the company they looked down on. "I like your work," says Timon to the painter as she tries to interest him in her probably dreadful portfolio. "And you shall find I like it." Music to her ears.

In the second scene, Timon gives an extravagant dinner for notables from Politics, Finance and the Arts. The play calls for a "*masque of Ladies as Amazons*." I ask Edward Watson of the Royal Ballet to create a contemporary Amazonian *pas de deux* for two tall ballerinas in leotards. Ed knows exactly what I mean: arty soft porn. He's danced plenty of it himself, worn the leotard, been to the parties, sat next to the sponsors. His *pas de deux* is ice-cool. At the end, there's an onstage standing ovation: "*The Lords rise from table, with much adoring of Timon.*" Dinner is served by young people in sexily tailored black shirts and trousers, the obligatory waiter's uniform at upmarket parties. They are drama students, many of whom have worn the same uniform and served the same dinner at real upmarket parties where ice-cool dancers have provided the entertainment.

Timon is unique among Shakespeare's protagonists in having neither family nor lover nor friends. He appears to have no inner life whatsoever, which is red meat to Simon Russell Beale, who sets out to discover why. Money, we think, must be Timon's armour against the world: a way of buying the world's gratitude without having to engage with it. He stands bail for a young protégé and springs him from jail, he receives a gift of two greyhounds from a powerful politician and responds with an even better gift, he hands out lavish goody bags at the end of his parties. Money oils the wheels of his network. But Timon shrinks from physical contact: he can barely bring himself even to shake hands.

When Timon suffers his own personal liquidity crisis, his social value plummets. Nobody wants to know him. I remember the story of Alberto Vilar, the American investment manager, who showered money on the Metropolitan Opera, the Royal Opera House, the Salzburg Festival, any number of impeccable cultural causes. He had his own seat at the Met, on the front row of the Vilar Grand Tier. He sat there alone, night after night. The more he gave, the more he promised to give, until, with the inevitability of a satiric fable, it turned out the money wasn't his to give. It belonged to his investors, and he'd embezzled it to give it away. Alone in his prison cell, at the start of a nine-year stretch, what must he have thought of his erstwhile suitors as they rushed to chisel his name off the fruits of his fraudulent philanthropy? The Vilar Grand Tier at the Met, the Vilar Floral Hall at the Royal Opera House, the Vilar Young Artists Programme—all of them scrubbed clean.

Timon is warned he's run out of money by his steward, the one person who cares about him. The play has no interest in relations between the sexes: women are brought on stage only to dance or to be the object of Timon's misogyny after his fall. The bankers, politicians, artists and personal assistants in a contemporary Timon's world can as easily be women as men, so it isn't hard to achieve something approaching parity in the casting of it. Flavius the steward becomes Flavia, though in retrospect the name change seems unnecessarily pedantic. It's an opportunity to bring Deborah Findlay back to Shakespeare ten years after *The Winter's Tale*. She and Simon make as much of what isn't in the text as what is. Flavia loves Timon, but he is utterly incapable of being loved. She cares for him, but he refuses to be cared for. Both are trapped by what they can't say. Simon and Deborah make of an apparently loveless play a study of the barriers to intimacy.

When Timon's creditors threaten to pounce, and the recipients of his largesse refuse to help him out, he invites them to one last dinner, one last encounter with the sexy black-clad waiters: "*Enter Servants with covered dishes.*"

"All covered dishes," says a titillated senator.

"Royal cheer, I warrant you," says another.

But *"The dishes are uncovered and seen to be full of steaming water."* And Timon speaks at last from his withered heart:

> May you a better feast never behold,
> You knot of mouth-friends! Smoke and lukewarm
>   water
> Is your perfection. This is Timon's last,
> Who, stuck and spangled with your flatteries,
> Washes it off, and sprinkles in your faces
> Your reeking villainy.

A tiny textual tweek ("Smoke" becomes "Filth") and the scene is set for the most satisfyingly cathartic spectacle I've ever staged, Simon Russell Beale splatting the fat cats with shit, the least they deserve in 2012.

After the interval, Timon's discovery of gold seems to come from a different play, or at least a different production. The satirical precision of the first half is reflected in Tim Hatley's caustic designs: when Timon tries to borrow money from the banker Lucullus, his offices are in Canary Wharf with a view over the HSBC building. But in the second half, satirical comedy changes with a lurch to moral fable. In a wilderness outside the city, the homeless, hungry Timon digs for roots and finds buried treasure: as if by magic, he's rich again, and all the bloodsuckers come back to ask him for money. Tim designs an urban wasteland, left behind perhaps by some failed property development. Simon, pushing his belongings in a shopping trolley, rains maledictions on humanity.

But I always look away when, after a little light digging, he finds a trapdoor and gold light floods from it as if we are suddenly in an Indiana Jones movie. When he clambers into the trap and pulls gold ingots out of it, I want to fire the director. I would happily fire the playwright, too, but I'd have to decide which one to fire. Because the source of the problem is that there are at least three: Shakespeare, his younger contemporary Thomas Middleton, and me.

There is no record of *Timon* ever reaching the stage during Shakespeare's life. Recent textual scholarship has demonstrated that Middleton wrote around a third of it. It's an unfinished first draft, full of inconsistencies, something that was never subjected to the rigour of an audience. Many of the stage directions, unlike anything else in the First Folio, feel like Middleton's memos to himself.

> *Hautboys playing loud music. A great banquet served in: and then enter Lord Timon, the States, the Athenian Lords, Ventidius which Timon redeemed from prison. Then comes dropping after all Apemantus discontentedly like himself.*

You can imagine Middleton scribbling down a precis of what he and Shakespeare agreed he'd write: halfway through the scene, bring on Apemantus, the philosopher, the malcontent, like himself, the way we agreed he'd be.

Middleton, like Jonson, was a go-to playwright for satirical comedy about contemporary London, a genre Shakespeare never attempted, which may have been why he needed help with *Timon*. Much of the London fat-cat material is Middleton's, and it's terrific. Timon's furious arias are Shakespeare's, as is most of the experimental second half, where Timon spits venom at everyone who visits him. He cools down only to excoriate the world with the philosopher Apemantus, played at the National with passionate contempt by Hilton McRae. Despite the wild vigour of the verse, the play sinks under its weight. You can see why they put it to one side, unfinished.

So we finished it, cutting large chunks, adding others to make more sense of what was left. We granted ourselves some of the translator's licence. Many productions of Shakespeare in translation appear to be freer and more radical than our own. In another language, you can bend the text to your will, cut it and rewrite it when it contradicts the story you want to tell, or—in the case of *Timon of Athens*—the story the playwrights tried but failed to tell.

The final visitors to Timon in his wasteland are a delegation of Athenian senators, who ask him to return to Athens to lead their army against an insurrection led by the rebel Alcibiades. Ten minutes before the end of the play, with no warning, we're asked to believe that its protagonist is a military genius.

FIRST SENATOR: Therefore so please thee to return
　　with us,
　　And of our Athens, thine and ours, to take
　　The captainship, thou shalt be met with thanks,
　　Allowed with absolute power, and thy good name
　　Live with authority. So soon we shall drive back
　　Of Alcibiades th'approaches wild,
　　Who like a boar too savage, doth root up
　　His country's peace.
SECOND SENATOR: And shakes his threat'ning sword
　　Against the walls of Athens.
FIRST SENATOR: Therefore, Timon—

This is unforgivable dramaturgy, and if it arrived on my desk from
a living playwright, I'd send it straight back with a frosty suggestion
that it needed more work. This time, I did the work myself, and
decided that the senators should want what everyone else who visits Timon wants: his money—in their case, to finance the defence of
Athens from the rebels.

LEPIDUS: Therefore so please thee to return with us,
　　And to our Athens, thine and ours, to bring
　　Thy gold.
　　So soon we shall drive back
　　The wild approach of Alcibiades
　　Who like a boar too savage, doth root up
　　His country's peace.
ISIDORE: And leads his threat'ning rabble
　　Against the walls of Athens.
LEPIDUS: How shall we defend them without gold?
　　Therefore, Timon—

It's not great, some of it doesn't scan, it smooths out a perfectly comprehensible inversion ("Of Alcibiades th'approaches wild"); and the
invented extra line ("How shall we defend them without gold?")
betrays a bad writer's fear that the audience won't get the point unless

it's beaten into submission with a mallet. But it's an improvement on what made it into the First Folio.

We raided *Julius Caesar* and even *As You Like It* to plug some narrative gaps, though few people noticed besides Ralph Fiennes, who visited Simon in his dressing room after the show and quoted back to him all the lines we'd stolen from *Coriolanus*: he'd just made a movie of it. But for most of the second half, Timon's alienation is so profound that Shakespeare abandons him outside the boundaries of the action and lets him howl. That Simon managed to shape the howl into something worth watching was the show's most remarkable feature.

❧

Everyone has ideas, everyone's a director. Hamlet is rarely so confident as when he directs the Player King. Racked with doubt about more or less everything else, he knows for certain what actors are for: "to hold as 'twere the mirror up to nature: to show virtue her feature, scorn her own image, and the very age and body of the time his form and pressure." He tells the Players how to act, too, which never goes down too well with them in a properly observed production. One thing to be said in Timon of Athens' favour is that he doesn't try to tell the poet and painter how to write or paint. "I like your work" is about as far as he goes, which for most artists is as close to criticism as they'll take from their patrons. "I like your work very much" would be better. "I like your work much more than I like anyone else's" would be best.

But Hamlet knows what the point of doing Shakespeare is: in his plays, you discover not just the image of virtue, but the age and body of the time. If you direct Shakespeare, you must decide whether you're aiming for a reflection of his world, your world or a theatrical distortion of them. You start in the study, and you go into rehearsal with a sense of the whole, but you leave yourself room to be surprised, because the actor playing Gertrude may suddenly bolt up a road you never noticed. You must know how to use the stage, to manipulate space, to move actors across it. You need to impose, or evolve, a common approach to what holding the mirror up means, to how much you require of the audience's imagination, to what constitutes real, to how to deliver the text. You're sometimes teacher, like I was with the young cast of *The History Boys*; but there's nothing you can teach Simon Russell Beale and Deborah Findlay, so you're sometimes coach, editor or sounding board. You're the one who reminds them, when you're rehearsing a scene with them, that they mustn't know what happens next.

"The word that keeps pinging out of Iago's soliloquies," says Rory Kinnear, who needs no reminding, "is 'now.' He works on instinct, in the moment." We're working through the first act of *Othello,* and we've noticed that Iago has no master plan. He's been passed over for promotion by a general at whose side he's fought many times and whom he thought he could trust: Othello, played by Adrian Lester. Iago knows the general is secretly about to marry Desdemona. His plan for revenge, such as it is, is to ruin the general's wedding night, to "poison his delight" by letting the bride's father Brabantio know the name of the hotel they've eloped to. Iago fails in this, as he fails in nearly everything he tries to do in Venice, where he's out of his depth. Events overtake him, and Othello is given command of the Venetian army. Iago has no strategy. He's an opportunist who takes control only when the environment suits him, which it does when the action moves to an army base in Cyprus. He isn't Lucifer. He isn't Machiavelli. He's a soldier.

Shakespeare requires his fellow actor to be large enough in his imaginative and empathetic capacities to track a psychologically and emotionally plausible path through the play. Rory had no interest in a diagnostic approach when he played Hamlet; nor does he want to identify in Iago a specific personality disorder, and define his cunning and callousness as symptoms of psychopathy. He doesn't want to distance himself from the role and present a case study. He allows himself to be surprised by what happens to Iago, a man who has perfectly good reasons to be what he is at the start of the play, who isn't fully in control of what happens next, to whom the action of the play occurs spontaneously, as life happens to all of us. Rory invites us not to observe a disordered alien, but to imagine what it would be like to be Iago, so consumed by hatred and envy that he allows them to run out of control.

The received wisdom is that *Othello* is a play best suited to a studio theatre. It seems to have had its first performance at James I's court, in relative intimacy. Most of the action unfolds in small rooms, it prefers the domestic to the epic, and it is tightly focused on its four or five major protagonists. But National Shakespeare is public Shakespeare, so *Othello* is in the Olivier.

The Olivier Theatre is of its time. For twenty or thirty years in the middle of the twentieth century, architects drew their inspiration from the theatres of ancient Greece, and audiences relished their uninterrupted sight lines and democratic openness. You can see why the builders of a new National Theatre would reject the stratified auditoria of the Victorian West End, the sight lines as cramped as the seats, the gallery accessible only via a special outside entrance to keep the plebs away from the grandees in the stalls and circle. The Olivier, based on the ancient theatre at Epidaurus, is a thrilling place to watch a show if the play, the production and the actors are up to it. The problem is that for nearly 2,500 years, between around 500 B.C. and 1970, nobody wrote plays for huge semicircular theatres on the Greek model. Even the Globe, to which Shakespeare's company transferred *Othello* after its Whitehall premiere, had a chaotic inn-yard familiarity. Still, I never lost my relish for commissioning or staging plays for a theatre that insisted on "making a large appeal to the whole community," a central plank of Harley Granville Barker's original manifesto. I enjoyed wrestling the Olivier to the ground, and the most effective throw was always to work with actors who had the personality and technique to pull 1,150 people towards them. But to abandon those actors for an entire evening on what could feel like a football field never did them any favours, so I always advised directors new to the Olivier to think of creating a much more defined acting space within it.

Designing *Othello,* four years after *Hamlet,* Vicki Mortimer had to enclose Iago and Othello in a small office, Desdemona and Othello in a small bedroom, Iago and the troops in a small barrack room. On the other hand, we didn't want to deny the communality of the Olivier, or the epic sweep of its stage. So two enclosed rooms, the size of shipping containers, moved alternately from the far corners of the stage into the centre, opening to provide small, bleak military accommodations. Pulled back again to the corners they formed part of the perimeter of a vast parade ground: the central public area of the army base that is the setting for most of the play. The most intense scenes, like Iago's destruction of Othello's marriage and the murder of Desdemona, all played out on a tiny fraction of the Olivier stage. They were fuelled by epic passions, but were physically confined as much as they would have been in a tiny pub theatre.

It barely occurred to us to play *Othello* as anything other than a contemporary play, nor to unmoor it from its roots in the real world. It is devoid of fantasy. The reflection in the mirror is pin-sharp: soldiers stationed abroad, waiting for orders after going into a war that never happened. But I needed help with the army, a world about which I knew nothing. A mutual friend introduced me to Jonathan Shaw, who had recently left the British army after thirty-two years in the Parachute Regiment. He'd served in the Falklands, Cyprus, Northern Ireland, Bosnia, Kosovo and Iraq, where he commanded the British-led division in Basra. We met after he'd read the play for the first time since school.

"Well, I know exactly where Iago's coming from," he said as we sat down to lunch, which was a bracing start. He quoted a truism about the military hierarchy: that every career bar one ends in failure. He said that many ex-military personnel would sympathise with how Iago feels about Othello's betrayal of his trust when, before the play starts, he promotes Cassio, a well-born university graduate, over him. Trust, said Jonathan, is the basis of all soldiering. Othello and Iago have fought together and faced death together. They've probably trusted their lives to each other. Betrayal, the most heinous of military sins, is the last to be suspected. It was no surprise to Jonathan that Othello trusted Iago over his wife.

For Jonathan, *Othello* was a piece of detailed social realism about his own world, though it has next to nothing to say about armed conflict. Othello is employed by the Venetian Senate to fight the forces of the Ottoman Empire for control of Cyprus. But within seconds of Othello's arrival in Cyprus, only half an hour into the play, the Ottoman fleet is sunk in a storm. "Boiled down to the basics," wrote

Jonathan in the *Othello* programme, "armies have traditionally been designed to kill people and break things." Now Othello and his army must stew in barracks instead of carrying out the task for which he's best suited. Iago, cheated of his revenge in Venice, has Othello and Cassio at his mercy in a barrack-room hot-house which is much more the NCO's element than the general's. Jonathan Bailey, transparently honest as Cassio, was never better than when he blamed himself for trashing his own reputation: all Iago's doing. "And into this context of operational turmoil," wrote Jonathan, "Shakespeare introduces sex. Civilian spouses and partners do not go on operations with their partners, based on the long-held view that the two strongest human urges—for sex and violence—should be kept apart." Desdemona is only there because Othello, newly married and besotted, exploits his political masters' urgent need for his services by insisting that if he accepts command, his new wife comes too. It turns out to be a huge mistake, another fault line that Iago can exploit, busking his way from stratagem to stratagem as he tears Othello apart.

A man without a plan must watch with preternatural concentration for his chances, and if an actor is entirely absorbed in what's unfolding in front of him, he can impose his vigilance on the audience. Spotting the disgraced Cassio lurking with Desdemona outside the office, Rory starts drip-feeding suspicion into Othello: "Ha? I like not that." Finding his wife, Emilia, with Desdemona's handkerchief, he forces her to give it to him and within a couple of minutes he is improvising an elaborate proof of Desdemona's adultery around the handkerchief. But, instinctively, he knows not to move too quickly, and keeps back the physical evidence until he can use it most effectively. Flying by the seat of his pants, he leaves it in Cassio's room, and waits for his break. Then he persuades Othello to hide in a toilet cubicle to overhear him engage Cassio in crude locker-room banter about the local woman he pays for sex. When the woman herself appears with the handkerchief that Cassio has found and given to her, Rory's eyes nearly pop out of his head: he can hardly believe his luck. But he pounces like a cat, and the audience is onto it with him, entirely implicated in the escalating malevolence of an ordinary man with a grievance who lets it run out of control. As he has no exit strategy whatsoever, the flood of dishonesty inevitably washes him away in its wake. You can see Rory start to panic as it engulfs him. As he is led out of Othello's quarters by the authorities at the end of the play, he turns back to look at the three corpses on the bed, stunned at the apocalyptic issue of what started as a sordid act of petty revenge.

⸙

Othello's disintegration, in Adrian's hands, is as terrifying as anything I have witnessed on stage. To a high degree, his life until his collapse is a performance, but whose isn't? There is much in Othello's background that seems remote to most of us: he was a slave, then a child soldier, and has since been commissioned from the ranks and reached the very summit. But anyone who has ever felt out of their depth at the top table will recognise what he does with the Venetian Senate to buoy up his performance:

> Rude am I in my speech,
> And little blessed with the soft phrase of peace . . .
> And therefore little shall I grace my cause
> In speaking for myself.

Surrounded by those born to rule, he apologises for himself before going on to speak in a manner so extravagant that you know it's a cover. Adrian's Othello, though a mighty general, is all of us. His construction of himself is a reminder of how shaky are the foundations of the self we send out into the world. He gives Iago a lot to work with.

He's also black, but Adrian and I agreed from the outset that his race is only part of his identity. We rejected centuries of performance tradition that insisted that race, or even racism, is the play's primary subject. The Venetian Senate appoints as its commander-in-chief an African general without even pausing to comment on his race: Venetian oligarchs always appointed a foreign mercenary to command their forces as they were wary of giving too much power to a member of their own elite. The same Venetian Senate, in *The Merchant of Venice,* allows Portia to stitch up Shylock. The same Venetians ascribe everything bad about Shylock to his being a Jew, and can barely let a moment go by without spitting out the word Jew as a term of abuse. But when they refer to Othello as the Moor, they use the term chiefly as a descriptor, the way Hamlet is called the Dane. There are racist characters in *Othello,* but all three have good reasons to hate Othello. Iago hates him because he's passed him over for promotion. Roderigo hates him because he's married his girl. Brabantio was once Othello's friend and colleague, and is the father of the teenage girl whom Othello has secretly and suddenly married. All three express their hatred in terms that now seem unpardonably ugly, but their racism appears not to be part of the social fabric.

By the nineteenth century, race had become virtually the play's only subject. Critics and audiences assumed that everything Othello is and does is because he is black. The National Theatre's 1964 production of the play still accepted that Othello's murderous jealousy was a return to his innate African barbarism. Old traditions die hard. Several recent productions, mired in the nineteenth century, have presented Othello as the exotic other, ear-ringed, with a thick African accent. At the Hamburg Schauspielhaus in 2005, he was a white actor in grotesque black-face, strutting through a series of horrible racist stereotypes, now James Brown, now Michael Jackson, a portrayal offered as an ironic commentary on the play, but still fixated on the colour of Othello's skin.

This isn't what Shakespeare wrote. Othello is vulnerable to Iago and insecure in his marriage for many reasons. He's a career soldier, never before married, unable to see in his young wife anything other than perfection. Women are a mystery to him. Desdemona is less than half his age. She's from the ruling class, and he is ill at ease with Venice and its inhabitants, "super subtle Venetians," as Iago calls them. He's a soldier among civilians, a stranger among Venetians, a middle-aged bachelor in a whirlwind romance with a teenager, and also a black man among white men. When he starts to have doubts about Desdemona's fidelity, he lists some of his insecurities:

> Haply, for I am black,
> And have not those soft parts of conversation

> That chamberers have, or for I am declin'd
> Into the vale of years (yet that's not much)
> She's gone.

In his first attempt to understand what's happening to him, he worries about being black, but no more than he worries about being a crude conversationalist and about being (not very) old.

Adrian and I wanted to return *Othello* to a world where it wasn't bizarre or unimaginable for a powerful soldier to be black, and to restore the emphasis of the tragedy as much onto Othello's internal landscape as on the tension between him and the world he has worked so hard to be part of. As Rory kicked away everything that supported Adrian's self-assembled identity, as Adrian writhed on the washroom floor, he returned to a barbarism that was not innately African but innately human. He was capable of murder not because he was the other, but because he was us.

❧

The naturalism and immediacy of both Adrian and Rory were in part the consequence of their readiness to open themselves entirely to the extremes to which we are all capable of being driven. They were also a function of their command of the medium through which they told their stories. Both have the physical and vocal capacity to express whatever they think, whatever they feel. And they have the same basic approach to the speaking of Shakespeare's text, an approach that I encouraged in all the actors who joined the National to play Shakespeare.

There is no mystery about it. "Verse speaking" is not a special skill distinct from acting or speaking comprehensibly, neither of which come easily without training and experience, but both of which can be torpedoed by fear of the iambic pentameter. Shakespeare demands what should be habitual fixations for any actor: relish for what you speak, delight in your own imagination, belief in your own articulacy and the emotional capacity to take yourself apart. He asks you to think before you feel: emotion is the consequence of thought.

Nobody cares how deeply you feel if you get stuck in an emotional rut: we'll be bored if you aren't as volatile as your character is. Very often, you'll find that Shakespeare helps you by using a clear rhetorical structure, or by writing a smooth five beats a line, and when the sense of what you're saying pulls against the regularity of the beat, he's helping you by allowing you to exploit, if you want to, the tension between the sense and the rhythm, because only an idiot would say to *be* or *not* to *be* that *is* the *question*.

So understand what you're saying, say it like you mean it, and use the rhythm if it's there. It doesn't matter if you don't know what a caesura is, because you'll probably be observing a short break in the middle of the line anyway, by speaking the sense of it. Don't make a meal of it: you'll have heard how important it is that every line should be "new-minted," as if you're discovering it for the first time, but if you stop to find the thought every time you want to say something, we'll be here all night. On the other hand, don't speed through it as if speed is inherently virtuous. Give yourself time. Life ebbs and flows. If you go fast just because you've been told to go faster, we won't understand what you're saying, and we'll be bored. Make sure you can be heard, but don't shout. Acquire and beget a temperance that gives smoothness to your passion, suit the action to the word, the word to the action, and all the other relentlessly quoted balancing acts that Hamlet urges on the Players: he may be an amateur but he's right. He never mentions "verse speaking," by the way, because whatever else he is, he's never pompous.

In Act 3 of *Othello* Shakespeare writes this bleak little exchange for Iago and his wife, Emilia:

IAGO: How now? What do you here alone?
EMILIA: Do not you chide: I have a thing for you.
IAGO: You have a thing for me? It is a common thing.
EMILIA: Ha?
IAGO: To have a foolish wife.
EMILIA: O, is that all? What will you give me now for the
same handkerchief?

IAGO: What handkerchief?
EMILIA: What handkerchief?

It's a close-up of an abusive marriage, in entirely naturalistic prose that's almost Pinteresque in the way it catches the cadences of the bully and the bullied. Scarcely five minutes later Othello is swearing vengeance on Desdemona:

> Like to the Pontic sea,
> Whose icy current and compulsive course
> Ne'er feels retiring ebb, but keeps due on
> To the Propontic and the Hellespont,
> Even so my bloody thoughts with violent pace
> Shall ne'er look back, ne'er ebb to humble love,
> Till that a capable and wide revenge
> Swallow them up.

The second follows from the first, the grubby theft of the handkerchief leading to the volcanic flow of Othello's jealousy, the blunt prose of the loveless marriage morphing into extravagant iambic pentameters. They call for the same acting process. Rory and Lyndsey Marshal as Emilia found their monosyllabic muttering in a loveless relationship. Adrian had the voice, the range, the long, long breath control for his extravagant oath; but the language scorched because he was immersed entirely in a self-invented man who reached spontaneously for a wild Homeric simile. It was the inevitable consequence of the performance Othello gives to the world, which includes the projection of himself as classical hero. When he can no longer sustain the performance, the words stop coming, language comes apart, and Othello loses consciousness:

Lie with her? Lie on her? We say "Lie on her" when they belie her. Lie with her! That's fulsome: handkerchief—confessions—handkerchief...It is not words that shakes me thus. Pish! Noses, ears and lips. Is't possible? Confess? Handkerchief? O devil! (*Falls into a trance*)

Othello ends with an act of shocking domestic violence: on the Olivier stage in the cramped bedroom of a bleak Corimec prefab. Othello and Iago both murder their wives before Othello stops the play for one last symphonic deluge of words that climaxes in his suicide, his final act of self-invention. But the two wives in *Othello* die as victims, cut off mid-flow as they struggle vainly to force their husbands to accept the truth. In yet another play about soldiers, the fourth I'd done at the National (*Henry V* and *Henry IV Parts 1 and 2* were the others), the women are collateral damage in the collision of two men.

At least they have voices independent of their husbands, an advance on the other three plays, even if their worlds are circumscribed by their marriages. In Olivia Vinall and Lyndsey Marshal as Desdemona and Emilia they had interpreters who refused to be mere sacrifices. Sharing a beer outside the prefab on the night of Desdemona's death, they spoke not just as resilient army wives but as defiant survivors of abuse. "How goes it now?" asked Lyndsey as Emilia. "He looks gentler than he did." Only a few hours after she saw Othello hit Desdemona, she wanted to tell her that she knew what it meant to be stuck in a violent relationship. They allowed the night to envelop them, then Olivia asked:

> Dost thou in conscience think—tell me Emilia—
> That there be women do abuse their husbands
> In such gross kind?

Are you kidding, of course there are, and a good thing too, the men deserve it, said Lyndsey. Though in fact she said:

> There be some such, no question . . .
> Let husbands know
> Their wives have sense like them . . .
> Then let them use us well: else let them know
> The ills we do, their ills instruct us so.

But such was the command of these two actors over the text, that the audience heard it with kitchen-sink immediacy. They also heard it as it was: the 400-year-old conversation of two tough, articulate and exceptional women. Bridging the gap was what we aimed for every time we did Shakespeare.

⌖

I am fonder of *Much Ado About Nothing,* which I did in 2007, than any of the Shakespeare I have ever done, maybe because Leonato's house in Messina is an almost testosterone-free zone. Locker-room machismo only arrives with Don Pedro's army: a band of mercenaries, presumably recruited from all over Italy, commanded by a Spaniard on behalf of the Spanish crown, billeting itself temporarily before further action. The first instinct of Leonato's Sicilian household is to throw a party: you don't get the impression that it is in any way incomplete before the army arrives. It seems content and at ease with itself. It's quite hard to negotiate through the first forty-five minutes of the play without repeated gales of phoney stage laughter.

On the one hand, I said to Vicki Mortimer, this is the least fantastical of all Shakespeare's comedies: no fairies, no forest, no separation of twins by tempest. But on the other hand, if we bring too much of the reality of the present into it, we'll have to ask too many questions about the war this army has just fought. The play isn't about war; it isn't even much about soldiers. Don Pedro's army is a narrative convenience, a way of bringing unattached men into a house full of women. It needs a real household.

And Vicki and I were very taken with what Peter Holland pointed out to me about the three-way pun in the title. It's much ado about nothing, as in nothing worth making a fuss about. It's much ado about nothing, as in no thing, the Elizabethan slang for vagina. And much ado about nothing, as in noting, one of the ways the Elizabethans pronounced nothing. None of this will be much ado to a contemporary audience, but the third pun is a big clue. The failure to note properly, to look properly, to listen properly is what the play's about. Virtually every man in the play gets it wrong: Antonio, Borachio, Leonato, Benedick, Don Pedro and Claudio all think they see something, but they're not looking carefully enough. The main plot is about the terrible consequences of not looking, not engaging: the young officer Claudio proposes to the beautiful Hero, daughter of Leonato, after a whirlwind romance, and then throws her over at the altar after he thinks he sees her at her bedroom window making love to another man. It never occurs to him to ask her about it. The subplot, the more famous romance, is between Beatrice and Benedick, who apparently despise each other, but they learn to see each other warts and all, and so love each other.

The National's *Much Ado* came from one of my frequent conversations about Shakespeare with Simon Russell Beale. Our warm friendship seems often to exist through Shakespeare, even though we've done only two of his plays together. Either one of us could have suggested it, and I have no memory which of us it was. We knew we'd try to persuade Zoë Wanamaker to do it with us at the same time as we knew we'd do it. We knew that, although there's nothing in the text to suggest what age they are, Beatrice and Benedick would be in advanced middle age, and that the play would to some degree be about us. I knew that once again Shakespeare would hold the mirror up not just to nature, but to myself. Simon knew the same thing. Neither of us would deny our Shakespearean solipsism. We know ourselves through Shakespeare.

Beatrice and Benedick, like everyone in Shakespeare, are as much a revelation of their actors as they are of the playwright, who gives them far less to play with than you'd imagine after seeing a decent production. Benedick has 161 lines and Beatrice has 111. Hamlet has over 1,000, and that's still not enough for him to let us know all the stuff that an actor must decide for himself. The actors playing Beatrice and Benedick have to create a whole history for themselves, as the playwright says almost nothing about the origins of the palpable pain that they cause each other by being in each other's presence.

This isn't faulty playwriting: it's another of Shakespeare's sure-footed acts of trust in his actors to complete the job for him. Zoë and Simon built a detailed past for themselves, based partly on the hints about it that are dropped in the play, partly out of their own intuition and experience. They assumed that theirs was a long friendship;

that at some stage Beatrice read their deepening friendship as blossoming love; that she pushed too hard and that Benedick did a runner. Benedick, we assumed, was a greater coward than Beatrice. And the memory is still raw. These secret histories are essential actors' tools, never intended to be legible to an audience, but the foundations for suggestive, fully human performances. Zoë and Simon's history kicked in from their first exchange, which is often and effectively played as a public performance, the opening sally in a prototypical battle of the sexes.

> BEATRICE: I wonder that you will still be talking, Signior
>   Benedick: nobody marks you.
> BENEDICK: What, my dear Lady Disdain! Are you yet living?
> BEATRICE: Is it possible disdain should die while she hath
>   such meet food to feed it as Signior Benedick?

Ha, ha, ha goes the company, to let us know how much they all enjoy the way these two always take a pop at each other. But not this time. Zoë and Simon found each other in a corner away from the crowd, in a private acknowledgement of the disdain that masks deep hurt.

The world was Sicilian, late sixteenth century, with a relaxed modernity about it: Vicki and I decided this time to follow Shakespeare in his cavalier treatment of period and location. An ancient Sicilian courtyard enclosed an elegant contemporary belvedere: slatted timber walls divided the vast Olivier revolve into four enclosed playing areas, and provided all of them with positions where eavesdroppers could hide, and overhear, and fail to note, but remain visible to the audience. At the last moment, just before Vicki finished the set model, I asked her whether she could dig a hole in the middle of one of the four playing areas.

"The scene where Benedick hides from Don Pedro, Leonato and Claudio, and they know he's hiding, but he doesn't know they know, so they talk ostentatiously about how much Beatrice loves him to trick him into declaring his love for her—when he hides, it should bring the house down. Give me a deep pool, and he'll jump into it."

I've always trusted Vicki's rigorous intelligence to put the brakes on my excesses, but her eyes lit up.

The show started before the audience came in. Leonato's house is an image of domestic contentment. My own private image of paradise has always included breakfast under a fig tree outside a crumbling French or Italian farmhouse, fabulous coffee, apricot jam and conversation. What the hell, I thought, it's my show, I get to decide what contentment is, it starts with breakfast, and breakfast starts half an hour before the show goes up. When I watched, I used to arrive well before curtain up and wish I was at the table with them.

Breakfast ends when Don Pedro's army arrives in Messina, and within minutes Claudio has his eye on Hero. They are barely allowed by the playwright to talk to each other, but once Claudio has made sure that Hero is Leonato's heir, he quickly proposes to her. He's making a conventional, sensible marriage, and everyone's happy, so they decide to try to get Beatrice and Benedick together too. The battle between them is less a battle between the sexes than a refusal to come clean with themselves. Like so many of Shakespeare's protagonists, they construct performances for themselves to conceal real selves too painful to acknowledge. They play resident wit in their respective worlds: they make happier people laugh from the lonely corners they've painted themselves into. Their banter is a front for their emotional dishonesty. So Don Pedro decides on a therapeutic trick to make them admit to the "mountain of affection" they have for each other, by manoeuvring them into overhearing their friends gossip about how much the one secretly loves the other. It's time for them to take the plunge.

Simon was alone centre stage with a book, taking into his confidence an Olivier audience he assumed to be made up of confirmed bachelors like himself, protesting his determination never to fall in love, when Don Pedro, Leonato and Claudio came in. Not wanting to be disturbed, he took himself off to another part of the garden, only drawn back when he overheard their scripted conversation. "Come hither, Leonato," said Don Pedro. "What was it you told me of today, that your niece Beatrice was in love with Signior Benedick?" Simon stalked them as they strolled through the garden, stunned by the confidences they seemed to be divulging, despite their patent lack of subtlety.

> CLAUDIO: I did never think that lady would have loved any
>   man.
> LEONATO: No, nor I neither, but most wonderful that she
>   should so dote on Signior Benedick, whom she hath
>   in all outward behaviours seemed ever to abhor.

And at the key moment, as they turned down the wrong path, threatening to walk smack into him, he panicked and hurled himself into the pool and disappeared beneath the water with an enormous splash. They waited for as long as Simon could hold his breath. The longer he held it, the louder became the rolling laugh that started with the enormous splash. Eventually his head slowly surfaced over the edge of the pool.

I get a disreputable kick out of building to and delivering a big laugh. In my defence, when I started seeing Shakespeare's comedies in the late 1960s, the general assumption seemed to be that they were funny only to the extent that their extraneous comic business was funny. They relied on comic props, pratfalls and routines. The splash was my only indulgence, and both its victims made the most of it. Simon, after his tormentors finally left the stage, still bobbing like an inflatable pool toy, thought over what he'd heard about Beatrice:

> Love me? Why, it must be requited.

His hair plastered to his head, his moustache dripping, his eyes wide, he went his own way with the punctuation:

> Love me? Why???

If there was an enormous laugh at his incredulity, there was also a flood of sympathy. Simon is an actor as loved as he is admired because of his honesty: when he unfolds himself, he reveals painful reserves of self-doubt. Why would anyone love him? Why would anyone love any of us? Zoë, listening from the water to the much harsher censures of her cousin and friends, found the truth harder to bear. "She cannot love" was like a dagger to her, a spur to prove them wrong.

Vicki's pool turned out to be a place of baptism. Beatrice and Benedick took the plunge, and emerged from it reborn. When I was later invited by the British Psychoanalytical Society to talk about Shakespeare, I claimed that this was the original idea. Perhaps it was.

As Beatrice and Benedick edge towards each other, the misunderstandings that drive the rest of the plot are the responsibility of Don Pedro's malevolent brother, Don John, who hates Claudio and uses his cronies to set up an elaborate scam that convinces Claudio that Hero is involved with another man. There is nothing in the play to explain the source of Don John's hatred. Once again, the actor is left to fill the gaps. And it's hard to imagine a draft of the play that fleshes out Don John, explores his inner life, and spends valuable stage time providing him with a history that motivated his malevolence. Shakespeare knows where his plays give off heat and where they don't, where it's worth hanging around and where it's best to move on. There's too much else of interest in *Much Ado* to make more space for Don John. He's plainly jealous of Claudio, and as Iago hates Cassio for the daily beauty in his life, so Don John hates Claudio for being the most popular officer in the mess. But nobody says why. Andrew Woodall decided that Don John had once made a pass at Claudio, and that Claudio had brusquely rejected it. It felt right that Don John was eaten up with self-loathing and fury that he'd allowed Claudio to note him. There's no textual evidence for it, but it allowed the actor to give emotional flesh where the playwright has provided a functional theatrical skeleton.

Claudio turns on Hero at the altar. The evidence of their own eyes seems to favour Claudio and Don Pedro. Leonato impulsively takes their side against his daughter. Beatrice's instinctive refusal to believe them is based on something truer than the evidence: she has a genuine capacity to know, or to note, those around her. She knows Hero. The church empties and she's left alone with Benedick, the first time she's been with him since she heard her friends say he loved her.

"Surely," he says, "I do believe your fair cousin is wronged." He's the only man in the play who does. Then:

> BEATRICE: Ah, how much might the man deserve of me that would right her.
> BENEDICK: Is there any way to show such friendship?
> BEATRICE: A very even way, but no such friend.
> BENEDICK: May a man do it?
> BEATRICE: It is a man's office, but not yours.

The great heart-stopper that follows is like so many of the best moments in Shakespeare, straightforward and prosaic, not a whiff of fancy when he wants to cut to the quick:

> BENEDICK: I do love nothing in the world so well as you. Is not that strange?

It acknowledges both an evident truth, and the genuine strangeness not of a *coup de foudre*—they happen all the time, and aren't particularly strange—but of his capacity to love without narcissism. He and Beatrice have discovered how to note the other, and love the other not as a projection of romantic perfection but as who the other actually is.

Hero pretends to be dead, Don John's malicious subterfuge is discovered, and Claudio is left to mourn the consequences of his blind haste to condemn her. His remorse is underwritten, but when he visits what he thinks to be Hero's tomb, Shakespeare calls for music and ritual. Whenever he asks for music, you know that he recognises its insidious communicative power, so it's a chance to create an event that gives Claudio space for genuine contrition. In the final scene, after he finds out that Hero is alive after all, Claudio reverts a little to the locker room, but in nearly all his romantic comedies, Shakespeare insists on the possibility of repentance and forgiveness. He's realistic about how hard it is, but he thinks people can change. Maybe Claudio changes. Beatrice and Benedick certainly do. If you work on his plays, you think we can too.

At the end, there's a double wedding, and the play calls for music and ritual again. "Strike up, pipers!" is the final line, and the final stage direction is *Dance*. But while Messina partied, Zoë pulled Simon away to sit on a bench on the edge of the dance; as the lights faded and the rest of the world rejoiced, they had too much to say to each other to need to join the revels. It seemed to me to express perfectly what Beatrice and Benedick have found in each other. It was also a final image as self-indulgent as the breakfast at the beginning, as nothing makes me happier than to throw a party and choose to sit on the edge of it.

PART FOUR

Show Business

On the Bandwagon

MUSICALS

There's a wonderful MGM musical about putting on a musical called *The Band Wagon*. It's even better than *Singin' in the Rain,* which is also about putting on a musical. So is *A Chorus Line*: musicals are embedded in the American psyche. In *The Band Wagon,* Fred Astaire is a washed-up Broadway star. Against his better judgement, he's persuaded to work on a new show with a fancy British director, a veteran of the classical theatre, played by Jack Buchanan. The British director decides the show is much deeper than anyone realises, so he reworks it as *Faust,* and casts himself as the Devil. He brings in a distinguished prima ballerina, Cyd Charisse, and turns an unpretentious musical comedy into Art. Its out-of-town try-out is a fiasco. Fred Astaire takes over as director. Cyd Charisse trades ballet for jazz. Art hits the scrapheap. Musical comedy triumphs.

In recent years, a regiment of British directors have come at Broadway musicals like Jack Buchanan, the same way they'd come at *Faust*. "Show me the greatest tragic actor or the lowest red-nosed comic in burlesque and I'll show you an entertainer," says Jack to Fred at the start of the movie as he establishes his musical-comedy credentials. "We're all entertainers!" I've said the same thing myself. I've said it at intervals throughout this book. Here's the big difference: Jack Buchanan *can sing and dance*. He sings and he dances *with Fred Astaire*. He still ends up driving Fred and Cyd and everyone else crazy.

How many of his inheritors, brandishing their success on the London stage, can sing a note or dance a step?

⤬⤬⤬

I was still a year off my thirtieth birthday when the producer Cameron Mackintosh called. He'd enjoyed a summer burlesque I'd just done at the 1985 Chichester Festival: *The Scarlet Pimpernel*, an exuberantly staged show of no substance whatsoever. Cameron had barely started his ascendancy. *Les Misérables* and *The Phantom of the Opera* were in the future. He wondered whether I was interested in musicals. A young American director would have had them in his bloodstream. He'd have been in them at high school, seen them at his local theatre, taken dance classes, learned all the great standards by heart. I'd watched the movies at the Manchester Gaumont with my gran. Cameron asked whether I knew Stephen Sondheim's *Follies*. I had all Sondheim's musicals on LP, so I said I knew it very well.

Follies is more than an American musical about musicals: it is haunted by the ghosts of the theatrical past as our lives are haunted by grief and regret. It was directed on Broadway by Hal Prince and choreographed by Michael Bennett, who were steeped in the theatrical history it referred to, and knew no limit to its expressive possibilities. Stephen Sondheim came to *The Scarlet Pimpernel*, which was smart and funny as far as it went, but he could see nothing in it that qualified me to direct *Follies*. He politely asked Cameron to move on, and he did me a huge favour: I was young, inexperienced, and I wouldn't have got within spitting distance of it. Such is Sondheim's genius that I've since seen his musicals survive London productions even more tone deaf than mine would have been. But I'm glad he saved *Follies* from me, and have enjoyed his company and hospitality many times, free of the embarrassment that would have been the consequence if I'd been let loose on his masterpiece.

Cameron cheerfully accepted Sondheim's verdict, and a couple of years later he was back. He had a new show from Alain Boublil and Claude-Michel Schönberg, the writer and composer behind *Les Misérables*. He showed me the poster, and sent me away with the script and a demo of Claude-Michel singing in French at the piano. *Miss*

Saigon was a contemporary reinvention of the story of *Madame Butterfly*. An American marine falls for a Vietnamese bar girl; they take part in a ceremony that as far as she's concerned makes her his wife. He's forced to abandon her when the North Vietnamese arrive in Saigon and he's evacuated from the roof of the U.S. embassy by helicopter. When he later learns that she has given birth to their child and escaped to Bangkok, he arrives with his new American wife to claim the baby. Like Madame Butterfly, she kills herself for the child's sake. It was popular opera on a huge scale, through-composed, with no dialogue and minimal dance. Most of my training had been in opera, so I reckoned I was on home territory.

Cameron is one of the great showmen of the age. Judged purely by the number of tickets he's sold, he may be the greatest showman of all time. He knows what he wants, even if he doesn't always know how to get it. The composer of a new musical once sat at the piano, playing him a number that wasn't making the grade. Cameron could barely contain his impatience. "No! No! No!" he cried, pushing the composer off the piano stool, and only when his hands were hovering over the keyboard, ready to show the composer how it should go, did he remember that he can't play the piano. I wish I'd been there so I could guarantee that it happened.

He knew exactly what he wanted from *Miss Saigon*: a vast, all-encompassing spectacle for the Theatre Royal, Drury Lane, that would move audiences to tears. He is entirely without cynicism. He loves the theatre he produces as much as the most refined classicist loves Sophocles. His taste is specific but passionate, and he doesn't bother to produce anything outside of it. He's demonic in his enthusiasm for what he produces.

John Napier, the designer, had been hired before me, so the priorities were clear enough. Drury Lane has always cried out for extravagant staging: in 1909, at the climax of a spectacular called *The Whip*, there was an onstage horse race, with real horses and real jockeys. When I met John for the first time, before the score for *Miss Saigon* was finished, there was already a helicopter, a sensational piece of engineering. Around it, he created a space of poetic delicacy, where romance blossomed and hearts broke. It was that kind of show. In

Claude-Michel and Alain, Cameron had found his ideal theatrical collaborators. Their work was unabashedly melodramatic and totally sincere.

There was, literally, a global search for someone to play the title role. We flew around the world, to New York, then to Los Angeles, Hawaii and Manila. In a rehearsal room in the basement of the concert hall Imelda Marcos built, an eighteen-year-old called Lea Salonga asked Claude-Michel and Alain to sign her copy of *Les Misérables*. Then she sang from it. She had a fabulous voice and astonishing poise. She came to London with her mother, and turned out to be the kind of star who seems to be lit from within. She wasn't even intimidated by a scintillating Jonathan Pryce, who played her pimp.

On the way back from Manila, some of us stopped off in Bangkok, which felt like a good opportunity to check out the bars and brothels which occupied long stretches of the show. I wandered through the red-light district, drinking glumly at bars where girls pulled strings of razor blades from their vaginas, cheered on by sweaty drunks to whose fantasies they were apparently catering. Mystified, I thought I'd cheer myself up at the gay end of the street. I ordered a beer. At the corner of the bar, a disgusting old white guy leered at a boy who couldn't have been more than twelve, and slithered his arm around him. I fled and found a taxi. "You want girls?" asked the taxi driver. I said I didn't. "You want boys?" I said I'd take a pass on them too. "No problem," said the taxi driver, "I take you to nice gift shop, open all night, you buy present for your mother."

"Thanks, Dr. Freud, but the hotel will do fine," I said, every time I told the story.

I'm not crazy, in retrospect, about the scenes in *Miss Saigon* that conveyed, accurately enough, the putrid atmosphere of the bars. I hurled everything I knew about staging at a script that had very little in the way of stage directions; the result had a relish that sometimes crossed the line into vulgarity. Clubs, bars and brothels have become staples of musical theatre. Some shows are aware that they aren't necessarily good news for the women who are supposed to work there, but musicals always want it both ways. What's not to like, they say, about a beautiful chorus girl in a bikini? Though please feel free to deplore the men who pay for her.

Alain and Claude-Michel wrote initially in French; the American dramatist Richard Maltby Jr. collaborated on the English lyrics and brought to them an authentic anguish for the survivors, Vietnamese and American, of a catastrophic conflict. It was an achievement to make a massive piece of popular musical theatre out of wounds still fresh, less than twenty years after the end of the war. And in Jonathan Pryce's irresistible performance as the Eurasian bar owner who put poor Lea to work, there was a caustic savagery that elevated the whole show. When it was time to take it to New York, there was never any debate about who to take with it: Jonathan and Lea were integral to its success. Nobody anticipated the response of the American Actors' Equity Association, who refused to give Jonathan permission to appear on Broadway. "Equity believes the casting of Mr. Pryce as a Eurasian to be especially insensitive and an affront to the Asian community." Cameron threatened to withdraw the show. Broadway bigwigs, all of them white, blew out suffocating clouds of hot air. Should Shylock be played henceforth only by Jews? Should Caucasian actors never play Othello?

Damn right they shouldn't, would have been my answer to that in 1991, but I ducked behind the parapet, and nobody asked me. In London in the late 1980s, there were fewer actors of South East Asian descent than there are now. We persuaded ourselves that there was nobody more suitable to play the Engineer, a small-time Vietnamese crook with a European father and Asian mother, than European Jonathan Pryce. His success in the part spoke for itself, but it should have occurred to us that on Broadway, the much larger community of Asian American actors would want a crack at the part. I can't pretend I was torn: Jonathan was my friend, he was tremendous, and I didn't want to do the show without him. And meanwhile, more than thirty Asian American Equity members, already cast in other roles, stood to lose their jobs if Cameron cancelled the show. The union didn't hold out for long. Jonathan played the part and stormed Broadway as he had the West End. *Miss Saigon* ran in New York for ten years, but if Equity lost the battle, it won the war: Jonathan's successors as the Engineer on Broadway, and everywhere else the show played, were all Asian.

Twenty years later, at the Park Theatre in north London, I saw *Yellow Face* by David Henry Hwang, an articulate spokesman in 1991 for the Asian American theatre community. His 1988 play, *M. Butterfly*, was an ironic counterpoint to the orientalist fantasy that submits the exotic Eastern woman to the dominant Western male: the fantasy, it must be said, at the heart of both *Madame Butterfly* and *Miss Saigon*. In *Yellow Face* he replayed the *Miss Saigon* casting saga, and put a character called David Henry Hwang on stage to write a new play about it. By the end of the play, as sharp and provocative as anything I've ever seen about racial identity, he had asked the audience to believe that a patently white actor was in fact Asian, so that he could "take words like 'Asian' and 'American,' like 'race' and 'nation,' mess them up so bad no one has any idea what they even mean anymore." The least I could do was arrange for it to have a run at the National.

Some shows want to imitate reality, some create their own. During my first months at the National, Owen McCafferty wrote *Scenes from the Big Picture* about a particular community in Belfast, and Kwame Kwei-Armah wrote *Elmina's Kitchen* about a particular community in east London. At the top of the agenda of both plays was the authentic representation of their communities. They were cast accordingly. But the onus is on directors and producers to justify racially specific casting. The classics, in particular, belong to all of us and their performance is a collective act: a community of actors plays to a community of spectators. If a director decides that a play's naturalism is its defining feature, that *The Cherry Orchard* requires a literal and exact portrayal of early-twentieth-century provincial Russia, the production must make the argument for racially exclusive casting through its undeviating naturalism. But most productions of the classics aren't so rigorously naturalistic that they justify excluding actors merely because of their colour. If a production asserts confidently enough the principle that anyone can play anyone, the audience will have no difficulty accepting it.

And we can at least agree that a show where people sing and dance as a means of communicating with each other is playing fast and loose with reality. If merry townspeople dance ballet in the streets because they're happy that June is bustin' out all over, their stage world is hardly a literal reflection of the real world.

⌒๑)

So here I am back in New York in June 1992, a year after *Miss Saigon* opened on Broadway, in an apartment at the top of the Pierre Hotel (jacket and tie obligatory). Propped up on a sofa is Dorothy Rodgers, the ancient widow of the composer Richard Rodgers. Her daughter Mary, also a composer, sits beside her. The sons of Oscar Hammerstein, Bill and Jamie, both theatre directors, sit opposite. Mrs. Rodgers is breathing oxygen from a cylinder, and she's on the warpath, because she's found out that I've asked Clive Rowe to play the part of Enoch Snow in the National Theatre's production of *Carousel,* the most moving and beautiful of all the Rodgers and Hammerstein musicals. It's another attempt at a casting veto, but this time I'm leading the charge against it, swollen with self-righteous zeal.

Carousel is happening because Richard Eyre, the director of the National, sees no reason why the great musicals of Broadway's golden age shouldn't be treated the same way we treat Shakespeare: as classics, ripe for new discoveries every time they're done. I've asked to do *Carousel* because it's haunted me ever since I saw the movie at the Gaumont, and because I've already seen it completely renewed by Steven Pimlott, at the Royal Exchange Theatre, Manchester, so I know it will reward any amount of exploration. I've spent months casting it. It's been almost impossible to find someone to play its leading role, the fairground barker Billy Bigelow. But Mr. Snow, the fisherman, is a piece of cake. I've known Clive Rowe for ages, though never worked with him. He's warm, funny, plump, and he has a tremendous tenor voice.

But the Rodgers and Hammerstein families have discovered that Clive is black, and apparently they're having none of it. They think because Mr. Snow is an "insider," Clive would be "inappropriate." They think that the character's name would become a joke. So I do what Cameron Mackintosh did: I threaten to cancel the show if I can't have him, though in truth it would be Richard Eyre doing the cancelling and I'm riding a high horse as June blossoms all over Central Park outside poor Mrs. Rodgers's window. Mrs. Rodgers accuses me of blackmail: the oxygen cylinder is no handicap to her fierce indignation. But I'm Daniel, certain of my cause. It takes me a while to notice that there's only one antique lion in the den. Mary Rodgers and Jamie Hammerstein are beaming their approval. They couldn't be happier. Nobody has any problem with Clive except the furious octogenarian: Mary and Jamie can't wait for their fathers' shows to be claimed by a new generation. As Mary takes me to the door of the apartment, she tells me not to worry, they had to give the old lady a chance to say her piece. In fact, she promises me, her mother is looking forward to coming to London to see the show.

Clive Rowe gets to play Mr. Snow; his fiancée, Carrie Pipperidge, is white. A couple of columnists looking for copy try to make a fuss, but nobody sane has a problem, because Clive is irresistible in the part. It's not that people don't notice: of course they do, and they're not stupid, so they don't think we're trying to pretend that coastal Maine in 1900 was a multiracial paradise. Instead, they agree collectively to suspend their disbelief, which is one of the things that audiences like doing best. When the production is remade for Broadway in 1994 with an American cast, Mr. Snow is white but this time Carrie Pipperidge is black: a Juilliard graduate called Audra McDonald comes in to audition, and I know almost from the first note she sings that I'll never stop boasting about being in on the start of her career. Audra comes back to sing for Mary Rodgers and Jamie Hammerstein, takes a deep breath, and faints dead away. She recovers, and out pours a stream of golden sound, even more golden because she means it. Mary and Jamie are ecstatic.

But Mrs. Rodgers never makes it to London, because a few weeks after I steam sanctimoniously into her apartment to tell her how to do her husband's show, she dies.

෨෭

Carousel is based on *Liliom,* a strange, sardonic play from 1909 by Ferenc Molnár, set in and around a dilapidated amusement park on the outskirts of Budapest. Its hero, a fairground barker, beats his wife, dies in a failed robbery and faces his heavenly judges "in the beyond." He's sentenced to burn for sixteen years. Given a day back on earth to make amends for a wasted life, he beats his daughter. This bleak cynicism seems a million miles from the optimistic world of Rodgers and Hammerstein, corny as Kansas in August, and gaudy in Technicolor in the movie I'd seen with my gran. In fact, although they relocate Budapest to the picturesque coast of Maine, they stick closely to the dangerous passion of their source. Clive Rowe's and Audra McDonald's parts are lifted from *Líliom,* too: the complacent small businessman who marries his sweetheart and has seven kids. Rodgers and Hammerstein prefer to give Billy Bigelow a third chance of redemption, where Molnár bundles Liliom off to hell after he's failed his second. And they end the show with a reprise of its famous anthem, "You'll Never Walk Alone." But it doesn't wash, because much of the show pitilessly contradicts the song: you'll often walk alone, you'll often live alone. You'll die alone.

Like Jack Buchanan in *The Band Wagon,* I descended on *Carousel* to demonstrate that a masterpiece of American entertainment was in fact high art. It was both, of course, but I usually set out to dissolve the boundaries between high art and show business from the other direction.

The original 1945 Broadway production had performed the same balancing act. Its choreographer was Agnes de Mille, one of the great pioneers of American dance. In the middle of the second act, she was given an entire fifteen-minute sequence to herself. On his return to earth after his death and heavenly judgement, Billy Bigelow is forced to watch his teenage daughter ostracised by the local children, and fall for exactly his own kind of fairground rough trade. It's all danced: a vision of the future beyond speech. Who, I wondered, was as singular as Agnes de Mille? The greatest living figure in British ballet was Kenneth MacMillan. There wasn't a chance he'd be interested, but he agreed to meet. Although I loved ballet, I hadn't a clue how to talk about it. Wary behind dark glasses, he let me try. I heard myself making no sense, so I gave up. "Here's the thing about *Carousel,*" I cried. "It's about sex and violence!" The ice melted. "Well, that's what I do," said Kenneth. He was underselling one of the most radical careers in British performing arts: he pushed at the boundaries of ballet, spoke through classical dance about desires too dangerous, and love too complex, for words. And it turned out that he'd been waiting for someone to ask him to choreograph a musical. We worked for a year together to integrate our two worlds. Like most trailblazers, he was as bruised as he was bold. He'd grown a skin of mordant wit to protect himself from the keepers of the flame, who are everywhere, and particularly vituperative in the ballet world.

Carousel was designed by Bob Crowley. We spent a week driving down the Maine coast. June was bustin' out all over, as it often did during the preparation of *Carousel,* making "the bay look bright and new, sails gleamin' white on sunlit blue." There was blue everywhere, most gorgeous on the indigo ceiling of a Shaker meeting house in Sabbathday Lake, built in the early 1800s. A guide called Seth told us it symbolised heaven: Shakers used to dance and sing under it. Bob stole the blue for a vast empty box. It was big enough to make Billy Bigelow feel tiny. "What are we? A couple of specks of nuthin'." It accommodated visions of loneliness that recalled Edward Hopper and Andrew Wyeth. But the sap rose in it, too: an ensemble of horny young women and men sang, danced and collapsed on a sandbank, blissed out after a clambake. They were led in London by a renowned actor, Patricia Routledge, and in New York by a renowned opera singer, Shirley Verrett. Art or show business? Neither of them cared.

Julie Jordan was Joanna Riding, reserved, self-contained, lethally drawn to the strutting fairground barker. "What's the use of wond'ring if he's good or if he's bad," she sang with naked simplicity. "He's your feller and you love him, there's nothing more to say." The melody is gorgeous, the sentiment apparently uncomplicated. The insidious power of the show is that at the dark heart of an abusive marriage is love and forgiveness no less profound for being misplaced. We met some handsome actors with powerful baritone voices to play Billy. I tried to imagine them lashing out at Joanna Riding. I'd have hated them, and hated the show for asking me to care about them, and besides, as actors they weren't up to her. We went to New York, and met lots more handsome baritones. Several of them looked like fairground rough trade, but only one seemed open to salvation: Michael Hayden, who was short on vocal heft, but when he sang, there was wounded frailty behind the bravado. As Billy, he caused pain because he was in pain.

Every morning before rehearsals, I sat with Kenneth and watched the company take ballet class. I began to learn his language. I watched him create the dance for Louise, the daughter Billy haunts sixteen years after his death, and the wild fairground barker who reminds him of his former self. I watched an unhappy adolescent girl, hungry for love, crazed with desire, hurl herself at a sexed-up boy who sets her alight and throws her aside. Kenneth was the master of sexually charged *pas de deux* in ballets like *Romeo and Juliet* and *Manon*. Now I saw the infinite pain, the hard-won craft, the sweat and the imagination behind them: what art requires.

Kenneth seemed to work to a secret deadline, constantly pushing himself to get ahead. In the middle of the penultimate week of rehearsals, he said goodbye to us for a couple of days: he wanted to supervise the dress rehearsal and opening of a revival of his ballet *Mayerling* at the Royal Opera House. The night before he was due to return to us, I was listening to the midnight news on the radio, and heard that the great choreographer Kenneth MacMillan had died suddenly, backstage, during the ballet. I was poleaxed: I had known him for little more than a year, but it felt like he'd be a friend and mentor for years longer.

A few days later, his wife, Deborah, and teenage daughter, Charlotte, came to watch a run-through of *Carousel*, one of the bravest and most generous things I have ever witnessed. They helped a stunned company realise what we had: Kenneth had choreographed nearly everything, and in the magical Act 2 ballet, he never stopped speaking to us.

Kenneth's ballet wasn't the only thing in *Carousel* that reduced audiences to tears, nor was ours the only production to do so. It's an infallibly moving show. I've never heard such unrestrained sobbing in a theatre. During Billy Bigelow's short life, "If I loved you" is as far as either he or Julie Jordan are prepared to go in opening up to each other. She squeezes out "I love you" only over his corpse. When he comes back to earth, at last he replaces "if" with "how": "How I loved you." A thousand people every night told me I wasn't alone in devoting too much of my life to emotional self-defence. They wept as much as I did when a man found a way, if only after his death, to say what he never admitted, even to himself. As Joanna Riding forgave Michael Hayden, the audience wept for the pain they'd caused and for the pain they'd suffered. They recognised themselves and each other, which is one of the reasons they come to the theatre, and why theatre is worth making. "Two little people, you and I, we don't count at all," sings Billy, the first night they meet. But on stage, their little lives become legend.

The more shameful, then, that Billy Bigelow's absolution culminates in a lie. In *Carousel* as in *Liliom,* when he meets his teenage daughter, Louise, he loses patience with her and hits out. It doesn't hurt her, because although she doesn't know it, he's only a ghost. She tells her mother about it, and asks her, "Is it possible, Mother, for someone to hit you hard like that—real loud and hard, and it not hurt you at all?" Her mother replies: "It is possible, dear, for someone to hit you, hit you hard, and it not hurt at all." It's presented as a climactic act of grace, but it's bullshit. Why didn't I tell old Mrs. Rodgers, while I was on her case, that I wasn't going to be responsible for putting it in front of an audience? I suppose because I told myself that, like too many victims of domestic violence, Julie Jordan has no alternative but to lie to herself. But it's not just Julie saying that violence doesn't matter: it's the show. I should have cut it.

Carousel speaks of joy, too, particularly through the rapturous young New Englanders who keep it afloat as its protagonists fall apart. Sprawled on the beach after their real nice clambake, the New York company were all people who knew how to give you a real good time. One of them, a gentle Texan with brown eyes, used to look at me like he knew my secrets and none of them bothered him. He got to know a lot of them, and they didn't.

☙

"Why would you want to base a musical on so perfect a movie?" I asked the producer who approached me, a couple of years after *Car*-

ousel, about a new Broadway musical based on the 1957 movie *Sweet Smell of Success.* "How do you make a musical out of such a venomous story?" But I wanted to work with the great American playwright John Guare, who would write the book; and I wanted to work with Marvin Hamlisch, who with *A Chorus Line* had composed one of the soundtracks to my youth. My initial scepticism evaporated when I went to Marvin's apartment on Park Avenue to hear the opening number. The heavy curtains were drawn, apparently to keep out the afternoon sun, but as he started to play, a long leg snaked out from behind them, followed by another, and then a third. They belonged to three dancers, who sold Marvin's song as if they were already on Broadway. The number was fabulous. The dancers were fabulous. Marvin was fabulous: music made flesh. Sitting at the piano, he could have seduced the Pope. He probably did, as he was always flying off to play for some world leader or other. I was snared. The producer later did time for fraud, unrelated to *Sweet Smell of Success,* which took four years to develop and didn't make him a cent.

So in the autumn of 2001, a month after the attack on the World Trade Center, I was back in New York to begin rehearsals for what would be my third Broadway musical, though the first not to open in London. I thought I had a perfect right to be there: I was by now the grandly titled director designate of the National Theatre, and I thought American musical theatre was one of the things I could do.

Sweet Smell of Success is genuinely a replay of *Faust.* Mephistopheles is J. J. Hunsecker, a newspaper columnist who offers the world—in fact his column, but it amounts to the same thing—to a press agent Faust: Sidney Falco. Sidney needs publicity for his clients. J.J. wants Sidney to destroy his sister's jazz-singer boyfriend. The bargain promises Sidney infinite power in the world of 1950s New York cafe society. It ends in Sidney's ruin.

John Lithgow played J.J. with fabulous menace and terrifying charm; Brian d'Arcy James was a driven, desperate and vocally bewitching Sidney. On the opening night, the audience stood and cheered. The party was at the Waldorf Astoria. We arrived in high spirits. Twenty minutes in, I fought my way through the crowd to the bar, to find another glass of champagne. When I turned back round, the crowd had fled into the night. Someone had arrived with the morning papers. Nowadays, they check the reviews on their smartphones while they're standing and cheering, and if the show's a flop they give the party a miss. But I got to experience at first hand an essential part of Broadway folklore before it was made obsolete by technology. I made a defiant exit with the cast from the deserted ballroom of the Waldorf Astoria, to get hammered somewhere less cavernous. The show closed a couple of months later.

Twelve years at the National have made me sanguine about accounting for creative failure, and for the failure to engage an audience. They don't always go together. Maybe *Sweet Smell* failed at the Broadway box office for the same reason the movie failed at the box office. It is cynical, bleak, hard-edged: the New York it celebrates, and you can't do much else if you put New York on the New York commercial stage, is a "dirty town." I'd love to go back to the Stork Club of the 1950s and hear jazz while the air crackled with malice and violence, but six months after 9/11, the audience didn't. Perhaps it was always a bad idea to base a musical on a great movie that failed commercially but later acquired cult status. But I still think that Marvin, John Guare and the lyricist Craig Carnelia wrote something powerful and gripping, so maybe I was the one who screwed up. Maybe, in the end, like Jack Buchanan, I lack the visceral feel for the intoxicating cocktail of dialogue, song and dance that comes with growing up in the American theatre.

John Guare and John Lithgow both came to work at the National. John Guare wrote *His Girl Friday* for my first season in 2003. John Lithgow, whose performance in *Sweet Smell* was so dark with danger, came at last in 2012 to play the title role in Arthur Wing Pinero's Victorian comedy, *The Magistrate*. It is supposed to be an iron rule of comedy that it must be acted seriously, but the rule only works if the actors doing the serious acting have funny bones. John has played J. J. Hunsecker and King Lear. His face, which can congeal into immobility and ooze tyranny, turns rubbery with panic when he plays farce.

I last saw Marvin in London a few months before he died, far too young, in 2012. I forget which world leaders he'd come to play for.

The Broadway failure of *Sweet Smell* had hit him hard: he never wrote another musical. But he'd just seen a student production of it in New York, and he'd loved it. It sounded better than mine. The show is bound to resurface, and now that the barbarians have stormed the gates of American democracy, its cynicism about celebrity and power will be harder to dismiss. The CD is terrific: I recommend it to young directors, preferably American, looking to make a splash.

☙

A life in the theatre sometimes feels like it's on a loop. I asked a young New York choreographer to make the dances in *Sweet Smell*. Christopher Wheeldon was from Somerset and trained at the Royal Ballet School before dancing with New York City Ballet. He made his first steps as a teenage choreographer for a Royal Ballet workshop at the Riverside Studios in west London. In the audience was Kenneth MacMillan, who pulled him aside afterwards and told him he should take every chance that came his way to practise his craft. Chris's sinuous work on *Sweet Smell* became a mere footnote to a career on the cutting edge of classical dance, which I have followed as a fan and as a friend. Ten years later, he told me he wanted to make a three-act Shakespeare ballet for the Royal Ballet: they hadn't done a new one since the MacMillan *Romeo and Juliet*. I suggested *The Winter's Tale*. I thought that dance might be the ideal medium for its magical synthesis of loss and rebirth, its marriages of flesh and spirit, jealous fury and unbridled glee; and I sent him a synopsis of the play that imagined a completely different response to it than mine in 2001. In 2014, I took a group of actors, including Alex Jennings, Debbie Findlay and Julian Wadham—Leontes, Paulina and Polixenes at the National—to a Royal Ballet rehearsal studio. They read the play to the dancers who were working, with Bob Crowley as their designer, on Chris's ballet. It was different in every respect to my production of the play, which I could remember with renewed affection thanks to its brief revival in the ballet rehearsal studio. Chris's beautiful ballet will be revived much more often.

☙

A few years after *Sweet Smell of Success,* I'm watching *Family Guy* on TV with Steve Ochoa, the brown-eyed Texan from the *Carousel* clambake. Brian the dog and Stewie the baby have joined the army, and they're out running with their platoon. One of the many virtues of *Family Guy* is that its writers are show queens, so the platoon chants:

> *West Side Story, Anything Goes,*
> Two of my favourite Broadway shows.
> *Miss Saigon* and *Cabaret,*
> Overrated I should say.

I couldn't be more excited. Brian, Stewie and the platoon are singing about my show. Steve points out that they don't think it's as good as *West Side Story.* His first Broadway show was *Jerome Robbins' Broadway,* an anthology of musical numbers created by the American musical's greatest director. Steve was a Shark in scenes from *West Side Story,* directed by Jerome Robbins himself, who later promoted him to a Jet, so he agrees with the platoon. I tell him that they are nevertheless making a very important point. It is through musicals that the theatre finds a perfect balance between high art and low, and reaches the wider public: the public that watches shows like *Family Guy.*

But then I remember that much though I love musicals, fascinated though I am by the vast passions they release and the euphoria they breed, they squeeze a director dry. I know they are as disproportionately draining of a theatre's energy as they are exhilarating. At the National, I was wary of programming too many of them. And in the wake of the rediscovery of the great Broadway classics by Richard Eyre and Trevor Nunn, there was no shortage in London of theatres or producers eager to stage old musicals, so I was happy to leave them to it, and focus on new ones. I produced six new musicals, three of them imported from New York. The two that caused most of a stir owed least to Broadway. Neither *Jerry Springer—The Opera* nor *London Road* jumped on the bandwagon of American musical comedy, which I continue to love, and continue to think can do just fine without the good offices of Jack Buchanan.

That left open the question of how to break through to the audience that kept *Miss Saigon* going for ten years in the West End, so I was reassured when, a couple of years after he joined the army on *Family Guy,* Brian the dog wrote a play and Alan Bennett came to see it. The animated Alan was voiced by the real Alan. There are more ways to the wider public's heart than through favourite Broadway shows, and more ways to entertain them than with song and dance.

11

What They Best Like

❦

ENTERTAINMENT

In his short play *The Dark Lady of the Sonnets,* George Bernard Shaw imagined a midsummer night's rendezvous between Elizabeth I and Shakespear, as he insisted on spelling him, always on the lookout for an opportunity to get up posterity's nose. Shakespear "craves a boon" of the queen: the endowment of a National Theatre, "for the better instruction and gracing of Your Majesty's subjects."

"Are there not theatres enow on the Bankside?" asks the queen.

Shakespear tells the queen that these theatres are by no means enow, because they only exist "to give the sillier sort of people what they best like."

A century after Shaw made his high-minded case for the National Theatre, it seemed to me that the occasional provision of what the public best like was part of the deal, a fair exchange for the annual boon of several millions of pounds from the public purse. And besides, I liked giving it to them, though knew that what they best like is rarely what they liked last time they came to the theatre. They want to see what they haven't seen before: they want to be surprised to find themselves liking what artists want to give them.

Still, I knew they couldn't get enough of *His Dark Materials,* so contemporary literature for young people felt like fertile territory. I heard about Jamila Gavin's *Coram Boy* on a BBC Radio 4 book programme in 2004. It starts in Gloucester in 1742, where desperate mothers give their illegitimate babies to the "Coram man" Otis Gardiner, who instead of taking them to the Coram Hospital for Foundling Children, kills them and pockets the fee. He buries their tiny corpses not far from Gloucester Cathedral, where the choir sings Handel. Although the novel had won the Whitbread Children's Book Award, it had nothing like the profile of *His Dark Materials,* but I reckoned we had uncovered a hunger for ambitious family shows, and could risk a relatively unknown title. While we geared up for the second run of the Philip Pullman, I asked Tom Morris to oversee the development of *Coram Boy* at the Studio. It opened in the Olivier in November 2005, directed and co-designed by Melly Still and adapted by Helen Edmundson. We scheduled it for around fifty performances and put it in rep in the Olivier with a sure-fire hit, *Once in a Lifetime,* Kaufman and Hart's great comedy about 1920s Hollywood. The sure-fire truth about sure-fire hits is that they never are. *Once in a Lifetime* felt like it had been scheduled for no better reason than to be a hit, and limped through nearly twice as many scheduled performances as *Coram Boy,* which immediately seized the public's imagination because it had seized the imaginations of the team that made it.

Melly started her career as a designer. With a fraction of the budget of *His Dark Materials,* she conjured a macabre, Hogarthian England and told an exciting story with propulsive energy, sweeping up in its wake eighteenth-century folk songs, sea shanties and church anthems. Some parents were disturbed by the gruesome honesty of her storytelling, but their children relished the frisson of horror at the discovery of the skeletons of Otis's little victims. They knew that a steady gaze into the darkness is a precondition for a journey from dark to light, from wickedness to salvation.

Coram Boy had to come back for a second, much longer run in 2006. It started to feel as if we'd invented a genre. Like a movie studio, we could look for material, buy it, and commission playwrights to work for us, rather than waiting on their unpredictable inspirations. Long before *Coram Boy* opened, Tom Morris was looking for its successors. He stayed behind after a Wednesday planning meeting and said, "I think I may have found something. My mum was listening to Michael Morpurgo on *Desert Island Discs* the other day, and liked him so much that she went out and bought some of his books."

⁓

"Does the horse speak?"

"No, the horse doesn't speak."

"You said the book is written in the first person, as if by the horse. Do you promise he won't be Mr. Ed?"

"I promise," said Tom.

Tom's mum had told him about Michael Morpurgo's *War Horse,* like *Coram Boy* a winner of the Whitbread Children's Book Award.

"It's short," said Tom. "You'll read it very quickly. It's about a horse called Joey who belongs to a Devon farm boy called Albert. Joey is requisitioned in August 1914 and goes to the Western Front. The entire First World War is seen from the horse's point of view. He's captured by the Germans, he witnesses unimaginable horror, gets snared by barbed wire and hideously injured in no man's land. Meanwhile, Albert joins up and spends the war looking for him. They're miraculously reunited in Calais on Armistice Day."

"But if it's about the horse and the horse doesn't speak, how is there a show in it?"

"Have I ever told you about Handspring?"

Tom had brought the work of Adrian Kohler and Basil Jones, founders of the South African Handspring Puppet Company, to Battersea Arts Centre when he was its director. He showed me a video of their latest show, *Tall Horse,* about a giraffe presented as a gift by the viceroy of Egypt to the king of France in 1827. The Handspring giraffe was a living, breathing creature, visibly manipulated by his puppeteers and superbly charismatic: a real leading actor.

"Can we bring Basil and Adrian to the Studio and see whether there's anything in it?" asked Tom.

In January 2005 I went down the road to the Studio to see what Tom, Basil and Adrian had discovered. Sam Barnett, Posner in *The History Boys,* put a halter on another actor and led him round in circles.

"Good boy," said Sam.

Then both actors put cardboard boxes on their heads and tied tails of shredded newspapers around their waists. They did some more circles.

"We're onto something," said Tom.

If the enemies of arts subsidy had seen two actors walking in a circle with cardboard boxes on their heads pretending to be horses at the taxpayers' expense, they would have had a field day. But Tom, Basil, Adrian and the actors all seemed excited and convinced, so I was too.

"OK," I said. "Let's develop it some more."

Basil and Adrian went back to Cape Town and started work on Joey. Tom commissioned an adaptation from the playwright Nick Stafford that put a puppet horse centre stage. Joey couldn't speak, so he needed to share the limelight with someone who could: Albert, the boy who owned him. Joey's story was intercut with the story of Albert's family in pre-war Devon, Albert's comrades in the army, Albert's search for Joey. I asked Marianne Elliott if she'd like to direct it. After a second workshop she said to me that she needed a collaborator: "Why don't I co-direct *War Horse* with Tom?"

As it became clearer how big an undertaking *War Horse* would be, I started to interfere a little more and say yes a little less. When we commissioned an original play, our role as producer was to nudge it into being as good a version as possible of the play the playwright wanted to write. We were as responsible to the playwright as the playwright was to us. When we took material to a writer for adaptation, we worked more like a film studio: the director and producer take the lead, and the writer provides a play to support their needs. *War Horse* needed a text that left space for Marianne, Tom, Basil and Adrian to transfer much of the narrative and emotional burden away from what actors said onto the way puppets moved. It had to work more like a libretto for an opera or the book for a musical, which are pared back to make space for music to do the dramatic heavy lifting; or like a screenplay that leaves the camera space to tell the story. In the event, it took hundreds of performances in London and New York for *War Horse* to find its final shape, but between its second and third workshops, draft after draft landed on my desk.

"I'm not sure it's clear enough, or tense enough, or the stakes are high enough," I said to Tom, quite often. Clear storytelling and high stakes are always at the top of a producer's agenda. One problem with *War Horse* seemed to be that throughout the first forty minutes of the show, Joey and Albert are inseparable, but after he's requisitioned, they never appear on stage together again until the closing minutes of the show. The audience has to follow two entirely different storylines. They needed something to reassure them that both stories are travelling in the same direction, like a signpost: Story This Way. Tom relayed the note to Nick Stafford and came back with a line for Albert:

> I promise you, Joey, that we will be together again. We will be reunited. I promise you. You understand that? I, Albert Narracott, do solemnly swear that we shall be together again.

Tom's delight with the line was in direct proportion to its lack of subtlety. It's the kind of speech you might hear in a big-budget action movie, and for the same reason: the audience has no time to decode oblique or poetic dialogue when the principal means of communication is beyond words.

For the third *War Horse* workshop in June 2006, Basil and Adrian arrived with Joey. He was gauze stretched over bent cane with leather ears and tail. Three puppeteers, two inside him and one outside at his head, manipulated him. As they breathed, so did he. The play still needed work, but I was completely sold on the horse and gave Tom and Marianne the go-ahead.

"So it's horse-based programming?" said Tom.

"It's an outstanding horse," I said.

War Horse had its first preview on 9 October 2007 after three months of training for the puppeteers and seven weeks' rehearsal for the rest of the company. Tom and Marianne brought to it not just visual and musical bravura, but a seriousness of approach that treated puppetry as a mature theatrical art, and drew truthful performances from a huge cast. Joey and an even more impressive horse called Topthorn could not have carried the show without Luke Treadaway as

Albert. Luke made the foal Joey his friend with a delicacy and tenderness that belied the scale of what was happening around them. His fevered search for his horse over the long years in the trenches was as harrowing as the images of suffering summoned by emaciated horses hauling immense field guns. But the show left the audience cold. Among those who thought it was doomed were Nick Starr and Michael Morpurgo.

My notes on the first preview were as blunt and as obvious as my notes on the first drafts of the play: "Too long. Too slow. Not clear. Indulgent, long, pretentious scenes in German. A girl beside me got out her phone and started texting! Cut! Cut!" I wished I'd been tougher when I'd seen run-throughs in the rehearsal room, but there was still time.

I left them to it for a couple of days and went back to see what they'd done. Still too long, still too much German, still too many extraneous scenes, still not working. Marianne and Tom had avoided the tough calls. They worried about poor Ned the soldier who had a long, wrenching scene about shell shock.

"He'll lose most of his part if we cut it," they said.

"I don't care about Ned," I said. "We've spent hundreds of thousands of pounds on this show and scheduled nearly a hundred performances. Do what you said you'd do!"

It was a low blow to mention money. Like almost everyone I know in the subsidised theatre, Marianne and Tom took the bottom line very seriously. And I hesitated before hitting them so hard, wanting always to balance my responsibility to the National and its audience with my respect for the creative instincts of the artists who worked for us. But the imperative behind *War Horse* was not the inspiration of a single artist. It was produced in answer to our collective hunger for large-scale storytelling, so the balance shifted. The next day, poor Ned was reduced to the ranks. The Germans still spoke German, but nothing like as much of it. The story was clarified. The show lost fifteen minutes. By the final scene, when Albert rode Joey back to his Devon village, even the stoniest hearts in the house had melted.

War Horse was less transformed during its previews than released. The great show was always there, hiding behind the long, slow, confusing show. Afterwards, my colleagues looked to me to turn every ailing show around during previews with a few well-chosen words and a stern look. They looked in vain, as a producer's notes can't turn a bad show into a good one. I sometimes turned a bad show into a mediocre show, and a debacle into a merely bad one. But my job was never as satisfying as it was when I could give a great show a final nudge.

While *War Horse* was running in the Olivier, I used to sneak into the back of the stalls to watch the foal Joey fly apart and dissolve into the darkness to make way for the magnificent full-grown Joey. The three puppeteers who manipulated the rickety little foal literally pulled him apart as the great, magnetic star puppet reared up into the light to replace him, and Luke Treadaway vaulted onto his back and cantered off. Basil and Adrian had given Joey eyes that were as deep and expressive as human eyes. A single twitch of his ear was worth lines of dialogue: you seemed to have direct access to his soul. His three human handlers evaporated.

What started as large-scale storytelling for a family audience became art as much as entertainment: it embraced the hardships of rural England as much as its loveliness, and the simple decency of men under fire as well as their fear. The terrible beauty of some of its imagery—the cavalry charge at Mons, the abandoned horse careering petrified through no man's land—recalled *All Quiet on the Western Front,* or Britten's *War Requiem.*

It still felt like a category error when, in New York in June 2011, I accepted on behalf of its producers the Tony Award for Best Play. It beat Jez Butterworth's *Jerusalem,* one of the few undisputed masterpieces of the new century. *War Horse* was a superlative show, with a very effective script, but the greater part of the vision behind it was not the playwright's. It was the apotheosis of a new and vigorous strand in the National's repertoire that was the collaborative vision of directors, designers, puppeteers, musicians, videographers and choreographers, as well as writers. It wasn't Best Play, and I didn't understand why, even if it was, the producers should be lining up with the playwright to receive the prize, but I did my best to look solemn and grateful.

Awards ceremonies can only be survived on large quantities of alcohol-fuelled malevolence. They are a terrible advertisement for what we do. We are never more repellent than when dressed up and hysterical for the cameras. The best work is usually ignored, the meretricious often rewarded. You're furious if you lose, delighted if you win, then immediately consumed by self-loathing because you're furious that you wanted to win in the first place. Every awards ceremony tries desperately to pretend it's the Oscars. The only time I went to the Oscars they were just as desperate as all the others, but with more superstars.

☙

In a coffee shop on Old Compton Street, shortly after I was appointed director of the National, I asked Danny Boyle whether he fancied coming back to the theatre. He'd started at the Royal Court and I first met him at the RSC, when he was directing Tirso de Molina and I was directing Shakespeare. He said that one day he'd like to stage *Frankenstein,* that he and the playwright Nick Dear had an idea for it, but he had some films he wanted to direct first. I reminded him every now and then of how keen we were to have him, and after *Slumdog Millionaire* won the Oscar for Best Picture in 2009, he finally said he was ready.

Nick Dear's big idea for *Frankenstein* was simple and sensational: to tell the story from the Creature's point of view. Mary Shelley and all her adaptors see the Creature from Victor Frankenstein's point of view. Danny and Nick described a show that started with a heartbeat and erupted into life as the Creature burst from its frame. The audience, said Danny, would see the world as if for the first time as the Creature saw it, learn to walk and speak with the Creature, follow the Creature to Geneva to confront his maker. *The Modern Prometheus* is Mary Shelley's subtitle for the book; it could just as well refer to Danny's prodigious imagination.

The script, when it arrived in 2010, was disappointing. The stage directions for the long, wordless opening sequence were fine, and I'd heard Danny's hypnotic description of what he was going to do with them. But once they all started talking to each other, although the dialogue was less ponderous than Mary Shelley's, it lay heavy on the page. Danny reassured me that he'd sort it all out in rehearsal. At planning meetings, my colleagues were scathing. They said the script wasn't up to scratch, so we shouldn't do it. "That's as may be," I said, "but Danny's films are turbo-charged. He'll solve this script's problems. We're doing it."

Danny had other big ideas besides the switch in point of view. He wanted the actors who played Frankenstein and the Creature to rotate in their roles. This made conceptual sense: the creator and the created are two sides of the same coin. Beyond that, Danny knew how much extra excitement he could generate by alternating two great actors. And there may have been an ulterior motive. The Creature was the part actors would be fighting for. By offering both parts to both actors, he guaranteed that every night the Doctor would be as strong as the Monster. He already knew he wanted one of them to be Jonny Lee Miller, Sick Boy in *Trainspotting,* and just as powerful on stage as on screen. He started circling around Benedict Cumberbatch, who was at the National in Rattigan's *After the Dance.* Danny could see from the Rattigan how good Benedict would be as the educated Frankenstein, but didn't know him well enough to be confident that he had enough of the animal to be the Creature. Benedict was at a point in his career when he could do anything and was being offered everything, but he wanted to work with Danny and he wanted to play both parts in *Frankenstein.* He asked to audition for Danny.

I very rarely sat in on other directors' auditions, but Danny wanted me to watch Benedict with him in case he needed a second opinion. I told him I was certain that Benedict could do anything he was asked to do, but I was happy to watch. Danny described the opening sequence to Benedict: the birth of a fully grown adult who learns first to see, then walk, then talk in a fierce fast-forward of infancy.

"So it would be great if you could do that for us now," he said.

"Absolutely no problem," said Benedict.

He lay on the floor of the rehearsal studio and shut his eyes. A few seconds later he opened them. They grew large in amazement, as he saw the world for the first time. He started slowly to twitch his limbs. Slowly and painfully, he tried to hoist himself to his feet. His legs buckled from under him: his limbs were like jelly. He collapsed pain-fully, and grunted in shock. He repeated the noise he'd just made, and realised he had a voice. He tried to stand again, grunting, mewling, bouncing off the walls. Locked in a room with him, it was impossible not to share his birth-pangs. I started to sweat, hoping it would end soon, but Benedict had only just started, and out of the corner of my eye I saw Danny beaming with delight. On and on went Benedict: the Creature's agonies weren't going to stop until somebody pulled the plug. After about twenty-five minutes Danny finally thanked Benedict very much, so Benedict thanked Danny very much, and returned to his dressing room to get ready for Rattigan.

"He'll be great," said Danny.

When the audience walked into the Olivier for *Frankenstein*, a corpse was already strapped to a vast circular frame that revolved slowly around a stage hung with hundreds of flickering light bulbs. A great bell, cast in bronze, tolled above the auditorium. Through an unsettling soundscape by Underworld, a heart started to beat, louder and louder, until in a terrifying flash of brilliant white light, the corpse moved. Naked and bloodstained, abandoned by their creator, Benedict and Jonny led the audience through the dawn of their own consciousness, and stumbled through an early industrial world of pounding machinery, swirling fog and violent humanity. They escaped to the verdant countryside, cleansed by the rain and warmed by the sun: from dark satanic mills to green and pleasant land. They learned to eat, laugh, weep and talk. At the first preview in February 2011, I sat among an audience that had been drawn by Danny, Benedict and Jonny. Most of them seemed new not just to the National but to the theatre, and they were thrilled. So was I, at Danny's control of the stage, and at the effortless modernity of his journey into the Romantic past. But half an hour in, it started to feel like the first preview of *War Horse*: too long, too slow, too much talk. When Benedict and Jonny faced off in the Swiss mountains, which-ever way around they were cast, their savage charisma was enough to rivet the audience to the show's urgent concerns about scientific responsibility, love and loneliness, parents and children. But I felt the show slacken its grip whenever they weren't together on stage.

Danny could not have been more grateful for my notes: cut, speed up, tighten transitions, more underscore, less talk. "That's very interesting," he said. "I see exactly what you mean. Thank you. I'll think about what you've said carefully." But he'd seen off mighty Hollywood moguls, and he was more than a match for me. I gave him the same notes after every preview, and he warmly agreed with everything I said. Then he did what he wanted to do, and no more. By the time the show had its two opening nights, one for each rotation of the cast, I'd stopped watching its thrilling highs and could only see what I thought were its lows.

But nobody had come to see Best Play: they'd come to see Danny Boyle's *Frankenstein*. The script gave Danny what he needed, and he had a respect for Nick Dear's dialogue born of his training at the Royal Court. He has an iron grip on an audience. Adrenaline-fuelled highs rush through his movies, but he gives you time to come down from one before he drives you through another. The highs in *Frankenstein* were many and frequent; but he wanted the audience to listen to its arguments, too, so he slowed its pulse as much as he quickened it.

Frankenstein was one of our hottest tickets, and it turned out to be, at least in part, a dry run for Danny's next show. Eighteen months later, in August 2012, with the same two designers, Mark Tildesley and Suttirat Larlarb, he created the London Olympic Opening Ceremony for a worldwide audience of 900 million. It had images of awe-inspiring industrial might and verdant rural tranquillity. It had music by Underworld. It had the biggest harmonically tuned bell in the world, cast in bronze. It had heart-pumping highs and laid-back lows. It celebrated the past and looked with confidence to the future. It made the rest of the world like Britain and for a brief, shining moment it made Britain like itself. It was even more exciting than *Frankenstein*.

❧

You can't second-guess what the public will best like. Popular success is always the consequence of creative conviction. Creative conviction can't guarantee popularity, but the pursuit of popularity for its own sake stifles creativity. So you do what you believe in, and if you're running a huge theatre like the National, you also do what the artists around you believe in. When Simon Stephens brought us his adaptation of *The Curious Incident of the Dog in the Night-Time,* he, like the adaptors of *War Horse* and *Frankenstein,* had completely changed its point of view. Mark Haddon's novel is narrated by its protagonist, fifteen-year-old Christopher Boone, and its genius is in its appeal to the reader to see the world through the eyes of "a mathematician with some behavioural difficulties." Christopher's parents exist only as he sees them. Simon's play looked at all three of them, and embodied by actors, they all existed independently of each other. For the book's countless admirers, one of the play's many new perspectives was in its acknowledgement of how difficult Christopher was to live with. It asked us to identify with his parents' mistakes, the collapse of their marriage, his mother's disappearance, his father's violence and dishonesty.

The playwright and novelist met when both had short residencies at the NT Studio. The invitation to adapt *Curious Incident* came from Mark. Simon wrote it without a commission and showed it to Marianne Elliott, who showed it to me, and it felt like the work of a playwright working to his own vision rather than a producer's. Simon's long working relationship with Marianne gave him the confidence to ask her to find a theatrical correlative for Christopher's way of seeing the world. Neither novel nor play ascribe Christopher's difficulties to Asperger's syndrome, as neither novelist nor playwright claim to have expert knowledge about the autism spectrum. But both are drawn to the outsider, to surprising ways of looking at human experience. Together, Marianne and her designers made an entirely new world from Christopher's obsessions.

The theatrical virtuosity of *Curious Incident* was matched by its unsentimental honesty. It never ducked how nightmarish it can be to be Christopher, or to live with him; nor how difficult it must be to love someone who doesn't know how to be loved. But it asked the audience to love him nevertheless, not just because he's brilliant, but because he's impossible. What a piece of work is man, says the show, particularly this difficult, contradictory young man who has no interest whatsoever in his fellow men. It's an unlikely premise for a blockbuster hit (two years on Broadway and more than four in the West End), but no less unlikely than the adventures of a puppet horse or eight A-level history students.

⁊⁌

What the sillier sort of people really like is comedy, and I'm with them on that, though many of my associates were wary of it. Whenever we looked together at the rep chart, and the programme for the year ahead looked unrelentingly serious, it would be to me that they turned. I grumbled, though in fact little made me happier than sitting in an audience that I'd helped render helpless with laughter. I relish working with the writers and actors I know to be funny, though most of them, if asked exactly how to be funny, shrug: you're either funny or you're not.

Harish Patel is one of Bollywood's leading comic stars, and a veteran of the Mumbai theatre. He'd never appeared on the London stage before *Rafta, Rafta . . .*, Ayub Khan Din's gorgeous celebration of close-knit Indian family life in a terraced house in Bolton. Ayub is an ex-actor, so he knows how to write funny parts from the inside, but Harish had the audience laughing before he'd spoken a line. Because he's tubby? Because he has huge eyes which he knows how to roll into the back of his head? Because, like so many tubby actors, he's absurdly light on his feet? He played opposite Meera Syal, another actor who is inherently funny. Maybe there were territorial negotiations before they settled on the comic give-and-take that brought happy crowds to the Lyttelton, but nobody taught them to be funny. They just were.

Simon Russell Beale and Fiona Shaw, two great tragedians, are also natural-born comics, though before 2010 neither of them had been in a play quite as preposterous as the Victorian comedy *London Assurance* by Dion Boucicault, one of the great chancers of the British theatre. He was born in Dublin, and *London Assurance* was his first big hit. "It will not bear analysis as a literary production," he wrote in 1841, in his preface to the published edition of the play. "I completed this work in thirty days . . . I am aware that it possesses all the many faults, incongruities and excrescences of a hastily written performance."

Sir Harcourt Courtly is fifty-seven, admits to thirty-nine, and makes a reluctant trip to the country to bolster his bank balance by marrying Grace Harkaway, an heiress less than half as old as he claims to be. There he falls in love with Grace's neighbour, Lady Gay Spanker, a devotee of the hunt: "I look upon foxes to be the most blessed dispensation of divine providence." Alas for Sir Harcourt, Lady Gay is already married, and Grace falls in love with his own son, Charles, who has fled to the country to escape his creditors. Thirty days wasn't enough for Boucicault to bring much finesse to his plotting.

"Isn't your name Charles Courtly?" says Sir Harcourt when he runs into his son.

"Not to my knowledge," says Charles.

"Cool, is that my son?" Sir Harcourt asks his supercilious valet.

"No, sir," says Cool, "it is not Mr. Charles, but is very like him."

Simon, one of the foremost scholars of the British stage, is never more convincing than when playing a feather-brain.

London Assurance needs funny actors sufficiently at ease in its ludicrous universe to take it seriously, though Fiona started by taking it too seriously, as she'd been so long in the world of Euripides, Ibsen and Beckett. Lady Gay Spanker stands up to analysis less fruitfully than Medea. "Honestly, if you just go for it, it will be fine," we all said. Once she did, she enjoyed herself as much as we did watching her.

The play's own author advertised its literary shortcomings. More to the point, a lot of its humour is as obscure as Ben Jonson's, so I put a yellow marker pen over every line I thought should be funnier and handed it to Richard Bean. Half the biggest laughs were his. He preferred an almost unnoticeable credit just above the production photographer, so Boucicault got the plaudits, which would have suited him as much as our pragmatic determination to make a hit of his old play by improving it.

The director's job on a show like *London Assurance* is to create a stage world where it can follow its own crazy logic, and cast it with actors who can play it without pushing it. The best directors of comedy and the best comic actors can push too hard on their bad days; even on their good days, they push too hard for somebody. As the rest of the audience rolls in the aisles, who hasn't sat alone and sullen, seething at how unfunny a play is and how grotesquely it's overplayed? So you try to establish where the top is, and urge the actors not to go over it.

Simon's first entrance as Sir Harcourt, to the sound of Tibetan bells, in a huge brocaded dressing gown and plump in dyed-brown kiss curls, pitched the base camp quite close to the summit. Half an hour later, Fiona made her first entrance as Lady Gay, beside herself with the thrill of the chase, invisible hounds baying at her feet, and climbed closer to it, only to find Richard Briers already there as her ancient husband, Mr. Adolphus Spanker. There was plenty that an aspiring comic actor could have learned from Simon's vowels, as full as his waist; from the affected precision of his diction; from the imperceptible lift he gave his best lines. She could have learned from Fiona's "pell-mell, helter-skelter" speed of thought, her unabashed brio: "Horse, man, hound, earth, heaven. All, all, one piece of glowing ecstasy." But whatever it was that brought the house down when Richard Briers wobbled unsteadily onto the stage cannot be taught.

❧

The summer of 2011 looked particularly grim: Chekhov, Ibsen, Jacobean tragedy, the Ipswich serial killer. "No balance here," I said to the planning meeting. I'd just done *Hamlet,* so nobody saw why it shouldn't be my turn to deliver the laughs. I pretended to groan under the intolerable burden of giving people a good time. "It's time James Corden came back to the theatre," I said. "Does anybody have any ideas for him?"

During *The History Boys,* James showed me the scripts for a sitcom he'd written with his friend Ruth Jones, called *Gavin and Stacey.* It was quickly picked up by the BBC, adored by the viewers, and catapulted James onto the front pages as National Treasure. He went to a few parties, had a few drinks, and appeared in a bad movie. This was more than enough for the tabloids to turn on him. The *Guardian* devoted a full page to a solemn analysis of "one of the steepest and quickest falls from grace in showbiz history."

Sebastian Born, head of the Literary Department, suggested an eighteenth-century Venetian comedy by Carlo Goldoni, *The Servant of Two Masters*. I knew it well enough to feel my lip curling. I played the title role at school, dressed in the full chequered harlequin gear, in a production reverent of the conventions of *commedia dell'arte,* and insistent on the physical dexterity of the harlequin. I managed no more than a couple of cautious somersaults, and I didn't remember the play, or me, being very funny. Still, it was a classic of the Italian repertoire and it had a theoretically funny title role, so I uncurled my lip.

As I read *The Servant of Two Masters* for the first time since school, I thought: the farcical mechanics of this play are good, the central part's OK, the dialogue's lame, I'm not interested in re-creating the world of *commedia dell'arte,* I don't want to dress James as a harlequin, but there must be some way of doing it that would play to James's strengths. What, I wondered, was the English low-comedy equivalent of Italian low comedy? It could have a whiff of end-of-the-pier farce, and the *Carry On* films, and Ealing comedy. Goldoni has his two masters escape to Venice from Turin, because Venice has hotels where you can hide from the law and hole up for a dirty weekend. Maybe that's Brighton, in the 1950s or '60s. And it could have elements of the kind of variety show I used to see at the Manchester Palace Theatre in the 1960s, with Ken Dodd, Arthur Askey, or Morecambe and Wise.

I often direct a play because I have a hunch I'll discover it as I go along. This time, with my back against a wall, needing a comedy, I thought I had a big idea.

The idea itself wasn't funny: it was just an idea. I called Richard Bean, with the play, the idea, and James. He wasn't at first wild about any of them, but he said he'd give it a go.

Then I called James. "I have this play, it's an old Italian comedy—"

"Yes," he said.

"You don't want me to tell you what it's about?"

"I'm in," said James.

By now I had my shtick ready about the common roots of all the great European comic traditions, Plautus, music hall, Max Miller, slapstick, panto. None of it added up to funny. I can cast it, I thought;

I can ask Mark Thompson to design an end-of-the-pier pastiche; but I can't do the physical stuff, I can't even turn a proper somersault. So I called Cal McCrystal, who made shows for Spymonkey, a company that traded in exactly the kind of controlled physical anarchy that I couldn't create by myself.

In *The Servant of Two Masters,* Beatrice flees to Venice from Turin disguised as her brother Federigo, who has been killed by her lover Florindo. Beatrice's servant, Truffaldino, loiters hungrily outside the inn where she's staying, when Florindo arrives and offers him a job. Truffaldino accepts it, and spends the rest of the play trying to keep his two masters apart.

> FLORINDO: What's this inn like?
> TRUFFALDINO: Very decent, sir. Comfortable beds, good
>   mirrors, excellent food. The smell from the kitchen
>   makes my heart lift.
> FLORINDO: And what do you do for a living, my good man?
> TRUFFALDINO: I'm a servant, sir.

Richard Bean's first draft arrived not long after he reluctantly agreed to have a go. Rachel Crabbe flees to Brighton from London disguised as her psychotic twin brother Roscoe, who has been killed by her posh boyfriend Stanley Stubbers in a gangland brawl. Her minder, failed washboard player Francis Henshall, is hanging hungrily outside the Cricketer's Arms, where she's staying, when Stanley arrives with an enormous trunk.

> STANLEY: What's this pub like?
> FRANCIS: Groundbreaking. It does food.
> STANLEY: A pub? That does food? Buzz-wam! Whoever
>   thought of that? Wrap his nuts in bacon and send him
>   to the nurse! What are the rooms like?
> FRANCIS: World class.
> STANLEY: Not that I care. I'm boarding-school trained. I'm
>   happy if I've got a bed, a chair, and no one pissing on
>   my face.

I know how to do this kind of crazy, I thought. Find the right toff, put him in a rehearsal room with James, and make sure they don't go over the top. Meanwhile, the toff offers Francis a second job, and he takes it:

> FRANCIS (*Aside*): I've got two jobs, how did that happen?
> You got to concentrate ain't ya, with two jobs. Kaw!
> I can do it, long as I don't get confused. But I get
> confused easily. I don't get confused that easily. Yes
> I do. I'm my own worst enemy. Stop being negative.
> I'm not being negative, I'm being realistic. I'll screw
> it up. I always do. Who screws it up? You, you're the
> role model for village idiots everywhere. Me?! You're
> nothing without me. You're the cock-up! Don't call
> me a cock-up, you cock-up! (*He slaps himself.*) You
> slapped me!? Yeah I did. And I'm glad I did. (*He
> punches himself back.*) That hurt. Good. You started it.
> (*A fight breaks out, where he ends up on the floor, and going
> over tables.*)

No problem here either. Cal McCrystal will show James how to pick a fight with himself and beat himself up.

Richard had given his version a title by the time rehearsals started: *One Man, Two Guvnors*. The next six weeks brought to mind what the Victorian actor Edmund Kean said on his deathbed when somebody asked him how he was feeling: "Dying is easy, comedy is hard." As you work your way through *Hamlet* you take endless pleasure in the discoveries you think you're making about the human condition. As you work through a farce, a company of funny actors will be funny the first time they read through a funny scene. It's less funny second time through, and third time it's torture. A lot of the rehearsal process is a fevered attempt to rediscover what made it funny in the first place. The possibility that the audience won't laugh looms larger and larger. If they don't laugh, you can't accuse them of failing to see the play's higher purpose. If it's only there to make them laugh, and they don't, it's a stinker.

"You've written too many words. It's like Ibsen," said Cal to Richard after the first read-through.

"Are you sure about him?" Richard asked me.

Cal is a precision engineer. He arranged James's fight with himself with scrupulous exactitude. Richard likes anyone who knows what he's doing, so relations improved.

Among Richard's additions to Goldoni was a skeletal eighty-seven-year-old waiter with the shakes, who helps Francis serve soup at the Cricketer's Arms in the big set-piece scene where he serves dinner to both guvnors simultaneously. The guvnors occupy private rooms on either side of the stage, neither of them aware of the other's existence. Alfie the waiter delivers food to Francis, who delivers it to the guvnors.

"Can we imagine it's at the top of the pub? Can you put a stairwell in the middle and can they all enter from below?" I asked Mark Thompson. "We can keep pushing the eighty-seven-year-old waiter downstairs. That's funny."

Cal spent hours working out with Tom Edden, the hilarious young actor playing cadaverous Alfie, how to fall backwards downstairs and bounce back like a rubber ball, while I negotiated with Oliver Chris, another hilarious young actor, who played posh Stanley Stubbers. Oli and I disagreed where the top was, so I thought he went over it a little too often.

"But we had fun, didn't we?" I asked him over dinner, a couple of years later.

"Except when you told me I was guilty of literally the most disgraceful piece of acting you'd ever seen in your life," said Oli.

"Did I really say that?"

"Yup, and I didn't do it again. Though it would have got a laugh."

"But I get an enormous laugh by it, Mr. Gilbert," said George Grossmith, the original Koko in Gilbert and Sullivan's *Mikado*, about some vulgar piece of business or other.

"So you would if you sat on a pork pie," said Gilbert, and vetoed the business.

"Stop laughing! Nobody's allowed to laugh anymore!" I cried one day at the loyal gang of understudies who sat in the corner of the rehearsal room, laughing indiscriminately. "I'm the arbiter of funny! I get to decide!"

"Reliance on actors' laughter is the furthest reach of self-deceit," wrote Moss Hart in his wonderful Broadway memoir, *Act One*. Somebody must draw the line, to balance tight control and loose spontaneity. Somebody has to throw out the rancid pork pies.

The composer Grant Olding put together a four-piece skiffle band, called it the Craze, and wrote a series of hit songs to hustle the show along. "Some of them could be funnier," I said to Grant. "Let's see what we can find online." Lying in wait on YouTube were the novelty acts that peppered the variety shows and pantos of my childhood: xylophone players, idiots playing car horns, accordionists and steel drummers. We filched everything that caught our eye: daylight robbery sustains many directorial careers. Before long, everyone in the cast had a novelty act except Daniel Rigby, who played Alan Dangle, Roscoe's girlfriend's boyfriend. "Do you want a novelty act? What can you do? Could you open your shirt and do a percussion solo on your chest?" Danny is effortlessly funny. He played his chest like he was Buddy Rich.

A few days before we opened, we invited fifty schoolkids into the rehearsal room to watch a run-through. They were particularly partial to Jemima Rooper as Rachel aka Roscoe Crabbe, "that tiny, weird-looking, vicious, short-arsed runt of a criminal." They loved Suzie Toase as Dolly, the woman of Francis's dreams: "He's like a big kid. I've always liked that in a man, immaturity." They roared at Tom Edden as the antique Alfie. The laughs for Oli were dangerously enthusiastic, but he stayed the right side of the top and sat on no pies. And, of course, they enjoyed James, who played them like a master and was as physically nimble as a gymnast. But the show didn't take off. "Maybe they're confused by you," I said to James. "They know who you are, they know how clever you are. Francis is a simpleton."

James was ahead of me. "I was like a smart-arse stand-up. I can fix it."

A couple of days later, another fifty kids arrived for another run-through. James staked out his territory from the start: hapless, bewildered, hungry, stupid. But not guileless: three hundred years on, he rediscovered the native cunning of the harlequin, though the delirious schoolkids couldn't have cared less about that.

The first preview was almost as heady as *The History Boys*, but everybody had to hold their nerve through the first five minutes. One of the director's jobs is to let the audience know as quickly as possible what kind of show they've come to see. They got the hang of it almost as soon as the curtain went up: end-of-the-pier farce, *Carry On* film, low comedy. So why, they wondered, are we watching this old rubbish at the National Theatre? The ice started to thaw when Danny Rigby told them why he loved his girlfriend: "She is pure, innocent, unspoiled by education, like a new bucket." And when James came on as Roscoe's minder, stole a peanut, threw it in the air, and tumbled backwards over an armchair to catch it in his mouth, they surrendered. It was the kind of old rubbish they secretly liked better than Ibsen. By the time James asked for volunteers to come up and help him carry Stanley's trunk into the Cricketer's Arms, he'd led them into a seaside-postcard Arcadia.

War Horse and *Curious Incident* were triumphs of a collective vision. *One Man, Two Guvnors* had the funniest script I've ever been given, so the triumph was above all Richard Bean's, with substantial supplementary ad libs by James. And I couldn't have directed it without Cal, nor would it have lifted off without innately funny actors, who never lost their balance on the comic tightrope that stretches between control and chaos.

But comedy is hard. "Has anyone any idea what it's like to be THE FIFTH FUNNIEST ACTOR in *One Man, Two Guvnors*?" one of them used to shout in the wings.

"This will be a very different crowd to the London crowd," I said to James during rehearsals for the Broadway run. "When you bring the volunteers up to carry the trunk, you *must not touch them*." James had an unerring instinct for selecting from the front two rows the two men most likely to give him what he needed to set the rest of the audience alight. In London, he used to pat their bottoms as they carried the trunk offstage, which lit up the audience some more.

"Don't go anywhere near their bottoms," I told James sternly. "Americans are a very litigious people. They'll sue you."

"Of course," said James, "I won't go near their bottoms."

At the packed public dress rehearsal, he brought up two sweet-looking young men, and when he asked them to tell the audience what they did, they said they were in *The Book of Mormon,* the famous hit musical.

"Oh my God, have you any tips? This is all completely new to me," said an apparently awestruck James, the opening shot in his campaign to conquer first Broadway and then the whole of American show business. As the Mormons carried off the trunk, he squeezed their bottoms like they were his gay best friends. The boys were thrilled, and so was the house.

"Sorry," said James afterwards.

"Forget everything I told you," I said.

A few days later, when he asked for help with the trunk, he spotted a man in a big blond wig, who seemed very eager to be selected. James brought him up.

"What's your name, sir?" he asked him.

"Donald," said the man, whose wig may have been a combover. The audience jeered: Donald didn't have many fans on Broadway.

"And what do you do?"

"I'm in real estate, and I'm the host of TV's *The Apprentice,*" said Donald, swelling with needy self-delight. James patted his bottom as he carried the trunk into the Cricketer's Arms. The Broadway audience laughed indulgently: they thought Donald was a joke, entirely inconsequential.

These days I watch James on YouTube, and catch up with him when he's in London. I tell him he must come back to the theatre before too long, and I think he will, because he's a creature of the stage. And when he sings in the car with Stevie Wonder, or Adele, or Michelle Obama, he's the same gleeful seraph who beat himself up for being the role model for village idiots everywhere, the singular talent who brought a thousand people a night to an uproar of comic ecstasy, giving them what they best like.

12

One Night Only

PACKING THEM IN

Early in *The Madness of George III,* the king has his weekly audience with the prime minister.

> KING: Married yet, Mr. Pitt, what, what?
> PITT: No, sir.
> KING: Got your eye on anybody, hey?
> PITT: No, sir.
> KING: More to the point—anybody got their eye on you, hey hey?
> PITT: Not to my knowledge, sir.

One night in New York, after a run of two years in London, Julian Wadham's mind was elsewhere, as must have been William Pitt's during his many routine interviews with the king.

"Married yet, Mr. Pitt, what, what?" said Nigel Hawthorne as the king.

"Yes, sir," said Julian, superb in his frosty hauteur.

Nigel's eyes narrowed.

"Who to, Mr. Pitt?" said Nigel.

Blind panic.

"The daughter of the Duchess of Huddersfield, Your Majesty," said Julian, rewriting history and inventing an entirely new branch of the aristocracy.

Nigel moved in for the kill.

"What's she like, Mr. Pitt, what, what?"

After a stricken pause, the king moved smoothly back to the warrant he was signing, leaving Mr. Pitt in a flop sweat, a departure from history, as the real Pitt only fell apart when he was drunk.

A live show happens for the audience gathered on the night, on one night only. It never happens the same way twice. At all other performances of *The Madness of George III,* Mr. Pitt was a confirmed bachelor. So when you go to the theatre, you are among the uniquely advantaged few. The trickiest balancing act of all is to reconcile that exclusivity with the thirst to share it as widely as possible. When I applied to run the National, I fretted about the retreat into tiny black-box studios, but compared to James Corden's YouTube millions, the difference between fifty people in a room above a pub and 1,150 in the Olivier seems negligible.

It was always worthwhile to run a show that people wanted to see for long enough for them to see it, even if no two houses see exactly the same show. But here was another conundrum. We wanted the National to be full, but that often meant closing a show before we'd exhausted its appeal. The only way of knowing we'd exhausted it would have been to keep it running until it started to fail at the box office, but we didn't want to play to half-empty houses. The traditional solution was to make partnerships with commercial producers and send successful shows into the West End. This allowed more people to see the show, but the commercial producer, who shouldered the financial risk of remounting it, also took the lion's share of the profits.

I assumed, when we started, that there was a rule that publicly funded theatres weren't allowed to risk their own capital. Nick Starr soon discovered we were required only to make "best use" of our resources. In 2006 we had in *The History Boys* a major hit that, despite more than three hundred performances in the Lyttelton, had nowhere near satisfied the public hunger for tickets. We didn't see why we should allow a commercial producer to earn large profits by bearing the almost negligible risk of presenting it in the West End. We spent hours in each other's offices, winding ourselves up into enjoyable furies about the money we didn't want to give away. The difference between us was that Nick had the financial acumen to present a case to a wary National Theatre board that the best use of our resources was to invest them in a West End transfer of *The History Boys*.

After a long national tour, *The History Boys* opened in the West End in December 2006 for a three-month run. It was packed, quickly earned back what we'd invested in it, and made us a handsome profit. At the end of its run, we closed it. We told ourselves that our remit was to find the widest possible audience for our work, so we toured it to twenty-seven different regional venues, before bringing it back to the West End for another limited run. Touring is expensive, and made us no money. Only after the tour ended did we ask ourselves why we'd been so determined to take it off in the West End. We could have run it indefinitely, made lots more money for the National, and put together another company to tour it to the rest of the country.

The widest possible audience was sometimes not very wide at all: an experimental multimedia production of fragments from a difficult novel by Dostoevsky was never going to appeal to the *War Horse* crowd. But we believed in both, and looked for the audience that would share our belief. When the widest possible audience could be numbered in millions, it was a pleasure as well as a responsibility to sell tickets to them.

War Horse started with workshops at the Studio, just as Katie Mitchell's Dostoevsky started at the Studio, and in the same spirit of investigation. To an outsider, Tom Morris's workshop with the two actors who put cardboard boxes on their heads would probably have looked more experimental than Katie's. Even if we'd ditched *War Horse* at the last moment, the two years of exploratory work wouldn't have been wasted. Everybody involved would have extended themselves as artists and taken what they'd learned into their creative futures. The scale of its success took us by surprise, but this time we knew what to do with it. After a second run at the National, we put it into the West End and left it there. *War Horse* ran at the New London

Theatre for seven years, toured the UK for two years, ran in New York, Toronto, Berlin, Amsterdam, Beijing, Cape Town, and toured the U.S., Canada and Australia. It played to over 7 million people, and by the time it closed in London, its global success had returned more than £30 million to the National Theatre. Later we did the same with *One Man, Two Guvnors* and *The Curious Incident of the Dog in the Night-Time.*

In 2003, public funding accounted for forty percent of a total income of £37 million. By 2015, turnover was £117 million, of which fifteen percent came from the public purse. Our commercial profits were enough to compensate for large cuts in public funding, and invest besides in the redevelopment of our building, and the production of new work for young audiences. The desire to widen the audience for our work found one outlet in the numbers we could attract to our productions in the commercial sector; and another in what we could do with what we earned to attract new audiences at low prices to the National itself.

❧

"I know it won't be perfect, and I know it isn't really theatre, but I keep thinking about how much I'd have loved to see Laurence Olivier at the Old Vic in my local cinema when I was a Manchester teenager."

Every Friday morning, I met with Nick Starr and Lisa Burger. "You've been talking about cinema for long enough," said Lisa one day, as we were looking at the 2009 budget. "I've found the money for it. Let's just do it." Lisa, subtle as finance director and super-subtle as chief operating officer, used to listen to my streams of consciousness, tell me what I wanted, and then make it happen.

The Royal Opera House had for years broadcast opera and ballet on television, but televised theatre has always been problematic. Opera works on television because its only point of reference is opera: you don't expect opera singers to give performances scaled down for the cameras. But when you watch actors on TV, your unconscious points of reference are television and film. You expect them to reveal themselves subtly to the camera, so when they reach out and include the house, you wonder why they're shouting. Somewhere in the background, you hear the theatre audience laugh, and you feel left out, so you switch over.

But I remembered that my 1998 production of *Twelfth Night* at Lincoln Center Theater in New York had been broadcast live on PBS television. On the night, the actors, all of them experienced in television, tried at first to play inwardly for the cameras. But they quickly realised that if they didn't communicate to the audience in the theatre, the show evaporated; so imperceptibly they opened it out to include them.

I watched it on TV, expecting to hate it. But it worked, partly because it was shot with skill and sophistication, but mainly because it was live across America. Its liveness, the fact that wherever you were, you were watching the same event at the same time as the audience in the theatre, made it less like television drama and more like an outside broadcast. You knew it wasn't the real thing, but as you couldn't be there at the big match, you were glad the cameras were there to capture it for you. It didn't matter that the actors were a bit sweaty and a bit shouty, because, like footballers, they were sweating and shouting live, in the moment.

I was still bothered by the mismatch between the small screen and the stage, and I missed being part of an audience. But I was excited when the Royal Opera House started to relay big-screen opera and ballet to huge crowds in Covent Garden and Trafalgar Square. Then, in 2006, the Metropolitan Opera started broadcasting live opera to cinemas across the world. And public demand pointed in the same direction as technology: although we sold 750,000 tickets every year at the National Theatre itself, there were many thousands more who wanted to see us.

The entire operation was masterminded by David Sabel, a young American who trained in mime at the Jacques Lecoq School in Paris. He discovered that there was a glut of red-nosed clowns plying their trade on the boulevards, so he found work as a pastry chef. Tiring of that, he crossed the Channel and did a business degree. Live satellite relays of theatre to cinemas were no more of a challenge to him than a perfect millefeuille.

We were ready to go by the middle of 2009, and had coincidentally already scheduled to open Racine's *Phèdre* in June, with Helen Mirren in the title role. Eighteen months after she'd won the Oscar for her performance in *The Queen,* there was no actor more likely to attract audiences to see theatre in cinemas. Always a pioneer, she was immediately enthusiastic, and completely unconcerned about how much she was risking her reputation by performing live on the big screen in an untried experiment. Helen was a more obvious first port of call than Racine. It would be hard to think of a less cinematic form of theatre than French neoclassical tragedy. Strictly bound by the unities of time, place and action, *Phèdre* unfolds on one set, has no jokes, ruthlessly excludes everything except the central agony of the woman who falls passionately in love with her chaste stepson Hippolytus, and drags him, her husband and herself to ruin. It had one advantage: if Racine worked live on screen, there'd be nothing in the repertoire that wouldn't.

On 25 June, *Phèdre* went out live to seventy-two cinemas in the UK, and live or delayed by a few hours to 120 cinemas in the rest of the world. If Helen was nervous, she didn't show it. Margaret Tyzack, who played Oenone, Phèdre's old nurse, remembered doing live TV in the 1950s and '60s, so it was no big deal to her.

I watched it in the BFI cinema, next door to the National. I had kept from everybody a residual fear that it would look like a bad movie. But you almost forgot you were in a cinema. You knew you were watching a play, so you expected theatre performances: you wanted the actors to reach out to you as if you were in the middle of the stalls. I was probably the only person who noticed that in the heat of her passion for Hippolytus, Helen skipped a key line of Ted Hughes's free-verse translation: "I am in love." It didn't matter: she was saying it with every fibre of her body, so nobody missed it. But I was secretly thrilled by how graphically her tiny lapse exposed the precipitous danger of the whole event.

Seventeen thousand people watched *Phèdre* in UK cinemas. After its international and encore screenings, 63,000 people had seen it, more than doubling its audience in the Lyttelton. During the party after the broadcast, David Sabel circulated the excited emails and tweets that arrived from all over the country; later they arrived from as far afield as Reykjavík and San Francisco. As the cost of the equipment necessary to receive and project our broadcasts fell, the number of cinemas that took them rose, and soon included small local arts centres and village halls from Cornwall to the Shetland Islands. When we screened *Frankenstein* two years after *Phèdre,* more than 600,000 people saw it on 1,500 screens.

NT Live will never replace the thing itself, nor does it discourage audiences from going to their local theatre: if anything, the cinema experience acts as a spur. It was driven, like our commercial operations in the West End, by the contradictory ambition to make theatre for the privileged few on the night, and to spread that privilege as widely as possible: the impossible balancing act.

Two weeks after screening in cinemas across the world, *Phèdre* played twice at the ancient theatre of Epidaurus. Helen and the rest of the cast ramped it up a little, but essentially they gave the same performance to the 28,000 people who saw in the flesh as they gave to the cameras. At the second performance, I watched from the very back of the vast, semicircular auditorium. The acoustics at Epidaurus are miraculous, so it was perfectly audible, though I couldn't see much of what was going on in Helen's eyes. At the BFI cinema, of course, I missed nothing.

But at Epidaurus, when Helen cried "I am in love," Venus reached out from Olympus across the Peloponnese and held the entire audience in her lethal embrace. Twice only.

◦❧◦

"Are you Nicholas Hytner?" Every so often, I was recognised front of house, or out and about in London, by enthusiastic theatregoers. "We just wanted to say how much we love the National Theatre."

"It's very kind of you." I would look forward to them telling me how moved they'd been by *Othello* or *Curious Incident.*

"Well, we love it. There are no queues for the women's toilets at the interval. You're doing a brilliant job."

Or: "The Terrace restaurant is such good value. Exceptional meatballs."

Or: "The cheap tickets—amazing! And the legroom in the Olivier Theatre—incredible!"

Or, a particular favourite: "There's nowhere like the National. Superb underground car park."

"And apart from all that, Mrs. Lincoln," I never quite said, "HOW DID YOU ENJOY THE SHOW?"

But packing them in makes you responsible for what happens to them before and after the show, so I learned to be as happy to hear about interval activity in the women's toilets as I was to hear about the play.

When Denys Lasdun designed the National Theatre, the site was a dead end: a wharf separated it from the rest of the South Bank. He did not foresee that it would quickly look as if the theatre had turned its back on the river. At the end of the twentieth century, London rediscovered the Thames; you could finally walk almost uninterrupted along the South Bank from Vauxhall Bridge to Tower Bridge. But where the National should have been showing its best face to the world, Lasdun had put the goods entrance and rubbish bins; 17 million people walked past them every year. I moaned about them endlessly.

By 2010, we knew we needed to spend about £10 million on keeping the existing plant up to scratch. Better, said Nick and Lisa, to raise £70 million for a scheme that promised a massive overhaul of the building than £10 million for rewiring and new generators. John Rodgers, the phlegmatic head of development, which is what arts institutions call fundraising, took it on the chin.

Lloyd Dorfman, whose company Travelex continued to sponsor hundreds of thousands of cheap tickets, was one of the first to step forward. He gave us £10 million, which immediately gave the scheme credibility with other major donors, and the renovated Cottesloe Theatre became the Dorfman Theatre. The naming of arts buildings for the philanthropists who back them has long and inspiring precedent: Tate, Courtauld, Carnegie, Whitworth, Guggenheim. The family of Lord Cottesloe, a political grandee and first chairman of the South Bank Theatre board, was sympathetic to the renaming.

Development increases in importance as public funding diminishes. Directors of American theatres, who receive almost nothing in government funding, spend nearly as much of their time courting donors as they spend on what happens on their stages. Their French and German counterparts spend no time on it at all, as public subsidy accounts for as much as ninety-five percent of their income. In the absence of American tax incentives, and the pervasive American culture of charitable giving, it will never be possible for our cultural organisations to raise as much as their American counterparts. Nor would it be desirable: the cushion of public subsidy encourages both creative innovation and the strong ethos of public service that lies behind our determination always to widen our audience.

But the arts are over-dependent on a small number of committed philanthropists. Apart from Lloyd Dorfman, the chief donors to NT Future—Guy and Charlotte Weston, Stewart Grimshaw of the Monument Trust, Dame Vivien Duffield—were supporting the National before I became its director. Their successors have yet to emerge. Fortunes have been made on Wall Street and in the City of London during the last twenty years, but the super-rich of London do not feel the social pressure that opens wallets on Wall Street for an entire spectrum of charitable and cultural causes.

Still, between 2003 and 2015, John Rodgers and his department increased annual fundraising from £3.7 million to £8.3 million, and raised £50 million towards the redevelopment of the building. Another £7.5 million came from *War Horse*. We built a new education centre, new workshops, new dressing rooms, and opened the building to face the river. Where rats once feasted from the overflowing rubbish bins, there is now a cafe and bar. The National looks at last like it wants you to come in and have a good time; and as the annual income from the bar is several hundreds of thousands of pounds, the provision of a good time to as many people as want to share it has once more turned out to be to the theatre's commercial advantage.

❧

A few days after the formation of the coalition government in 2010, the new Secretary of State for Culture, Media and Sport, Jeremy Hunt, invited a group of artists and producers to meet him at the Roundhouse in north London. He promised "a golden age for the arts," based on a huge increase in charitable giving, which he vowed to facilitate. He then presided over a thirty percent cut to the Arts Council's budget, did nothing to encourage philanthropy, got chummy with Rupert Murdoch, and moved on in 2012 to work his magic on the NHS. Thereafter, the arts were cut less aggressively than other spending departments, though outside London, theatres were hit hard by cuts to local authority funding. I much preferred Jeremy Hunt's successors as Secretary of State: none of them pretended that they could do much for us, or that they knew as much as Ed Vaizey, the excellent Minister of State for Culture until 2016.

Meanwhile, Joey the War Horse became a poster boy for what we learned to call the creative industries, eventually travelling with the prime minister to China for a special appearance at a state banquet. He was more comfortable in the company of the queen. She saw him first on a rare visit to the West End, and he was swiftly invited to Windsor, where she made a great fuss of him, and was expert in her assessment of his equine verisimilitude. When she came on an official visit to the National to mark our fiftieth birthday, she greeted him like an old friend.

The most significant devotee of the arts was the man who did the cutting. The Chancellor of the Exchequer, George Osborne, came regularly to the theatre, and was a connoisseur of opera, ballet and the visual arts. Few of the artists whose work he enjoyed can have had much time for his economic policies, but they were spared the worst of them: a different Chancellor might have done more damage. He invented, in the theatre tax credit, a way of giving back to us some of what he'd taken away. The tax credit is more useful to big-spending theatres than it is to companies who are strapped for cash, but it's impossible to avoid the awkward reality that the arts were not hit as hard as, for instance, welfare.

Every society chooses how much it values art. It can look to its government to sustain its artists and to make their work affordable. It can look to the market to identify the art that most people want to buy, and to the goodwill of its rich to support the rest. It can trust to a balance between the patronage of the public, the state and the wealthy. But for centuries, powerful patrons of the arts have wanted something back: prestige, the company of the artist, sex with the dancers, a marble tomb. When I started in 2003, what the Labour government wanted back was greater access to the arts. The Secretary of State for Culture, Tessa Jowell, loved the theatre, and wanted as many people as possible to find out about it. After 2010, diversity and inclusion were lower on the agenda. In 2013, Jeremy Hunt's replacement, Maria Miller, candidly asked artists for help in making the economic case to the Treasury for "arts investment." Nick and I made it in a sober, boring piece in the *Daily Telegraph*. The Tories were also keen on international pre-eminence, so we gave them evidence for that, too.

Arts journalists frequently grumbled that we never learned to make the arguments for public funding, but their complaints were unfounded. Successive Labour governments responded to us with handsome increases in funding. We convinced George Osborne to spare us the worst of the cuts, and in 2015, he announced the first rise in arts spending since the big-spending days of New Labour. Everything we said was true: investment in the arts amounts to 0.1 percent of public spending but delivers four times that in gross domestic product; publicly funded art is the bedrock of a creative economy that in 2016 was worth £84 billion and is growing at twice the rate of the rest of the economy; British creativity is admired across the world and is a source of disproportionate "soft power"; the arts boost tourism; they draw communities together; they are an unparalleled educational tool. There are legions of articulate arts leaders who make the arguments daily to public funding bodies, corporate sponsors and philanthropic trusts.

But none of these are the reasons why I came into the theatre, and they aren't why George Osborne comes to see it, or why the Elizabethan audience thronged to the South Bank, or why Queen Elizabeth brought the Lord Chamberlain's Men to court. Nor are they the reasons why the Germans spend three times as much each year on the arts as the coalition government spent in total over its five-year term. The most eloquent argument is the one that can only be made by the art itself. Inspired, moved, outraged, cast down, cheered up, entertained or infatuated by a good performance, the audience cares nothing for GDP.

The theatre has never been more popular, in rooms above pubs, in abandoned factories, in ornate West End theatres, in concrete culture palaces. Maybe the most significant consequence of the digital revolution is not that it has opened the door to widespread digital distribution of live performance, but that it has led to a resurgence of the real thing. The instant availability of everything you want at the click of a mouse turns out not to include the thing you want most: human contact. You want to be there when it happens, for one night only.

A failed washboard player beats himself up for being an idiot; a woman falls in love with her stepson; a man could be bounded in a nutshell and count himself a king of infinite space, were it not that he has bad dreams. You reach out across the void and touch lives you seem to have led. Or you live vanished lives, strange lives, the lives of others. You are part of a community that, by an act of collective empathy and imagination, rejects the low dishonesty of the age, and insists that no one exists alone.

❦

Every Friday at 10 a.m. there's a company meeting in the canteen. It lasts about fifteen minutes and it's usually standing room only: actors, stage crew, painters, lighting, finance, IT, anyone who wants to turn up. We're given the low-down on last week's box office. We hear about the death-defying acts that will play outside on Theatre Square during the summer: acrobatic identical twins from Poland, artistic hairdressers from Barcelona, the Whalley Range All Stars' Pig. The canteen manager tells us that she's had enough of whoever's nicking the stainless-steel cutlery so she's going over to plastic. I announce additions to the programme and the latest casting.

It was at a Friday company meeting in the spring of 2013 that I announced I'd step down as director in March 2015. After ten years, I said, it's time to let someone else think about what the National should be doing. Theatres need regular reinvention; their directors must make way for new generations. It's someone else's turn to decide what it means to give the audience a good time.

But this Friday in November, not much more than a year before I'm due to leave, is the day before the fiftieth-birthday show, and I'm already feeling wistful about my departure. I tell the company how the show's going, though most of them are involved in it, so they know already. Then I riff about the mighty actors from the National's past who have joined us, and what it means to be the National Theatre. I ask myself what I'll do with all my stories when I don't have a weekly captive audience. I think that maybe I'll have to write a book.

At the end of the company meeting, instead of going back to the press office, Lucinda Morrison walks upstairs with me. She's just had a call from one of the Sunday papers. They have information that the rabbit roulade served in the Terrace restaurant uses meat from rabbits kept in shocking conditions on a Spanish farm. This is news to our kitchens, but they immediately remove the roulade from the menu. This doesn't stop the Sunday paper running the story, with a big photograph of happy diners on the terrace of the National Theatre next to a bigger one of sad white rabbits with brown ears and pink eyes.

It's unnaturally quiet in my office, but the silence is broken by the saxophonist who plays "Moon River" to the passers-by on the South Bank. No longer content merely to play badly, he now walks a rickety tightrope at the same time, so not a single note comes out in the right order.

On my desk is the rep chart. There's a thick line under March 2015, which is when my time's up. There are one or two gaps in the schedule, but none of them can accommodate the very good new play that arrived yesterday, whose fate now rests with my successor. Lyn Haill comes in with the programme for tomorrow's show, packed with memories of the last fifty years. Lyn, who has edited our programmes for as long as anyone can remember, worked for Olivier at the Old Vic. She points me to something Sir Laurence said, which she's printed in big bold letters:

The National Theatre can never be what the public wants if it isn't allowed sometimes to be what the public doesn't want.

Niamh tells me that they're ready to continue the technical rehearsal in the Olivier. I spend the rest of the day finessing transitions from scene to scene, from *Antony and Cleopatra* to *Angels in America,* from *Mourning Becomes Electra* to *Jerry Springer—The Opera.* In the evening, there's a public dress rehearsal. Some of the biggest laughs go to Penelope Wilton and Nicholas Le Prevost, who perform a scene from Alan Ayckbourn's *Bedroom Farce.* They're in bed with a plateful of pilchards on toast, and they're as precise about the consumption of the pilchards as Baryshnikov would be about a multiple pirouette. But they also seem totally spontaneous: one more perfect balancing act.

Before the performance the following night, I go backstage. There are five floors of dressing rooms facing each other around a central light well. "It's like a women's prison," says Maggie Smith when I knock on her door. Actors are leaning out of the windows, shouting encouragement and obscenities to each other. Plumes of illicit cigarette smoke curl from Michael Gambon's window. Frances de la Tour also has a cigarette. She's never come across a rule she doesn't want to break, so she's smoking for the revolution.

I go from room to room to thank everyone and wish them good luck, and I'm in with Alex Jennings and Simon Russell Beale when the stage manager calls beginners to the stage. Softly at first, the room starts to shake. I look across the light well, and see that in every dressing room, actors are banging with their palms against the windows. It's what happens at the beginners' call on every opening night, and it carries with it the terror of prisoners on death row, hammering at their cell doors in tribute to the condemned on his way to execution. But tonight, it's as if the starting gates have opened on the Derby, and a hundred thoroughbreds are thundering towards the finish.

I stand with Alex and Simon and everywhere I look are the actors who have marked my life at the National, in a frenzy of drumming. So I start drumming with them.

And I think: I'm going to miss this.

Prologue

At my leaving party in the new scenic workshops, I owned up to breaking the pass door at the back of the Olivier stalls on the fiftieth birthday, because I was locked out of the backstage celebrations. During the whole of my last day as director, I was locked out of the workshops, because they wanted them to be a surprise. When I arrived for the party, I was immediately surrounded by hundreds of old friends and colleagues, so had no time to admire the battered furniture, faded costumes and props: mementos of all my shows, beautifully hung like a vast gallery installation. They'd made life-sized cut-outs of Nicholas Hytner, so that people could have their photos taken with him. Some people had their photos taken with the real thing, but eventually I joined the pack having their photos taken with the cut-outs, and had mine taken with Nicholas Hytner too. He's probably still around, stacked against a wall somewhere.

Lisa Burger, Alex Jennings and Frances de la Tour made speeches: Alex talked about our twenty-five-year friendship, Frankie said that she was my wife. I drank too much, danced a little, and stole a joke from Alan Bennett for my own speech: how proud we can all be, I said, of the contribution we have made together to show-business history, by playing a small part in the inexorable rise of James Corden.

"What's past is prologue," says Antonio in *The Tempest,* often quoted as an inspirational maxim, though in fact he's trying to persuade Sebastian to turn his back on the past and murder his brother. The National's past is always prologue, if not to murder then at least to new directions. Eighteen months before I left, the board, chaired by John Makinson, appointed my successor, Rufus Norris. He has a stirring vision for the National, and the respect and devotion of the artists who will realise it for him. Some of them came to my leaving party straight from rehearsals for his first show as director. Lisa is now executive director, Nick Starr's old job. I love going back and seeing what they're up to. No longer responsible for what's on stage, I'm free to have a really good time.

Not long before I told the board that I thought my time was up, Nick suggested that we went on working together after we both left. He had an idea that we could raise the money to buy or build our own theatre. I was immediately up for it, and we started to think about where we wanted to be.

We are both immune to the allure of the West End, where the theatres will always be constrained by their architectural heritage. They are perfect for the kind of shows that they were originally built for, most of them around a hundred years ago, and many of them are beautiful and atmospheric. But my heart beats faster at the National, at the Manchester Royal Exchange or in a disused warehouse than it does on Shaftesbury Avenue. I prefer theatres that can be knocked around to suit the show to theatres that force me to knock the show around to fit the space. And London has changed. Audiences will go wherever you invite them if the invitation is worthwhile.

We knew that whatever we did had to work as a business. There'd be no public funding: we've had our turn. We'd try to make bold, popular theatre. We'd commission ambitious plays that could run long enough to pay for themselves, and build an environment for them that would be exciting, flexible and welcoming, with plenty of legroom, and lots of women's toilets.

I went out and talked to playwrights, while Nick went out and talked to property developers. And then, as we always have, we went to each other's meetings. One of Nick's new friends told him about a development nearing completion on the Thames, between Tower

Bridge and City Hall, five minutes' walk from London Bridge Station. The local authority, Southwark, had made substantial cultural provision a condition of its planning consent.

Six months after I left the National, we made a deal for 45,000 square feet of empty space, big enough for a 920-seat theatre and a foyer with breathtaking views over the river and the Tower of London. Our old friend Steve Tompkins has designed a beautiful, flexible auditorium. We'll make shows behind a proscenium arch, on a thrust stage, in the round, or we'll take out all the seats and have the audience stand in the pit: whatever's best for the play. The money to build it and to produce what happens in it comes from a small group of investors who are interested both in making theatre and in making money. So were the first businessmen who built theatres south of the river more than four hundred years ago, and although none of our investors would compare themselves to Shakespeare, we hope to make for them as handsome a return on their investment as Shakespeare took with him on his retirement to Stratford.

The Bridge Theatre will open in the autumn of 2017. We'll produce around four shows a year in it, and I'll direct half of them. Maybe we'll stick at one theatre; maybe we'll build others. Whether we succeed or fail, it will be another balancing act, and this book is its prologue.

Cast and Creatives

This book does not record everything that happened at the National Theatre between 2003 and 2015, and cannot come close to acknowledging everyone who made it happen. I have devoted too little space to the shows that I didn't myself direct, because I remember less about them than the shows I lived with in the rehearsal room. I wish I could pay tribute to them all.

Everybody involved in *National Theatre 50 Years on Stage* deserves applause. I have only scratched the surface. Benedict Cumberbatch and Kobna Holdbrook-Smith were needle-sharp in Tom Stoppard's *Rosencrantz and Guildenstern Are Dead.* In addition to playing Mrs. Sullen, Maggie Smith appeared in a clip from Noël Coward's *Hay Fever,* directed by Coward himself: nobody doubted that they'd seen a comic miracle. Deborah Findlay was the matron in Peter Nichols's *The National Health;* forty-five years after it opened, Charles Kay occupied the same bed. Gawn Grainger and James Hayes, two other Olivier-era veterans, were also on the ward. Clive Rowe stopped the show in *Guys and Dolls,* as he always did. Andrew Scott and Dominic Cooper were deeply affecting in *Angels in America.* Roger Allam's lament as Walter Heisenberg for his ruined German homeland in Michael Frayn's *Copenhagen* was heart-stopping. Helen Mirren flew in from a film set in France, and in a wild burst of adrenaline murdered

Tim Pigott-Smith in O'Neill's *Mourning Becomes Electra*. The show was superbly designed by Mark Thompson and lit by Mark Henderson.

On a typical Monday, the casting team included over the years Charlotte Bevan, Alastair Coomer, Juliet Horsley and Charlotte Sutton. In the Literary Department were at various times Chris Campbell, Sarah Clarke, Ben Jancovich, Tom Lyons, Clare Slater and Brian Walters. Among the stage-management team were Fi Bardsley, Rosemary Beattie, Angela Bissett, Barry Bryant, Ian Connop, Ben Donoghue, Cynthia Duberry, Ian Farmery, Val Fox, Peter Gregory, Sara Gunter, Harry Guthrie, Nik Haffenden, Ernie Hall, Janice Heyes, Anna Hill, Emma B. Lloyd, Eric Lumsden, David Marsland, Kerry McDevitt, Neil Mickel, David Milling, Trish Montemuro, Jo Neild, Alison Rankin, Brew Rowland, Andrew Speed, Jane Suffling, Shane Thom, Lesley Walmsley and Julia Wickham. The marketing team was led first by Chris Harper, then by Sarah Hunt and finally by Alex Bayley. Nick Starr and I often took advice from my brother, Richard, who was deputy chairman of Saatchi & Saatchi and is now a global advertising guru. The front-of-house team was led by John Langley, catering and commercial operations first by Robyn Lines and then Patrick Harrison. The genius production managers included Jason Barnes, Katrina Gilroy, Tariq Hussein, Igor, Sacha Milroy and Di Willmott. In the workshops, the head scenic artist was Hilary Vernon-Smith, the head of props was Nicky Holderness; Paul Evans was head of scenic construction. Carol Lingwood was head of costume, and head of wigs was first Joyce Beagarie and then Giuseppe Cannas. Almost all the American (and British) donors were delightful, none more so than Barbara Fleischman, a nonagenarian whose politics are as radical as her enthusiasms.

❧

I joined English National Opera in 1978 as a staff producer, which was what they called an assistant director, at £55 a week. I learned most from John Copley, who trained as a dancer until he was told one day by Dame Ninette de Valois, the founder of the Royal Ballet, that he'd never make it, so she was having him transferred forthwith to the Opera. There was no aspect of the performance of opera that he hadn't learned at the coal face. He stood in for Maria Callas when she withdrew to her suite at the Savoy, and played Tosca at the stage rehearsals of the famous Zeffirelli production opposite Tito Gobbi's Scarpia. He still needs no encouragement to sing Act 2, particularly in restaurants. I followed him from wardrobe to prop shop, from paint frame to rehearsal. I watched him light a show, and move the vast chorus over the stage as if he were painting with them, all the time entertaining them with stories of his wicked adventures in the world's fleshpots. In 1979, I was approached out of the blue by Norman Platt, the founder of Kent Opera. He needed a late replacement for Harold Pinter whom he'd hoped to be able to persuade to direct Britten's *The Turn of the Screw*. Being second choice to Pinter didn't seem like a problem to me. Nor did *The Turn of the Screw*, which always works: I've never seen a bad production of it. The opera itself was one stroke of luck. Another was Norman himself, an ex-singer with stronger opinions about how opera should be staged than the fiercest German deconstructionist. He insisted above all on truthful acting and vivid music-making. It was impossible to imagine offering him ideas that were sloppy, self-serving or merely fashionable. My education continued at the old Leeds Playhouse, then run by John Harrison, a model artistic director. He shared with me both his theatrical know-how and his determination to put it primarily at the service of his audience. He knew exactly how to take the community with him.

Don Carlos was at the Manchester Royal Exchange, where between 1985 and 1988 I was an associate director. Ian McDiarmid was King Philip II, a performance of suppressed ferocity. Michael Grandage was a watchful Don Carlos. Ian McDiarmid was also Volpone at the Almeida. His passionate intelligence had a big influence on me. Joshua Sobol's play *Ghetto* was an overwhelming record of the destruction by the Nazis of the Yiddish Theatre Company in Vilna, Lithuania.

Cressida had splendid performances from Anthony Calf, Matt Hickey, Lee Ingleby, Charles Kay and Malcolm Sinclair. In *Orpheus Descending*, Val Xavier was played by Stuart Townsend. In *Twelfth Night*, there were beautiful performances from Kyra Sedgwick, Max

Wright, Brian Murray and David Patrick Kelly. Helen Hunt was Viola and Philip Bosco was Malvolio. In *The Winter's Tale* Phil Daniels performed a miracle with the often intolerable Autolycus: he left you wanting more. Ian Redford as the princess was perfect in *Mother Clap*. So was Paul Ready as the apprentice Martin, never better than when required to make pig noises while Con O'Neill went at him. Iain Mitchell gamely wore a leather harness and jock strap in the Act 2 sex party. Maggie McCarthy was the cunning old brothel-keeper. All the mollies were divine.

⟅∽⟆

The serpentine archbishop in *Henry V* was William Gaunt. Peter Blythe was a model of establishment civility as Exeter. Robert Blythe was Llewellyn; Ian Hogg was the king of France; Felicité du Jeu was his daughter Catherine. In the tavern, Jude Akuwudike was Pistol and Cecilia Noble was the hostess, sticking around to be Ruta Skadi, queen of the Latvian witches in *His Dark Materials*. *Edmond* was deftly staged by Edward Hall. The *Jerry Springer* cast was led by Michael Brandon as Jerry, and included David Bedella as Satan, Benjamin Lake, Loré Lixenberg, Vlada Aviks, Andrew Bevis, Wills Morgan, Sally Bourne, Alison Jiear and Marcus Cunningham. Their singing was refined; their performances were right out there.

Elmina's Kitchen was uncommonly well acted by Shaun Parkes, Paterson Joseph, Emmanuel Idowu, Oscar James, George Harris and Doña Croll, and directed by Angus Jackson. Kwame Kwei-Armah wrote two more equally powerful plays for the National: *Fix Up* (2004) and *Statement of Regret* (2007). At the centre of *Democracy* were profoundly moving performances by Roger Allam and Conleth Hill. *The Pillowman* was quite brilliantly acted by Jim Broadbent, Adam Godley, Nigel Lindsay and David Tennant and directed by John Crowley. The cast of *His Dark Materials* all deserved awards for courage under fire. Among numberless exceptional performances in roles whose very names will thrill Pullman aficionados were Niamh Cusack as Serafina Pekkala, queen of the Lapland Witches, Danny Sapani as Iorek Byrnison and Tim McMullan as Fra Pavel of Geneva and the Gallivespian Lord Roke. The fantastic costumes were by Jon Morrell, the puppets were by Michael Curry, and the magical score was by Jonathan Dove.

The 2003/4 season was completed by *Power*, an elegant new play by Nick Dear about the young Louis XIV, and revivals of two terrific shows from Trevor Nunn's last season: Matthew Bourne's *Play Without Words*, and Roy Williams's *Sing Yer Hearts Out for the Lads*, a potent exposé of racism, set in a pub during an England/Germany World Cup qualifier.

❧

Over twelve years, the cast for the Wednesday planning meeting revolved often. It included: Nick Starr, Lisa Burger, Howard Davies, Marianne Elliott, Katie Mitchell, Tom Morris, Rufus Norris, Ben Power, Bijan Sheibani (associate directors); Jack Bradley, Sebastian Born (Literary); Lucy Davies, Purni Morell, Laura Collier (Studio); Pádraig Cusack, Paul Jozefowski, Daisy Heath, Robin Hawkes, Jo Hornsby (Planning); Toby Whale, Wendy Spon (Casting); Matthew Scott (Music); Chris Harper, Sarah Hunt, Alex Bayley (Marketing); Mark Dakin (Technical); John Rodgers (Development); David Sabel (Digital); Jenny Harris, Stephanie Hutchinson, Alice King-Farlow (Learning).

In *Stuff Happens,* Joe Morton was Colin Powell, Adjoa Andoh was Condoleezza Rice, Dermot Crowley was Dick Cheney, Nick Sampson was Dominique de Villepin and Angus Wright asked the audience to consider its own complacency. The speed-dating session at the Studio that gave birth to *London Road* was organised by Purni Morell. Its phenomonal cast was Clare Burt, Rosalie Craig, Kate Fleetwood, Hal Fowler, Nick Holder, Claire Moore, Michael Shaeffer, Nicola Sloane, Paul Thornley, Howard Ward and Duncan Wisbey. *Paul* was directed by Howard Davies and designed by Vicki Mortimer. Adam Godley was Paul, Lloyd Owen was Peter and Pierce Quigley was Yeshua. In *The Seafarer* were Ron Cook, Conleth Hill, Karl Johnson, Michael McElhatton and Jim Norton, all of them sensational. *England People Very Nice* was designed by Mark Thompson;

the wicked animations were by Pete Bishop. The skipping teenager in *To Be Straight With You* was the kinetic Ankur Bahl. In *Dara,* Zubin Varla and Sargon Yelda played the warring sons of Shah Jahan. Nadia Fall directed in a gorgeous set by Katrina Lindsay.

Anna Chancellor was Matt Charman's election observer. Lloyd Owen was the CIA operative at the centre of *Blood and Gifts.* Nikki Amuka-Bird and David Harewood were the rival presidents in *Welcome to Thebes,* which was magisterially directed by Richard Eyre. Sahr Ngaujah brought the audience to its feet as Fela Kuti in *Fela!* In a significant first, its director Bill T. Jones ripped off his shirt and danced on stage with the cast at the first-night curtain call. I was never tempted to follow his example. *3 Winters* was one of Howard Davies's best productions, which is to say it was one of the best things we ever did. The actors who created *Two Thousand Years* with Mike Leigh were Caroline Gruber, Allan Corduner, Ben Caplan, Adam Godley, Alexis Zegerman, John Burgess, Nitzan Sharron and Samantha Spiro. Olivia Williams was Kitty in *Happy Now?* The superb damaged children in *The Last of the Haussmans* were Rory Kinnear and Helen McCrory. *Market Boy* was Rufus Norris's first production at the National: he occupied the Olivier stage as if he owned it. The pitmen painters, all regulars of Live Theatre and all first rate, were Deka Walmsley, Christopher Connel, David Whitaker, Brian Lonsdale and Michael Hodgson; Ian Kelly was their tutor. Jeremy Herrin directed *This House* with great panache. Walter Harrison was Philip Glenister, Jack Weatherill was Charles Edwards: they and the entire cast were knockout. *Great Britain* was designed by Tim Hatley, and the projections were by Leo Warner, the founding director of 59 Productions, who have been at the forefront of the transformation of video as a theatrical medium. Robert Glenister was the editor, Dermot Crowley was the proprietor and Oliver Chris was the assistant commissioner, all of them lethally funny. *Collaborators* was designed by Bob Crowley, with a nod to Russian constructivism. Mark Addy, always bullseye, was the KGB man; Jacqueline Defferary was Yelena Bulgakov; George Fenton wrote a score that Shostakovich would not have disowned. Billie Piper and Jonjo O'Neill were the couple at the centre of *The Effect,* in a searing production by Rupert Goold. Billie is Lucy Prebble's muse, which is good news for both of them. The *James Plays* were given a thrilling design by Jon Bausor. It's hard to believe that any of the real Stuart kings were as charismatic as James McArdle, Andrew Rothey and Jamie Sives as James I, II and III. Queen Margaret was an incandescent Sofie Gråbøl. In *The Hard Problem,* dazzling Olivia Vinall was in bed with sharp-witted Damien Molony. They wore their high intelligence lightly. So did Parth Thakerar, Jonathan Coy, Rosie Hilal, Lucy Robinson, Anthony Calf and Vera Chok. I regret having no space to mention many other excellent new plays.

❧

Jeremy Sams composed the enchanting score for *The Wind in the Willows.* In its first cast were David Bamber as Mole, Richard Briers as Rat, Griff Rhys Jones as Toad, Terence Rigby as Albert the horse and Michael Bryant as Badger. It was the only time I worked with Michael, the National's adored mainstay during the directorships of Peter Hall, Richard Eyre and Trevor Nunn. He was indulgent of the younger actors' approach to animal characterisation, and agreed to take home a video of badgers going about their nocturnal business. He returned it the following day. "I've studied these badgers very carefully, and discovered an extraordinary thing. They all move exactly like Michael Bryant." He was particularly fond of two newcomers to the National: Tim McMullan as the chief weasel and Adrian Scarborough as his sidekick, Norman. Tim went on to become almost as valuable to the National as Michael, giving a succession of perfectly observed performances. Adrian became an Alan Bennett regular: he was promoted to Mole in *The Wind in the Willows,* played the king's page Fortnum in *The Madness of King George,* the gym teacher in the movie of *The History Boys,* and Humphrey Carpenter in *The Habit of Art.*

Charles Kay was literally mesmerising as Dr. Willis in *The Madness of George III.* James Villiers was Lord Chancellor Thurlow: his Cordelia was the least convincing in theatre history. Among many other smashing actors was Cyril Shaps as Dr. Pepys, who spent the play peering into the king's chamber pot, transported by the consistent perfection of his stool. *The Lady in the Van* was the only one of my collaborations with Alan Bennett not to be produced at the National. Maggie Smith has never cared for the Lyttelton, and wanted to perform it eight times a week in the West End. The two Alan Bennetts were Kevin McNally and Nicholas Farrell, both perfect. Robert Fox was the producer, his wit and urbanity a throwback to the days when the West End was glamorous.

I was on a panel with Simon Callow when he quoted Shakespeare's Banished Duke, so my use of the same quotation is a direct steal. I have forgotten the sources of many of this book's purloined insights, and I apologise for failing to acknowledge them. Bob Crowley's set for *The Habit of Art* was a replica of Rehearsal Room 2. Stephen Wight was Stuart the rent boy and John Heffernan was the Assistant Stage Manager. They were both spot on. The superlative cast of *People* included Linda Bassett, Selina Cadell, Nicholas Le Prevost and Miles Jupp.

❧

About half of the cast of *The Madness of King George* had been in *The Madness of George III*. Among those who hadn't were Helen Mirren as Queen Charlotte, Ian Holm as Dr. Willis and Rupert Everett as the Prince of Wales, all of them sublime. Helen was nominated for an Oscar, as were Nigel Hawthorne, Alan Bennett and Ken Adam, who won, as he had for *Barry Lyndon*. He wasn't even nominated for *Dr. Strangelove* or *Goldfinger,* which says all you need to know about awards. Stephen Evans and David Parfitt were the two British producers of *The Madness of King George*. The producers of *The Crucible* were Arthur Miller's son Robert, and David Picker, a Hollywood heavyweight. As president of United Artists, he worked with Bergman, Fellini and Truffaut and he shared stories about them without ever once making me feel small. Salem village was the creation of the production designer Lilly Kilvert. The make-up designer Naomi Donne became one of my best friends. Both *The History Boys* and *The Lady in the Van* were produced by Kevin Loader and Damian Jones. They were backed by BBC Films and my old friend Tom Rothman. All the scores were composed by George Fenton.

❧

David Bradley played the King in *Henry IV*. Sinking under the burden of power, still haunted on his deathbed by the violence he had unleashed, he gave a great performance. The mostly male cast included, in addition, excellent performances from Susan Brown as Mistress Quickly, Naomi Frederick as Lady Percy and Michelle Dockery as a servant. Adrian Scarborough memorably doubled Poins and Silence. The designer Mark Thompson was always the perfect collaborator on a low-budget Travelex show, able to conjure whole worlds with minimal resources. The cast for *King Lear* was amazing: Estelle Kohler, Sally Dexter and Alex Kingston as Goneril, Regan and Cordelia, Norman Rodway as Gloucester, David Troughton as Kent, Linus Roache as Edgar, Ralph Fiennes as Edmund, Paterson Joseph as Oswald and Linda Kerr Scott as the tiny, rubbery Fool. In *Hamlet,* Patrick Malahide was Claudius and James Laurenson doubled the ghost and the player king. Both were remarkable. Horatio was Giles Terera, Laertes was Alex Lanepikun, Fortinbras was Jake Fairbrother, Rosencrantz was Ferdinand Kingsley and Guildenstern was Prasanna Puwanarajah.

❧

The cast of *The Importance of Being Earnest* included Margaret Tyzack as Miss Prism and Richard Pearson as Chasuble. Alex Jennings and Richard E. Grant were Jack and Algernon; Susannah Harker and Claire Skinner were Gwendolen and Cecily. It was produced by Robert Fox. In *The Country Wife,* Cheryl Campbell was irresistible as Margery Pinchwife; Alex Jennings glittered as Sparkish, the fop. Bryan Dick and Amit Shah were touching dupes in *The Alchemist.* The scam was uncovered by Tim McMullan as Pertinax Surly, in yet another needle-sharp performance. Samuel Adamson made many excellent amendments to the text. Jonson's contemporaries were lucky in Melly Still's macabre production of Middleton's *The Revenger's Tragedy* and Joe Hill-Gibbins's iconoclastic staging of Marlowe's *Edward II*.

In *Saint Joan,* there were silver-tongued performances by Oliver

Ford Davies, Paterson Joseph, Paul Ready, Michael Thomas and Angus Wright. The startling choreography was by Hofesh Shechter. Paul Ready, a frequent and outstanding company member, was Major Barbara's fiancé; her mother was Clare Higgins, on top form; her brother was John Heffernan, who was just as good in *After the Dance*, which was directed by Thea Sharrock and designed by Hildegard Bechtler. The astonishing cast included Nancy Carroll, Benedict Cumberbatch and Adrian Scarborough. Dervla Kirwan, Adrian Dunbar and Peter McDonald were outstanding in *Exiles*; it was directed by James Macdonald. *Men Should Weep* was directed by Josie Rourke with a great set by Bunny Christie. Sharon Small and Robert Cavanah led a company that rose to its wild poetry. Martina Laird, Jenny Jules, Danny Sapani and Jude Akuwudike were part of an impressive cast in Michael Buffong's production of *Moon on a Rainbow Shawl*. Opposite Zoë Wanamaker in *The Rose Tattoo* was an exuberant Darrell D'Silva. James Baldwin was magnificently served in a production of *The Amen Corner* by Rufus Norris with Marianne Jean-Baptiste, Sharon D. Clarke, Cecilia Noble, Lucian Msamati, Eric Kofi Abrefa and the London Community Gospel Choir.

The emperor in *Emperor and Galilean* was the protean Andrew Scott, an astounding performance, in eye-popping designs by Paul Brown. Ben Power made an engrossing three-hour adaptation of the eight-hour original. *The White Guard* had an unforgettable set by Bunny Christie. The awe-inspiring cast included many of Howard Davies's regulars: Richard Henders, Daniel Flynn, Justine Mitchell, Paul Higgins, Pip Carter, Kevin Doyle, Conleth Hill, Nick Fletcher and Anthony Calf.

Katie Mitchell also had a loyal repertory company of actors, among them Kate Duchêne, Michael Gould, Gawn Grainger, Sinead Matthews, Hattie Morahan and Justin Salinger. Ben Daniels was brilliant as Agamemnon in *Iphigenia*. There was more illustrious work on the Greeks in the Olivier. Jonathan Kent staged a gripping *Oedipus* with Ralph Fiennes and Clare Higgins; Polly Findlay directed *Antigone* with Jodie Whitaker and Christopher Ecclestone; Carrie Cracknell directed *Medea* with Helen McCrory and Danny Sapani.

The two fabulous dancers in *Timon of Athens* were Christina Arestis and Kristen McNally. The indefatigable Ben Power collaborated on the text. In *Othello* were several of the actors upon whose matchless work in supporting roles the National's reputation rests: Tom Robertson, Robert Demeger, William Chubb and Nick Sampson. The stunningly violent barrack-room brawl was arranged by Kate Waters. She also arranged the superb duel at the end of *Hamlet*. Mark Addy was hilarious as Dogberry in *Much Ado,* without a single piece of extraneous comic business. Julian Wadham was Don Pedro, Oliver Ford Davies was Leonato, Daniel Hawksford was Claudio and Susannah Fielding was Hero. The costumes were by Dinah Collin, and Rachel Portman wrote the ravishing music.

I have written only about the Shakespeare that I have myself directed, so may have given the impression that he was my personal fiefdom. Not so: there were fascinating productions of *Measure for Measure* by Simon McBurney; *All's Well That Ends Well* by Marianne Elliott; *Twelfth Night* by Peter Hall; and *The Comedy of Errors* by Dominic Cooke with dazzling performances from Claudie Blakley, Michelle Terry, Lenny Henry and Lucian Msamati. Sam Mendes and Simon Russell Beale did *King Lear* in 2014; it took eleven years to get them together, and it was worth the wait.

In the London *Carousel,* Janie Dee was a glowing Carrie Pipperidge. In New York, Sally Murphy was a heartbreaking Julie Jordan, and Eddie Korbitch was a captivating Mr. Snow. Jigger Craigin was sung as if by Popeye by Phil Daniels in London, and Fisher Stevens in New York, both tremendous. At Lincoln Center, the show was produced by André Bishop and Bernard Gersten, who could not have given us a better time. In *Sweet Smell of Success,* luminous Kelli O'Hara played J.J.'s sister, and Jack Noseworthy was her boyfriend. Besides *Fela!,* two other musicals came from New York. *Caroline, Or Change* had a book and lyrics by Tony Kushner and a thrilling, eclectic score—ranging from klezmer to Motown—by Jeanine Tesori. It was directed by the great George C. Wolfe. *Here Lies Love* in 2014 was based on David Byrne's concept album about the life of Imelda Marcos, made in collaboration with Fatboy Slim. Oskar Eustis, the artistic director of the Public Theater, shepherded it to the stage, a triumph of creative producing. Its brilliant director was Alex Timbers.

The designers of *War Horse* were a massive part of its success: Rae Smith did the set and costumes, Paule Constable lit it, video was by Leo Warner and Mark Grimmer of 59 Productions. The exhilarating score was by Adrian Sutton; the songmaker was the great folkie John Tams. Movement was by Toby Sedgwick. *Curious Incident* had a set by Bunny Christie, lighting by Paule Constable and video by Finn Ross. Movement was by Scott Graham and Steven Hoggett for Frantic Assembly. Luke Treadaway was Christopher, a beautiful performance; his parents were played with rare empathy by Paul Ritter and Nicola Walker. Among the very funny actors in *London Assurance* were Mark Addy, Michelle Terry, Paul Ready and Nick Sampson, whose snooty valet Cool brought down the house. Among other large-scale entertainments were a lovely adaptation by Carl Miller of Erich Kästner's 1929 German classic, *Emil and the Detectives,* and an entirely fresh *Treasure Island* by Bryony Lavery.

Robin Lough was the camera director for *Phèdre*: his expertise was crucial to the success of NT Live. The admirable cast of *Phèdre* included Dominic Cooper, Stanley Townsend, Ruth Negga and John Shrapnel. Our touring programme continued to thrive. Most in demand were the big shows: *The History Boys, War Horse, Curious Incident* and *One Man, Two Guvnors.* Among many others that went on the road were *The Habit of Art, People, Hamlet,* Nicholas Wright's *Travelling Light,* Martin McDonagh's *The Pillowman,* Conor McPherson's *The Seafarer,* Katie Mitchell's *Waves* and Mike Leigh's *Grief.* The project manager of NT Future redevelopment was Paul Jozefowski. He and Rob Barnard know every corner of the building. The stars of the weekly company meeting were often Christine Paul, the canteen manager; Angus MacKechnie, head of Platforms; and Michael Straughan, head of box office, who was succeeded by Aidan O'Rourke.

❧

As I kept no diary, I asked a lot of old friends to reminisce. I want to thank Sam Barnett, Richard Bean, Alan Bennett, Lisa Burger, Oli Chris, Dominic Cooper, Bob Crowley, Frances de la Tour, Marianne Elliott, Nadia Fall, Deborah Findlay, Alex Jennings, Jonathan Kent, Lesley Manville, Tom Morris, Vicki Mortimer, Adam Penford, Ben Power, Lucy Prebble, Mark Ravenhill, Wendy Spon, Russell Tovey, Nick Wright, and above all Niamh Dilworth, who not only organised my life for the best part of twelve years, but remembered most of it too.

When I left the National, I was presented with a complete bound edition of Lyn Haill's peerless programmes. They were a priceless resource. So were the books she commissioned in the *National Theatre at Work* series, particularly Jonathan Croall's on *Mother Clap's Molly House*; Robert Butler's on *His Dark Materials* and *The Alchemist*; Bella Merlin's on *Henry IV*; and Mervyn Millar's on *War Horse*. Erin Lee spent days digging material that I didn't know existed out of the National Theatre Archive. To jog my memory, I sometimes searched for old reviews online, where the theatre criticism algorithm favours Michael Billington, Susannah Clapp, Charles Spencer and Paul Taylor. Most useful of all was Daniel Rosenthal's vast and indispensable book, *The National Theatre Story*. I am very happy to salute all of them.

I am indebted to all the playwrights whose work I have quoted, and acknowledge with gratitude those from whose plays I have taken long extracts: Richard Bean, Alan Bennett, David Hare and Tom Stoppard.

Simon Russell Beale, Peter Holland, Lucinda Morrison and Steve Ochoa read my early drafts: my heartfelt thanks to them for their advice. So, of course, did Nick Starr, without whom there would have been nothing to write about. I hope it's obvious how much I owe him. Stephen Grosz made some invaluable suggestions. I could not be more fortunate in my agents, Natasha Fairweather and Anthony Jones, or in my publishers Michal Shavit and Bea Hemming. Anthony suggested the title; they all gave me much better notes than I often give in my day job.

A large part of this book was written in a crumbling French farm-house uncannily like Leonato's in *Much Ado About Nothing*. Many of its protagonists drank rosé on the terrace while I wrote, and gave me some of my best material. Writing about the things we've done together was almost as much fun as doing them. I am immensely grateful to them, and I'm looking forward to lots more.

Index

A Note About the Author

Nicholas Hytner is a theater director and producer. He was director of London's National Theatre from 2003 to 2015 and cofounded the London Theatre Company, whose first theater, The Bridge, opened in October 2017.

A Note on the Type

The text of this book was set in Requiem, a typeface designed by Jonathan Hoefler (born 1970) and released in the late 1990s by the Hoefler Type Foundry.

Composed by North Market Street Graphics
Lancaster, Pennsylvania

Printed and bound by Berryville Graphics,
Berryville, Virginia

Designed by Betty Lew